# SUPPORTING
## THE SUCCESS OF ADULT
 ### AND ONLINE STUDENTS
#### Proven Practices in Higher Education

Edited by Kelly A. Flores, Kurt D. Kirstein,
Craig E. Schieber
and Steven G. Olswang

ISBN: 1533071586
ISBN 13: 9781533071583

# Table of Contents

# Preface

This book is the fifth and final volume in the Proven Practices in Higher Education series published by City University of Seattle. In the five years since the first volume was published, higher education has experienced some substantial changes. It is now commonplace, even for traditional institutions, to have programs offered entirely online. Competency-based programs and adaptive learning models and tools are influencing an increasing number of students at colleges and universities across the country. And improvements in Internet connectivity and communications technologies are transforming distance education to a format where synchronous, face-to-face interaction is, once again, an integral part.

Through these many transitions, one factor that has not changed is the need to support students through the educational process. This book focuses on student support. The chapters that make up this volume explore different proven practices when engaging with the nontraditional adult student.

Part I focuses on proven practices for supporting and teaching adult students. At times, it becomes useful for instructors to have a clearer idea of the psychosocial factors that influence an adult's ability and willingness to learn. To the extent that these factors present themselves as roadblocks to learning, an instructor may be required to provide social and emotional support to students to help ensure academic success. The practices included in Part I address social support, psychological support, and technological support for adult learners and offer strategies to support students, both directly and indirectly, through the learning process.

Part II shifts the focus to strategies for motivating and engaging adult students. One key characteristic of adult learners is that they are busy people; they have limited amounts of time and energy to dedicate to a large number of concerns. Any learning activity is competing with these other concerns. Thus, activities need to be carefully designed to reveal their relevance, or they will be left behind in short order. Learning that cannot be connected to practical value runs the risk of becoming useless drudgery that adult students will resist.

Motivating students requires instructors to establish a connection between the course content and factors of concern for the students; they have to see a personally relevant reason for extending the effort to learn. The strategies in Part II of this volume help faculty members make this connection. By addressing how best to motivate learning, in different formats and through varied subjects, the strategies presented in these chapters are useful for instructors who wish to engage their students at a higher level.

Part III addresses the process of advising students and the need to retain them. So much of what establishes the quality of the student experience is determined outside of the classroom. From the application process through to the first course and beyond, students work with different individuals, including support staff and advisors, who help them get to the right classes. Utilizing best practices in student support can make the difference as to whether a student will stay or not.

Once in class, the real work begins for many students who may struggle with a return to a structured learning experience after a long absence. Given the higher rates of attrition during the early stages of nearly every academic program, particular attention should be paid to strategies that can smooth the transition into classrooms in a manner that helps students recognize their potential success. Several of these retention strategies are presented in Part III of this volume.

This book, the last in the Proven Practices series, makes a significant contribution to the list of progressive educational strategies that have been described in all five books in the series. Book one focused on authentic instruction strategies that linked learning to real-world experience. Book two presented innovative methods for teaching adults. Book three focused on how to teach leadership principles to emerging leaders. Book four focused on advances in exemplary instruction. Book five focuses on best practices in student support.

Together, the Proven Practices series contains 102 chapters, each of which describes a method for improving the learning process for adults and online learners. The faculty, staff, and students at City University of Seattle have collectively generated these volumes to reflect a combination of the research, theory, and practice, and real-life experience, of highly effective teachers and leaders within the higher education sector.

Throughout the generation of this series, the intent has been to provide readers with proven practices that can be used to support and educate learners.

Lastly, if we are to believe that experience is a great teacher, then proven practices, developed through instructor experience, have much to offer both novice and veteran educators. The insights included in all five volumes in the Proven Practices series were shared with this goal in mind.

Kelly Flores
Kurt Kirstein
Craig Schieber
Steven Olswang

Seattle, WA
April 2016

# Part I

# Proven Practices for Supporting and Teaching Adult Students

1

# Lean on Me: The Importance of a Social Support Network for Adult Students

**Joel Domingo**

## Abstract

Social support and social support networks are important factors in creating positive feelings of self-efficacy and confidence and helping to mitigate negative feelings or behaviors. Typically used in health and wellness environments, their utility in academic settings to address issues of student persistence is an emerging practice that continues to show promise. This chapter outlines the history and impact of these supports from the context of student affairs and the behavioral sciences and shares emerging best practices for consideration. The chapter concludes with several key principles and characteristics of social supports that can help inform practices that educational leaders can consider when serving adult students in the most holistic way possible.

# Overview

For the typical adult learner, the completion of a degree or certificate program represents a type of accomplishment that has many facets. Along with the receipt of the degree is the collection of interesting stories that come along with such an endeavor. Many of these stories recount long hours of studying and the challenge of balancing school with occupational demands and family obligations, two defining characteristics of this population (Merriam, Caffarella, & Baumgartner, 2007).

Invariably, these stories also contain the memories of individuals along the scholastic journey who provided timely support and encouragement, much of which proved critical. As such, a gesture common at commencement exercises includes the public recognition of those family members and friends, thanking them for their support.

*Social support* or *social support networks* are critical factors in student success (Conner, 2015). Social supports can be defined as networks of relationships that a person has; they have long been used in the psychology literature as a mechanism for promoting resilience and well-being (Juliano & Yunes, 2014). In the context of education, research has pointed to several positive effects of social supports including mitigating student burnout (Chang, Eddins-Folensbee, & Coverdale, 2012) and helping increase degree completion rates (Jairam & Kahl, 2012).

Social support among adult learners is a critical aspect of student success. This chapter includes a list of practical ways that social supports can be fostered within the institution and apart from it. Furthermore, some of the positive auxiliary effects initiated by the institution resulting in informal social networks will be discussed. Institutions that recognize and understand the psychosocial aspects of adult learners are that much more prepared to help overcome barriers to completion for these students and thus create the excellent experience that they deserve.

# Review of the Literature

Foundations for an exploration in adult student success lie in understanding concepts found in both the student development and the psychological and behavioral science literature. Student development theory provides a basis for understanding the perspectives of self-identity, development, and other factors arising within the learning context (Evans, Forney, & Guido, 2009). Theorists such as Freud and Jung proved instrumental to the field of student development, which began simply as the practice of vocational guidance and preparation. Student development would evolve to include addressing complex student needs (Evans et al., 2009). Moreover, addressing students' needs required understanding students' sense of self-identity and their psychosocial stages of development. This new responsibility requires the university administration—the student services office—to be knowledgeable in psychological developmental theories such as those of Erikson (1959) and Chickering (1979), among others.

Common among the theories is the idea that there are stages of human development and associated needs therein. Erikson (1959) suggested that in certain stages of development, namely the young and middle adulthood stage where most adult learners are, success is linked to having comfortable relationships that can mitigate feelings of loneliness and isolation. Similarly, Chickering (1979) found several interrelated components that contributed to one's sense of identity, one of which was the importance of developing interdependence and interpersonal relationships. By all accounts, these developmental theories agree on the idea that identity is socially constructed and that environmental influences, the campus environment, and other external influences are critical elements to help students succeed (Torres, Jones, & Renn, 2009).

As increasing numbers of adult learners entered university studies, Knowles (1984) recognized the unique needs of adult learners and provided a framework for learning that emphasizes the process of instruction beyond the actual content. Adult learning is characterized by an emphasis on experience as the basis for learning; an immediate life or job relevance to the subject; active participation; and a focus on problem solving and solutions rather than just content (Knowles, 1984; Knowles, Holton, & Swanson, 2005). Building on these frameworks, Merriam (2004) found strong linkages between the way adults learn and changes in their personal dispositions and attitudes, both of which depend on a strong sense of personal, critical reflection. Chen (2012) found that self-reflection, meaningful connections, and strong interpersonal relationships were found to affect the development of other positive self-concepts. These interpersonal relationships provided a foundation for social support networks.

# Integration into the Student Experience

Researchers have historically explored the idea of social supports in studies of health and wellness (Eklund & Hansson, 2007; Low & Molzahn, 2007). Chaichanawirote and Higgins (2013) found that strong networks of social relationships with older adults resulted in increased receptivity to health-care interventions.

Wrzus, Hänel, Wagner, and Neyer (2013) conducted a meta-analysis of social support networks and life events across the life span and found that these networks vary according to the circumstances in a person's life. Within the educational experience, social support networks have been attributed to increasing a student's sense of self-efficacy and neutralizing the effects of student burnout. Rigg, Day, and Adler (2013) researched the impact of social support on graduate students and found that students who have supportive relationships both from within and outside the institution experience less exhaustion and strong feelings of self-efficacy and engagement. These effects can help adult students overcome barriers that prevent them from being successful in school and gain balance from juggling multiple roles in their lives.

The research on social support networks justifies a reexamination of the processes and relationships that occur in traditional graduate teaching experiences. Informal ties and relationships with faculty and others who provide encouragement have been shown to help students balance the demands of graduate study (Hunt, Mair, & Atkinson, 2012). Networks of collaboration within a supportive environment cultivate a sense of collective efficacy, which results in better student achievement (Moolenaar, Sleegers, & Daly, 2012). Institutions can affect student satisfaction, and improve student experiences, by cultivating an environment of positive support for students.

The notion of mentoring also falls within the sphere of support networks in education. Improving outcomes for students includes support structures and programs that mitigate the effects of burnout. Mentoring is one such avenue that has been shown to help prevent student dropout (Crisp, 2010). The traditional mentoring relationship commonly occurs between a mentor and mentee for help in such areas of career exploration and personal and professional goals. However, informal interactions of the mentoring relationship have also been found to be beneficial for students, especially those who would not otherwise seek a formal process or arrangement. Khalil (2008) explored this idea of informal mentoring, using a technology platform, for students with disabilities in higher education and found that the students experienced satisfaction with this innovative and informal arrangement.

## Student Support Networks in Practice

Fostering student success and a sense of community for adult students is a shared responsibility across the campus. Educational leaders in higher education, from the initial admissions and student services personnel to the faculty and other staff, must first know the needs of adult students to create a culture that is both welcoming and supportive, especially to those students who have been away from school for a time. Furthermore, traditional methods of support such as faculty office hours and advising appointments better serve traditionally enrolled students that may not have the complex characteristics and demands that adult students have.

Several valuable principles emerge from the adult learning tradition that can inform practices used today. One principle is establishing an environment where the university leaders, staff, and faculty are perceived to be approachable and exhibit sensitivities to student needs. By creating a learning community where instructors move from an authoritarian and dogmatic role to more of a knowledgeable guide and colleague, students are committed to working harder and being more engaged in learning (Barkley, 2010).

Encouraging students to develop their relationships and social networks outside the formal classroom setting is a common practice that has also been effective. For adult students especially, entering a different environment can be both exhilarating and intimidating; programs that provide social and academic support can serve as emotional buffers during periods of stress and anxiety. Who better to relate to the adult student than a fellow student experiencing similar stressors? For this reason, institutions commonly foster student support groups around a variety of issues connected to the topic of study or need.

One institutionalized practice includes formal programs that serve the needs of adult and returning students. The TRiO program is an example of a federal program designed to focus specifically on outreach to the returning adult, first-generation, low-income, and veteran students. Beyond the traditional offering of study skills interventions and tutoring,

TRiO programs have provided regular opportunities for students to share insights with each other in small group settings and other social opportunities to connect, improve self-efficacy, and build camaraderie, all contributing to student success (Grier-Reed & Ganuza, 2012).

## Lessons Learned, Tips for Success, and Recommendations

While formal and institutional support networks are helpful to many students, informal student support networks can be equally, if not more, important to adult students. Informal support networks include both topic-specific academic groups or practical nonacademic functions like book exchanges or babysitting support. Since most adult students do not have the time to participate in traditional forms of formal support activities, these ad-hoc-type events coalescing for a particular time and purpose are often welcomed.

O'Connor and Cordova's (2010) work provided several examples of theory applied to practice when it comes to the experience of adult students and the supports they need for success. These features included:

- regular attendance in external organizations such as churches that serve as an existing community and provide emotional support;
- the occasional "break" from school in the form of a semester off or a lesser credit load to deal with life challenges;
- support from employers who know that the employee is currently in school;
- methods of instruction that acknowledge students' life experiences and are matched to their particular learning styles; and
- opportunities for social events that focus on building community.

## Conclusion

The growth of the nontraditional and adult student population brings new challenges for institutions of higher education. The National Center for Education Statistics project enrollment for adult students to outpace that of traditional students (US Department of Education, 2015), and schools that recognize the unique features of this demographic and also create environments of support, whether formal or informal, will be a step ahead of those institutions that do not.

The history of student support and student services gives us a glimpse into this continuing evolution and desire to serve the "whole needs of the student," and student development theory provides a look into what possible specific interventions along the development cycle can be most effective to help bring about feelings of confidence and self-efficacy. It is that sense of confidence and self-efficacy that correlates to students finding meaning and purpose (Kramer, 2009).

The variety of positive effects resulting from social supports cannot be underestimated. While social supports typically address academic issues like writing and study habits, it is the informal social supports that have shown to influence the psychosocial dimension in adult students, mitigating the negative effects of burnout and exhaustion. Moreover, the external social supports such as empathy and encouragement from fellow students and family members, if combined with strong institutional and traditional programs of student support, show strong promise. Current and future leaders of these institutions would be wise to recognize and take advantage of these opportunities to create the campuses of the future.

# References

Barkley, E. F. (2010). *Student engagement techniques: A handbook for college faculty*. Hoboken, NJ: Jossey-Bass.

Chaichanawirote, U., & Higgins, P. A. (2013). The complexity of older adults' social support networks. *Research in Gerontological Nursing, 6*(4), 275–282. doi:http://dx.doi.org/10.3928/19404921-20130805-01

Chang, E., Eddins-Folensbee, F., & Coverdale, J. (2012). Survey of the prevalence of burnout, stress, depression, and the use of supports by medical students at one school. *Academic Psychiatry, 36*(3), 177-182. doi:10.1176/appi.ap.11040079

Chen, P. (2012). Empowering identity reconstruction of indigenous college students through transformative learning. *Educational Review, 64*(2), 161–180. doi:10.1080/00131911.2011.592574

Chickering, A. R. (1979). *Education and identity*. San Francisco, CA: Jossey-Bass.

Conner, M. (2015). Self-efficacy, stress, and social support in retention of student registered nurse anesthetists. *AANA Journal, 83*(2), 133.

Crisp, G. (2010). The impact of mentoring on the success of community college students. *Review of Higher Education, 34*(1), 39–60.

Eklund, M., & Hansson L. (2007). Social network among people with persistent mental illness: Associations with sociodemographic, clinical and health-related factors. *International Journal of Social Psychiatry, 53*, 293–305. doi:10.1177/0020764006074540

Erikson, E. H. (1959). *Identity and the life cycle*. New York, NY: W.W. Norton & Company.

Evans, N. J., Forney, D. S., & Guido, F. M. (2009). *Student development in college: Theory, research, and practice* (2nd ed.). Hoboken, NJ: Jossey-Bass.

Grier-Reed, T., & Ganuza, Z. (2012). Using constructivist career development to improve career decision self-efficacy in TRiO students. *Journal of College Student Development, 53*(3), 464–471.

Hunt, A. N., Mair, C. A., & Atkinson, M. P. (2012). Teaching community networks: A case study of informal social support and information sharing among sociology graduate students. *Teaching Sociology, 40*(3), 198–214. doi:10.1177/0092055X12441714

Jairam, D., & Kahl Jr., D. H. (2012). Navigating the doctoral experience: The role of social support in successful degree completion. *International Journal of Doctoral Studies, 7*, 311–328. Retrieved from http://ijds.org/Volume7/IJDSv7p311-329Jairam0369.pdf

Juliano, M. C. C., & Yunes, M. A. M. (2014). Reflections on the social support network as a mechanism for the protection and promotion of resilience. *Ambiente & Sociedade, 17*(3). http://dx.doi.org/10.1590/S1414-753X2014000300009

Khalil, M. A. (2008). Promoting success: Mentoring students with disabilities using new technologies in higher education. *Library Hi Tech News, 25*(1), 8–12. doi:http://dx.doxi.org/10.1108/0741905810877490

Knowles, M. (1984). *The adult learner: A neglected species* (3rd ed.). Houston, TX: Gulf Publishing.

Knowles, M., Holton III, E. F., & Swanson, R. A. (2005). *The adult learner: The definitive classic in adult education and human resource development.* New York, NY: Routledge.

Kramer, G. L. (Ed.). (2009). *Fostering student success in the campus community.* Hoboken, NJ: Jossey-Bass.

Low, G., & Molzahn, A. E. (2007). Predictors of quality of life in old age: A cross-validation study. *Research in Nursing & Health, 30,* 141–150. doi:10.1002/nur.20178

Merriam, S. B. (2004). The role of cognitive development in Mezirow's transformational learning theory. *Adult Education Quarterly, 55*(1), 60-68. doi:10.1177/0741713604268891

Merriam, S., Caffarella, R. S., & Baumgartner, L. (2007). *Learning in adulthood: A comprehensive guide.* Hoboken, NJ: Wiley.

Moolenaar, N. M., Sleegers, P. J. C., & Daly, A. J. (2012). Teaming up: Linking collaboration networks, collective efficacy, and student achievement: *Teaching and Teacher Education, 28*(2), 251–262. doi:10.1016/j.tate.2011.10.001

O'Connor, B. N., & Cordova, R. (2010). Learning: The experiences of adults who work full-time while attending graduate school part-time. *Journal of Education for Business, 85*(6), 359–368.

Rigg, J., Day, J., & Adler, H. (2013). Emotional exhaustion in graduate students: The role of engagement, self-efficacy, and social support. *Journal of Educational and Developmental Psychology, 3*(2), 138–152.

Torres, V., Jones, S. R., & Renn, K. A. (2009). Identity development theories in student affairs: Origins, current status, and new approaches. *Journal of College Student Development, 50*(6), 577–596.

US Department of Education, National Center for Education Statistics. (2015). *Digest of Education Statistics 2013.* Retrieved from https://nces.ed.gov/programs/digest/d13/

Wrzus, C., Hänel, M., Wagner, J., & Neyer, F. J. (2013). Social network changes and life events across the life span: A meta-analysis. *Psychological Bulletin, 139*(1), 53–80.

## Author Biography

Joel L. Domingo is an Associate Professor and Associate Program Director of Higher Education and Nonprofit Leadership at City University of Seattle and has a history of leadership and teaching in education, community, and civic organizations. His work focuses on exploring issues of leadership, developing strong communities and schools, disability issues, and creating socially transformative practices for education and the nonprofit sector. Dr. Domingo holds a BA from the University of Washington, an MA in theology from Fuller Theological Seminary, and an EdD in educational leadership from Argosy University.

# 2

# Students' "Dark Side" Personalities in a Classroom Setting

**Joyce Mphande-Finn**

## Abstract

This chapter includes an exploration of the dark side, and what it means to educators in the context of students in a learning environment. An in-depth description of the dark side is provided to assist educators in understanding the dark personality traits that students might present in a classroom setting. The chapter covers offensive and yet nonpathological personalities that students may present, including Machiavellianism, subclinical narcissism, and subclinical psychopathy, referred to as the Dark Triad. All three personalities share features of varying degrees of self-promotion, emotional coldness, duplicity, and aggressiveness. Everyday sadism is another dark personality described in this chapter. Consulting the literature on dark personalities, this chapter provides an educator with information and knowledge regarding student dark side behaviors in a learning environment.

## Overview

> This being human is a guest house. / Every morning a new arrival. / A joy, a depression, a meanness, / some momentary awareness comes / as an unexpected visitor. / Welcome and entertain them all! / Even if they're a crowd of sorrows, / who violently sweep your house / empty of its furniture, / still treat each guest honorably. / He may be clearing you out / for some new delight. / The dark thought, the shame, the malice, / meet them at the door laughing, / and invite them in. / Be grateful for whoever comes, / because each has been sent / as a guide from beyond. ("The Guest House" by Mewlana Jalaluddin Rumi)

When students come into a learning environment, they bring their individual personalities and behaviors that an educator honors and interacts with during the learning process. Students may have dysfunctional interpersonal dispositions such as dark side personality traits, which are socially undesirable attributes and that have been shown to predict career derailment across a variety of organizations, levels, and positions (Dalal & Nolan, 2009). In their research, Hogan and Hogan (2001) suggested that the dark side personality traits do coexist with functional interpersonal dispositions, including talent, ambition, and good social skills. When students present with dark side behaviors in the form of compulsiveness, passive-aggression, narcissism, and other personality issues, educators benefit from understanding the dark characteristics. Bohart (2013) reported that Freud, Rollo May, and others believed that individuals must consciously confront their dark sides to grow.

Johnson and Johnson (1999) suggested that creating positive classroom climates supports student learning. The students that present behaviors stemming from personality disorders can be supported by educators who understand the manifestations of the particular disorders. Mgbodile (1997) contended that the school environment should allow students to increase their feelings of satisfaction, belonging, identification, and achievement in present and future situations.

When dark side behaviors are acted out in a classroom setting, other students are affected, and negative consequences result. Educators would benefit from having a better understanding on how to deal with these situations.

In this chapter, dark side behaviors (compulsiveness, passive-aggression, narcissism) and other dark side personality traits will be explored and discussed in the context of students and educators in a learning environment. These behaviors manifest themselves in both group and individual levels, and these traits can influence how students respond or react in a classroom situation. This chapter includes further discussion on ways educators can respond to and handle situations that arise in the classroom, and the role of creating a safe place for students to confront their dark sides and allow for learning and growth.

## Review of the Literature

Several researchers believe that everyone has a shadow personality. Zweig and Abrams (1991) reported that every child naturally develops a personal shadow. Parents, siblings, teachers, clergy, and friends create a complex environment in which one learns what is kind, proper, moral behavior, and what is mean-spirited, shameful, and sinful. Zweig and Abrams (1991) also reported that the shadow will act like a psychic immune system, which defines what is *self* and what is *not self*. What falls into *ego* and what falls into *shadow* can vary depending on family and environmental factors. Zweig and Abrams (1991) stated "All the feelings and capacities that are rejected by the ego and exiled into the shadow contribute to the hidden power of the dark side of human nature" (p. XVII). The authors suggested that the personal shadow contains undeveloped, unexpressed potential. This personal shadow is the part of the unconscious that is complementary to the ego and represents those characteristics that the conscious personality does not wish to acknowledge. Instead, the conscious personality neglects, forgets, and hides these characteristics, only to have them surface in uncomfortable confrontations with others.

The study of dark personality and its impact is not new. Harms and Spain (2015) cited Kraepelin and Diefendorf's (1907) work, and indicated that the study of dark side personality began when Kraepelin detailed the nature of disturbed personalities. Kraepelin and Diefendorf (1907) described disturbed personalities as: (a) the morally insane, characterized by a lack of comprehensive reflection and foresight; (b) the unstable, characterized by becoming rapidly interested and disinterested in activities, moodiness, and irritability; (c) the morbid liar and swindler, characterized by high intelligence, deriving joy from successfully deceiving others, and prone to blaming others for setbacks; and (d) the pseudo-querulants, characterized by suspiciousness, defensiveness, and litigiousness. Harm and Spain (2015) summarized these personalities as modern labels of psychopathic, borderline personality, Machiavellianism, and paranoia.

Similarly, Paulhus, and Williams (2002) came up with the term *Dark Triads*, a constellation of three related, socially undesirable personality traits: Machiavellianism, narcissism, and subclinical psychopathy. In the recent years, a fourth trait, *everyday sadism*, was added to the roster. Ashby and Linda (2005) described compulsiveness as pathological since it involves extreme preoccupation with thoughts or activities, and also that it includes a tendency toward over-organization and difficulty making decisions. Paulhus (2014) referred to these dark personalities as a set of socially aversive traits in the subclinical range and considers these socially offensive traits falling in the normal or everyday range.

The DSM-5 (American Psychiatric Association, 2013) described narcissism disorder as:

> a pervasive pattern of grandiosity (in fantasy or behavior), need for admiration, and lack of empathy, beginning by early adulthood and present in a variety of contexts, which include the following: (a) a grandiose sense of self-importance (e.g., exaggerates achievements and talents, expects to be recognized as superior without commensurate achievements); (b) preoccupation with fantasies of unlimited success, power, brilliance, beauty, or ideal love; (c) belief that he or she is "special" and unique and can only be understood by, or should associate with, other special or high-status people (or institutions); (d) requirement of excessive admiration; (e) having a sense of entitlement (i.e., unreasonable expectations of especially favorable treatment or automatic compliance with his or her expectations); (f) being interpersonally exploitative (i.e., takes advantage of others to achieve his or her own ends); (g) lacking empathy: is unwilling to recognize or identify with the feelings and needs of others; (h) being often envious of others or believes

that others are envious of him or her; (i) shows arrogant, haughty behaviors or attitudes. (p. 669)

Further noted in the DSM-5 (American Psychiatric Association, 2013) is that vulnerability in self-esteem makes individuals with narcissistic personality disorder sensitive to injury from criticism or defeat. Although they may not show it outwardly, criticism may haunt these individuals and may leave them feeling humiliated, degraded, hollow, and empty. When narcissists feel this way, they may react with disdain, rage, or defiant counterattack (American Psychiatric Association, 2013).

Muris, Meesters, and Timmermans (2013) defined Machiavellianism, narcissism, and psychopathy in the following ways: Machiavellianism is the manipulation and exploitation of others, a cynical disregard of morality, and a focus on self-interest. Narcissism is concerned with a grandiose self-view, a sense of entitlement, and egotism. Psychopathy mainly has to do with callousness and a lack of personal affect and remorsefulness. Sadism is another trait that can be added to the list. Sadism involves the humiliation of others, patterns of cruelty and demeaning behavior, and harming others physically, sexually, or psychologically for personal enjoyment (Southard, Noser, Pollock, Mercer, Zeigler-Hill, 2015).

In recent studies by Jones and Paulhus (2011), the personality traits described are related to the Big Five personality factors, which include extroversion, agreeableness, conscientiousness, neuroticism, and openness. Muris et al. (2013) reported that Machiavellianism is positively correlated to neuroticism and negatively correlated with agreeableness and conscientiousness. Narcissism is positively correlated to extraversion and negatively correlated to agreeableness. Psychopathy is negatively correlated to both agreeableness and conscientiousness.

Researchers studying different personality traits have revealed that the Dark Triad traits have a significant negative impact on functioning in daily life (Muris et al., 2013). These authors believed individuals with high degrees of Dark Triad traits

- adopt more aggressive and forceful tactics at work;
- display more risky and less self-controlling behaviors;
- more often use aggressive and self-defeating humor styles;
- more frequently engage in bullying behaviors;

- show a stronger tendency toward short-term, exploratory mating and superficial intimate relationships; and
- exhibit higher levels of prejudice and racism.

These more aggressive, forceful tactics can also be demonstrated in a classroom environment, as evidenced by research that shows that threatened egotism among students with high self-esteem is associated with more aggression, especially when coupled with high narcissism (Vaillancourt, 2013). The Big Five personality traits provide a framework to understand individual differences and social relationships from the internalized and externalized symptoms that may be displayed by individuals, including students.

## Integration into the Student Experience

Students do not often display their personalities when they first come into a learning environment. Through the process of learning and the challenges that arise, educators may have a glimpse of some positive or negative behaviors exhibited by students. Research studies have indicated that the transition to college by students normally coincides with a period of development. Characteristics of this developmental period include instability, identity exploration, reduced parental monitoring, and a general lack of commitment to the familial and financial responsibilities and roles of adulthood (Nelson & Barry, 2005).

Educators can contextualize these characteristics within the Dark Triad traits (Machiavellianism, narcissism, and psychopathy) and sadism. Some students may present personality traits and socially deviant behaviors, including "a glib and superficial charm; egocentricity; selfishness; lack of empathy, guilt, and remorse; deceitfulness; lack of enduring attachments to people, principles, or goals; impulsive and irresponsible behavior; and a tendency to violate explicit norms" (Hare & Hart, 1993, p. 34). Rivers, Brackett, Omori, Sickler, Bertoli, and Salovey (2013) reported that, in general, a variety of maladaptive behaviors tend to occur as a result of decisions made under less than optimal conditions.

Students may present with maladaptive behaviors in a classroom, but educators should be cautious not to assume the behaviors are always negative. A student, for example, who has a high need for achievement and high levels of competitiveness could be narcissistic and exhibit a need for admiration and a lack of empathy. An educator should be aware of these behavior patterns in the student and focus on the positive aspects of these tendencies. Studies have shown that individuals who exhibit these narcissistic behaviors manage to survive, and even flourish, in everyday society. Zibarras, Port, and Woods (2008) reported the importance of encouraging such students to be innovative and creative, which means having self-confidence, high energy, independence of judgment, autonomy, and toleration.

## Proven Practices, Examples, and Results

By defining the dark side and recognizing what fuels the behaviors, educators can help students feel in control in a learning environment. Muris et al. (2013) showed that individuals with high levels of Dark Triad traits may demonstrate aggressive, forceful tactics; be bullish toward other students or the educator in the classroom; or express racial slurs or prejudice. Narcissism is demonstrated when the student is highly reactive to criticism, has low self-esteem, can be inordinately self-righteous and defensive, reacts to contrary viewpoints with anger or rage, projects negative qualities onto others, and demonstrates poor interpersonal boundaries. Such a student may challenge an educator on minor matters in class, all with the intention of undermining the educator's character and the qualification to teach, in front of other students.

It is important for an educator to understand that personalities of students are not necessarily constant across each person, since there are individual differences that distinguish them. Students may behave differently in different courses, and with different professors. The dark side personality tendencies might be different in some situations; for instance, perfectionistic students will most often be frustrated and disappointed with both themselves and other people who fail to meet their unrealistic expectations. Jones and Paulhus (2011) concluded that, in this case, such a student would be demonstrating impulsivity, and that both narcissistic and psychopathic individuals tend to show higher levels of overall impulsivity.

Each characteristic of the Dark Triad is correlated with different forms of impulsivity, and Dickman (1990) differentiated between *functional impulsivity* and *dysfunctional impulsivity*. He described functional impulsivity as being related to idea generation, enthusiasm, adventurousness, and the ability to make quick decisions. On the other hand, dysfunctional impulsivity is related to erratic disorderliness, distraction, and inaccurate decision making (Dickman, 1990). A student can present with enthusiasm in class, but can also be erratic and disorderly, which can distract others.

## Lessons Learned, Tips for Success, and Recommendations

Students learn best in an environment in which they feel a sense of trust, safety, and openness to different modes of learning, acceptance, and a basic sense of security. They also bring their personalities and egos. The students bring their light sides and dark sides, which educators interact with on a daily basis. The light side can be well tolerated by the educators and the other students in the classroom, whereas the students who act out their dark side personalities might create discomfort for other students, and even challenge and undermine the educator. Jones and Paulhus (2011) reported that the Dark Triad members have unique personality styles favoring different life outcomes. Each member is believed to have a unique social engagement style that might prove adaptive in some situations but maladaptive in others.

The concept of the shadow, as a portion of everyone's personality, and how it manifests in our personal lives through the unconscious as it spills into our self-defeating behaviors are important for educators to understand. Students enter the learning environment with baggage from their childhood, where they may have been blocked, oppressed, and denied permission for expressing themselves, thus they might struggle in an overcompensated way to break free from the strong grip of their family experiences by hiding in their shadow, or the dark side.

## Conclusion

The dark side behaviors, which may include compulsiveness, passive-aggression, narcissism, and other dark personality traits, were examined through exploration of the Dark Triad. The research discussed in this chapter reveals that educators must acknowledge and be aware that students in general have a dark side of their personalities. However, not all students will display dark side behaviors in the classroom unless triggered by specific circumstances.

Educators need to create a learning environment in which students feel safe, accepted, and respected and to understand students without stereotyping them as having darker personalities. This chapter shows an educator's understanding of the dark side that students bring into the classroom, and can improve their understanding of many propositions around narcissism, Machiavellianism, subclinical psychopathy, of which some of the dark side behaviors students may exhibit in the form of compulsiveness, passive-aggression, and narcissistic tendencies.

# References

American Psychiatric Association. (2013). *Diagnostic and statistical manual of mental disorders* (5th ed.). Washington, DC: Author.

Ashby, J. S., & Linda, P. B. (2005). Multidimensional perfectionism and obsessive-compulsive behaviors. *Journal of College Counseling, 8*(1), 31–40.

Bohart, A. C. (2013). Darth Vader, Carl Rogers, and self-organizing wisdom. In A. C. Bohart, B. S. Held, E. Mendelowitz, & K. J. Schneider (Eds.), *Humanity's dark side: Evil, destructive experience, and psychotherapy* (pp. 57–76). Washington, DC: American Psychological Association.

Dalal, D. K., & Nolan, K. P. (2009). Using dark side personality traits to identify potential failure. *Industrial and Organizational Psychology, 2*(4), 434–436.

Dickman, S. J. (1990). Functional and dysfunctional impulsivity: Personality and cognitive correlates. *Journal of Personality and Social Psychology, 58*(1), 95–102.

Hare, R. D., & Hart, S. D. (1993). Psychopathy, mental disorder, and crime. In S. Hodgins (Ed.), *Mental disorder and crime* (pp. 104–115). Newbury Park, CA: Sage.

Harms, P. D., & Spain, S. M. (2015). Beyond the bright side: Dark personality at work. *Applied Psychology: An International Review, 64*(1), 15–24.

Hogan, R., & Hogan, J. (2001). Assessing leadership: A view from the dark side. *International Journal of Selection and Assessment, 9*, 40–51.

Johnson, D. W., & Johnson, R. T. (1999*). Learning together and alone: Cooperative, competitive, and individualistic learning* (5th ed.). New York, NY: Allyn & Bacon.

Jones, D. N., & Paulhus, D. L. (2011). The role of impulsivity in the dark triad of personality. *Personality and Individual Differences, 51*(5), 679–682.

Kraepelin, E., & Diefendorf, A. R. (1907). *Clinical psychiatry; a text-book for students and physicians*. New York, NY: Macmillan.

Mgbodile, T. O. (1997). The nature and scope of educational administration and management. In N. Ndu, L. O. Ocho, & B. S. Okeke (Eds.), *Dynamics of educational administration & management, The Nigerian perspective* (pp. 48–52). Akwa, Nigeria: Mekslink Publishers.

Muris, P., Meesters, C., & Timmermans, A. (2013). Some youths have a gloomy side: Correlates of the dark triad personality traits in non-clinical adolescents. *Child Psychiatry and Human Development, 44*(5), 658–665.

Nelson, L., & Barry, C. (2005). Distinguishing features of emerging adulthood: The role of self-classification as an adult. *Journal of Adolescent Research, 20*(2), 242–262. doi:10.1177/0743558404273074

Paulhus, D. L. (2014). Toward a taxonomy of dark personalities. *Current Directions in Psychological Science, 23*(6), 421–426. doi:10.1177/0963721414547737

Paulhus, D. L., & Williams, K. M. (2002). The dark triad of personality: Narcissism, Machiavellianism, and psychopathy. *Journal of Research in Personality, 36*, 556–563. doi:10.1016/S0092-6566(02)00505-6

Rivers, S. E., Brackett, M. A., Omori, M., Sickler, C., Bertoli, M. C., & Salovey, P. (2013). Emotion skills as a protective factor for risky behaviors among college students. *Journal of College Student Development, 54*(2), 172–183. doi:10.1353/csd.2013.0012

Southard, A. C., Noser, A. E., Pollock, N. C., Mercer, S. H., & Zeigler-Hill, V. (2015). The interpersonal nature of dark personality features. *Journal of Social and Clinical Psychology, 34*(7), 555–586. doi:10.1521/jscp.2015.34.7.555

Vaillancourt, T. (2013). Students aggress against professors in reaction to receiving poor grades: An effect moderated by student narcissism and self-esteem. *Aggressive Behavior, 39*(1), 71–84. doi:10.1002/ab.21450

Zibarras, L. D., Port, R. L., & Woods, S. A. (2008). Innovation and the "dark side" of personality: Dysfunctional traits and their relation to self-reported innovative characteristics. *The Journal of Creative Behavior, 42*(3), 201–215. doi:10.1002/j.2162-6057.2008.tb01295.x

Zweig, C., & Abrams, J. (1991). *Meeting the shadow: The hidden power of the dark side of human nature*. New York, NY: TarcherPerigee.

## Author Biography

Joyce T. Mphande-Finn is an Associate Professor and Associate Program Director in the Master of Arts in Counseling at City University of Seattle. She spent 15 years practicing as a clinical mental health counselor in Montana and Oregon. She has been teaching in higher education for seven years. She holds a BA in education from the University of Malawi, a BS in business administration from Berea College, an MA in mental health counseling from the University of Montana, and an EdD in counselor education and supervision from the University of Montana.

# 3

# Person-Centered Approaches: Providing Social and Emotional Support for Adult Learners

**Ellen Carruth and Thom Field**

## Abstract

This chapter includes an overview of how instructors can establish and maintain working relationships with students and facilitate working relationships between students. The concept of person-centered learning will be explored from a theoretical standpoint, and then discussed in the context of adult learners in contemporary society. Applications in face-to-face instructional settings and online learning environments will also be examined. The benefits of person-centered learning will be listed, including more advanced critical thinking, a greater sense of personal agency and responsibility for learning, and motivation for self-directed learning. Finally, best practices for promoting person-centered learning will be offered.

## Overview

Over the past several decades, college teaching has transitioned from an instructor-focused to a student-focused learning environment. The objective of the instructor-focused learning environment is to transfer knowledge from a master to a novice. In this environment, the instructor primarily provides lectures to students with the goal of sharing information through direct transfer. In contrast, a student-focused learning environment is characterized by active student participation in the learning process and a focus on the unique phenomenological (or, idiosyncratic) understandings of students during the learning process. This new approach to learning requires the instructor to transition from the role of relaying information to facilitating experiences. This shift from modern conventional pedagogy to postmodern, constructivist andragogy is observable in learning environments. Including students in decision making related to the learning process, providing the opportunity for creativity and innovation, facilitating collaboration among peers and their instructor, and engaging students in out-of-class learning followed by prompts for self-reflection are all strategies of postmodern, constructivist andragogy. In the postmodern learning environment, the relationship between instructor/student and student/student takes on central importance.

## Review of the Literature

The person-centered approach to adult learning is influenced by several prominent figures from the field of psychology, most notably Carl Rogers and Albert Bandura. The following literature review describes the development of person-centered learning theory and the establishment of a nurturing atmosphere and its impacts on self-directed and collaborative learning and cognitive development.

## Importance of Social and Emotional Support in the Classroom

The establishment of a socially and emotionally supportive learning environment is necessary for the facilitation of learning. Over the last several decades, adult development theorists have focused on issues both inside and outside of academics that influence adult learners. For example, Bandura (1986) introduced the concept of *triadic reciprocal causation*, explaining that there are interacting forces between behavior, the environment, and personal factors, and that these forces affect learning. Additionally, Bandura described *self-efficacy* and revealed that some factors—mastery, modeling, social persuasion, and affective arousal—can influence a person's perception of his or her abilities in any given area (Bandura, 1997).

Bandura's (1986) social cognitive theory continues to influence researchers who are interested in understanding the ways in which social learning affects teacher self-efficacy (Mintzes, Marcum, Messerschmidt-Yates, & Mark, 2013) and the ways in which social learning can be integrated into virtual learning environments (Greener, 2009).

In today's classroom, whether face-to-face or virtual, the need for a sense of belonging continues, even though the nature of the learning and teaching relationship is changing (Greener, 2009). In his person-centered approach to psychotherapy, Rogers (1961) described unconditional positive regard as a central component of his theory; he believed that for a client to move toward psychological maturity, the client must experience the therapist as warm, positive, and accepting. In his later work, Rogers (1983) described a model of interpersonal relationships in teaching using his notion of "facilitative conditions of empathy, congruence, and positive regard" (p. 200). Just like with Bandura's work (1986, 1997), Rogers's work (1961, 1983) continues to influence contemporary thinkers. For example, Merriam and Caffarella (1999) equated Rogers's notion of client-centered therapy with student-centered learning. In both situations, the facilitator (either instructor or therapist) is concerned with learning that leads to personal growth. This type of learning places primary emphasis on the *process* of learning, above the *content* of what is to be learned.

## Self-directed Learning

Merriam and Caffarella (1999) claimed that being self-directed in learning is a natural part of life for adults. For this to occur, the establishment of a safe classroom environment is critical. This environment supports both the group's learning needs and the individual learner's needs, and is the ground from which self-directed learning can take place. Once the "ground" has been established, the adult learner may become actively involved in the construction of new knowledge. Self-directed learning is not passive learning; it is a process within which the learner plans, carries out, and evaluates learning (Merriam & Caffarella, 1999). Current research supports the idea of self-directed learning as an important focal area in adult education. For example, Conradie (2014) described a transferring of responsibility for the planning of learning—from the facilitator to the student—that takes place in the modern learning environment. As students assume more and more responsibility for their learning, facilitators are called to provide opportunities for collaborative learning that will serve to inform and support the construction of new knowledge.

## Collaborative Learning

In addition to the importance of a safe classroom environment for self-directed learning, a safe environment will allow students to work together as they construct knowledge. Moate and Cox (2015) stated that providing opportunities for active participation in the classroom may affect student learning and development. First, by creating a safe space, facilitators of learning are reducing the inherent power imbalance that exists in the traditional classroom. This shift away from a hierarchical structure allows students to take ownership in their learning, and to teach their peers what they've learned. Second, collaborative learning in the adult classroom may promote a deep, reflective approach to learning. Deep learning (as opposed to surface learning) occurs whenever facilitators have designed learning activities and assessments that require students to take on active roles in the creation of knowledge (Jayashree & Mitra, 2012). Students become more accountable for their learning whenever provided opportunities for collaboration, and collaboration encourages conceptualization and problem solving.

## Integration into the Student Experience

When construction of knowledge is placed centrally in the classroom, students are afforded the opportunity to struggle with their peers. Within the group, the learner is tasked with building upon prior knowledge, constructing shared meaning, and defending his or her beliefs. Constructivist thinkers have espoused the cognitive benefits of social learning for decades (Piaget, 1976), and current thinkers continue to explore the cognitive benefits of learning in collaboration. For example, Furr and Carroll (2003) described the benefits of collaborative or experiential learning for counselors in training, noting that experiential activities swayed cognitive development. More recently, researchers have discovered that argumentation and problem solving as collaborative skills are particularly important for higher-level cognitive development in online learning environments (Shukor, Tasir, Van der Meijden, & Harun, 2014). Social and emotional support in the classroom benefits students' cognitive development, provides opportunities for collaboration and self-directed learning, and promotes a sense of belonging, all of which will affect student success.

## Proven Practices, Examples, and Results

In 1968, Paulo Freire wrote a famous text on pedagogy entitled, *Pedagogy of the Oppressed.* Freire (1968) identified several problematic components of formal educational practices such as lectures. In modernist classrooms, student learning is understood to occur when the instructor directly transfers knowledge to the student. Freire (1968) called this the banking model of education. In this model, the institution of learning is the conceptual equivalent of a bank, and the instructor is the conceptual equivalent of a cash machine. In other words, the student need only approach the institution and pay for knowledge, for it to be dispersed proportionately.

Freire (1968) argued that such a conceptualization of education was outdated and inconsistent with how learning occurs. Learning is the product of student engagement with content, and can differ between students. In a classroom setting, student learning will differ within classrooms and between classrooms *even when the same content is being taught.* The postmodern classroom is founded on the principle of constructivism, which allows students to engage with material and form their own conclusions. Lectures, while useful, must be paired with experiential exercises such as discussions, role playing, and other creative activities to foster student engagement in the learning process. In other words, the banking model does not resonate with how learning occurs. If a student approaches an institution and pays for knowledge, different students will receive not only different amounts but also different currencies and different understandings of what their payout means!

So how do we motivate students to become self-directed learners? The person-centered approach to education can be helpful in this regard. Person-centered approaches to instruction in face-to-face classrooms and online classrooms are now reviewed.

## Face-to-Face Classrooms

The layout of the classroom is important in the facilitation of self-directed learning. Many classrooms feature all of the chairs facing front, for students to face the lecturer to provide the lesson. In person-centered classrooms, the room is set up to facilitate either large group or small group discussions, with students facing others and their instructor. For large group discussions, the most helpful table and chair configurations include variations of circles and semicircles. The "round" nature of seating provides students with more opportunity to interact. For small group discussions, the room could be divided into "pods," for pairs of students to sit facing each other (at least four students to a table) at various placements around the room. This structure again facilitates student dialogue and discussion.

Once the room has been arranged properly, the facilitator must seek to enhance student motivation toward self-direction. Following the person-centered model, the principles of congruence, unconditional positive regard, and accurate empathic understanding must be demonstrated by the facilitator for self-directed learning to occur.

Congruence (or genuineness) in the classroom is also known as authenticity. When the facilitator is congruent, it provides students with a model for how to be authentic with themselves and approach the material without a need to impress the facilitator or other students. It also enhances motivation by strengthening the relationship between the facilitator and the student. Congruence is demonstrated when the facilitator feels a certain emotion, and the facilitator voices the emotion out loud when appropriate. When the facilitator expresses emotions at appropriate times, they appear more human and "real" to students. In return, students feel more connected with their facilitator. Likewise, instructors appear more approachable when they acknowledge mistakes rather than appearing defensive. Another example includes acknowledging the lack of knowledge when feeling stumped by a student question, rather than pretending to know and promising to investigate further outside of class (or asking the student to research the question and bring an answer to class). This modeling establishes trust and safety, as students learn that it is acceptable to not know everything.

Unconditional positive regard in the classroom occurs when the facilitator expresses an appreciation ("prizing") of students, regardless of the quality of their work or their behavior. When students feel respected and valued, they contribute more to the classroom and their learning experience. Yet, unconditional positive regard is not an easy concept to apply in classrooms. For example, it is not uncommon for students to arrive late to class, to turn in assignments late or incomplete, or to turn in substandard work. In such cases, Rogers (1983) discussed the need for the facilitator to communicate acceptance and to value the person while also encouraging him or her to change problematic behavior. This dialectic allows the facilitator to express appreciation for the student (e.g., "I'm glad you made it to class; your presence in here is valued"), while also identifying problematic behavior that needs to change ("it would help your classmates if you could arrive on time because we miss your valued input and thoughts on this topic").

When facilitators must confront students, it is suggested that the best setting for this is a one-on-one meeting outside of class, so the student does not feel shamed in front of his or her peers. Likewise, the facilitator's tone during this meeting should be kind, and demonstrate a genuine concern and care for the student. The best outcome of such a meeting is for the student to feel respected and valued. When facilitators approach meetings in this manner, students feel that they are "worth" enough for their instructor to provide this feedback to them. This approach enhances trust and safety, which increases the student's comfort and engagement in the learning environment and provides the conditions for self-directed learning to occur.

Accurate empathic understanding is again a challenging skill to demonstrate in classroom settings. When the facilitator understands the student at a deep level, it leads to deep reflections on the student's experience, which can motivate self-directed learning. As an example, imagine a highly self-directed student who asks multiple questions about the same topic during the same class session. After a while, these questions keep the class stuck on the same concept during the lecture, when the class needs to move on. The facilitator has noticed over the course of several class sessions that the student asks questions perpetually when feeling anxious about the content. The facilitator intuitively senses that the student may fear "falling behind" and being unable to catch up. Meeting with the student at the break, the facilitator wonders if the student indeed feels this way, and asks how best to help. The student appreciates the concern. After problem solving, the student is willing to write down questions about content that he or she still does not understand, after asking a question in class, to share with the facilitator at the next break. Following this meeting, this self-directed student remains engaged in class, since his or her skill in asking questions has been reinforced by the instructor (at appropriate times), and the student knows the questions will be answered eventually.

## Online Classrooms

The concepts of congruence, unconditional positive regard, and genuineness can be used by facilitators of online courses. Online learning often contains both synchronous (real-time) and asynchronous (time-lag) communication. Differing student issues can arise depending on the communication type. Synchronous communication most often occurs with video interface programs that allow users to see each other and talk in real time. These video meetings are subject to similar issues as face-to-face communication. For example, acknowledging mistakes and lack of knowledge (congruence) and demonstrating unconditional positive regard and accurate empathic understanding are important when communicating in real time. However, asynchronous communication requires a different skill set, as the facilitator and learners communicate via written means rather than face-to-face dialogue.

One of the most-used communication platforms for asynchronous communication is the discussion board, where learners post responses to question prompts and to other students' posts about the topic being discussed. Facilitators of discussion boards must also learn to reinforce self-redirected learning by fostering safety and trust. For example, students should know that they will feel respected and valued, regardless of their behaviors or posted content.

Sometimes student disputes will arise in a discussion board exercise. The facilitator's job is to encourage students to work through the dispute using synchronous communication, and to attend the meeting, acting as a mediator if needed. The facilitator should demonstrate respect for each student, and approach the conflict as an opportunity for growth. Allowing students to work through conflicts using synchronous communication encourages self-directed learning, and the facilitator's presence as a potential mediator provides the necessary safety for learners to engage in the conflict-resolution exercise.

## Lessons Learned

Student motivation toward self-directed learning is greatly enhanced by collaboration; this is particularly true for facilitator-learner relationships. One method of enhancing collaboration for both face-to-face and online classrooms is to allot one class period per course for students to select the course topic to be explored that meets their interests. While this requires additional work by the facilitator, it encourages self-direction and often results in students taking ownership of their learning.

## Face-to-Face Classrooms

One of the benefits to face-to-face classrooms is the ability for students to engage in group work or project-based learning. Group work enhances self-directed learning by providing opportunities for direct task engagement through learners working together on a project with less input from the facilitator than occurs during direct instruction, such as lectures. During group work, students also learn the critical skill of how to work in teams to accomplish a significant task. Since most work environments require teamwork, learning this skill in the classroom setting can be beneficial as a training exercise.

Group work is most successful when the facilitator structures the activity in a way that not only identifies the task to be completed but also provides expectations for team member interactions. Providing guidelines on team member interactions is important because students often have negative experiences with group work, from the lack of structure provided. Identifying expectations for how to collaborate in groups provides learners with the trust that their peers will be similarly invested in the learning task. This commitment provides learners with enough confidence to take the risk of engaging fully in the team process, by trusting one another with the delegation of tasks. Without trust, the group task will be less successful due to unequal task delegating, resulting in low student engagement in the learning process by at least one member of the group.

## Online Classrooms

Collaboration in online environments is often more challenging to facilitate, though is possible through the use of both synchronous and asynchronous communication. Group work and project-based learning can still occur if students are required to communicate as a team through online mediums. Online collaboration is perhaps most easily facilitated through online web-based synchronous meetings. Asynchronous communication does not lend itself easily to collaborative exercises, though can still occur if students are provided with guidelines for teamwork and agree to communicate through mediums such as discussion boards and e-mail. As with face-to-face discussions, parameters and guidelines for group member interactions and collaboration can be useful to establish safety and trust in the group process. This enhances self-directed learning, as students collaboratively participate in direct task engagement with their instructor either absent or in a supportive role.

## Conclusion

Person-centered approaches to education aim to help learners discover and value themselves as people beyond the mere learning of knowledge and skills. Whether in a face-to-face classroom or an online learning environment, facilitators of learning can establish a socially and emotionally supportive learning environment with the use of congruence, unconditional positive regard, and genuineness. These characteristics set the stage for facilitators of learning to encourage collaboration and self-directed learning, which are critical in the workforce.

# References

Bandura, A. (1986). *Social foundations of thought and action*. Englewood Cliffs, NJ: Prentice-Hall.

Bandura, A. (1997). *Self-efficacy: The exercise of control*. New York, NY: W. H. Freeman and Company.

Conradie, P. W. (2014). Supporting self-directed learning by connectivism and personal learning environments. *International Journal of Information and Education Technology, 4*(3), 254-259. doi: 10.7763/ IJIET.2014.V8

Freire, P. (1968). *Pedagogy of the oppressed*. New York, NY: Continuum.

Furr, S. R., & Carroll, J. J. (2003). Critical incidents in student counselor development. *Journal of Counseling and Development, 81*(4), 483–489. doi:10.1002/j.1556-6678.2003.tb00275.x

Greener, S. (2009). E-modeling: Helping learners to develop sound e-learning behaviors. *Electronic Journal of e-Learning, 7*(3), 265–272.

Jayashree, P., & Mitra, S. (2012). Facilitating a deep approach to learning: An innovative case assessment technique. *Journal of Management and Organization, 18*(4), 555–572.

Merriam, S., & Caffarella, R. S. (1999). *Learning in adulthood: A comprehensive guide* (2nd ed.). San Francisco, CA: Jossey-Bass Publishers.

Mintzes, J. J., Marcum, B., Messerschmidt-Yates, C., & Mark, A. (2013). Enhancing self-efficacy in elementary science teaching with professional learning communities. *Journal of Science Teacher Education, 24*(7), 1201–1218. doi:10.1007/s10972-012-9320-1

Moate, R. M., & Cox, J. A. (2015). Learner-centered pedagogy: Considerations for applications in a didactic course. *The Professional Counselor, 5*(3), 379–389.

Palmer, P. J. (1998). *The courage to teach: Exploring the inner landscape of a teacher's life.* New York, NY: John Wiley and Sons.

Piaget, J. P. (1976). *The child and reality: Problems of genetic psychology.* New York, NY: Penguin Books.

Rogers, C. R. (1961). *On becoming a person: A therapist's view of psychotherapy.* Boston, MA: Houghton Mifflin.

Rogers, C. R. (1980). *A way of being.* New York, NY: Houghton Mifflin Company.

Rogers, C. R. (1983). *Freedom to learn for the 80's.* Columbus, OH: Merrill Publishing.

Shukor, N. A., Tasir, Z., Van der Meijden, H., & Harun, J. (2014). Exploring students' knowledge construction strategies in computer-supported collaborative learning discussions using sequential analysis. *Educational Technology and Society, 17*(4), 216–228.

Yammamoto, K. K., Stodden, R. A., & Folk, E. D. R. (2014). Inclusive postsecondary education: Reimagining the transition trajectories of vocational rehabilitation clients with intellectual disabilities. *Journal of Vocational Rehabilitation, 40*(1), 59–71. doi:10.3233/JVR-130662

## Author Biographies

Ellen K. Carruth is a Professor and an Academic Program Director in the Master of Arts in Counseling program at City University of Seattle. Dr. Carruth uses her experiences as a clinician to inform her practice as an instructor and her current research agenda. She has developed a unique perspective on the importance of action research for counselors, and her research interests now include examining the relationship between action research and social justice in counselor education. Dr. Carruth has spent her career helping others and has over fifteen years of experience working in human services and community mental health.

Thom Field is an Associate Professor and Associate Program Director in the Master of Arts in Counseling program at City University of Seattle. Dr. Field has ten years of counseling experience with over a thousand clients in a variety of settings, including inpatient psychiatric units, community mental health centers, outpatient private practice, and schools. He received his PhD in counseling and supervision from James Madison University in Virginia. His dissertation on implementing dialectical behavior therapy for adolescents at an inpatient psychiatric unit was awarded the 2013 Dissertation Research Award by the American Mental Health Counselors Association (AMHCA) Foundation.

# 4

# Supporting Learners in the Virtual Classroom through Instructor Presence

**Erin Noseworthy and Whitney Boswell**

## Abstract

The increase in online education in higher education institutions necessitates a shift in the practice of instruction. While teaching online is different from teaching face-to-face classes, the instructor role is still of vital importance. This chapter shares how instructors demonstrate presence before, throughout, and after an online course based on best practice and research.

## Overview

Online education continues to grow worldwide, increasing the need for instructors to embrace this new instructional modality (Allen & Seaman,

2015). The growing demand for online courses requires the development of instructors in best practices for online instruction. A key element of effective online instruction is instructor presence. Instructor presence is a combination of instructional design, facilitation of discourse, and direct instruction (Anderson, Rourke, Garrison, & Archer, 2001). The following chapter presents research, which supports the importance of the instructor's online presence and strategies for developing one's teaching presence in online courses.

## Review of the Literature

The Babson Survey Research Group (Allen & Seaman, 2015) reported that in 2013 over 70.7 percent of active degree-granting institutions offered some form of distance learning to over 2.25 million learners. These numbers have steadily increased since the advent of distance education as more learners seek flexible pathways to earning a degree. While the opinions of academic leadership on the effectiveness of online instruction are progressively improving, instructor acceptance of this modality has decreased since 2007 (Allen & Seaman, 2015).

Fish and Gill (2009) asserted that instructors' perceptions of online learning correlate to their experiences teaching online; those with less experience had more negative perceptions of online instruction, while those with more experience were more likely to believe that online instruction was equal in quality to traditional classroom instruction. The authors stated that "quality online instruction is dependent upon faculty not subscribing to the myths of online learning" (Fish & Gill, 2009, p. 2) that may color their perceptions.

Li and Akins (2005) discussed several myths about online learning, including the concerns that it will make the teacher redundant, promote isolation and lack of community, and be limited to content learning. However, research has shown the opposite to be true. Courses with high learner and instructor satisfaction scores promote interaction between learner, instructor, and content (Bolliger & Wasilik, 2009). Furthermore, instructor presence has been shown to be the catalyst for social presence within online courses and is essential to creating opportunities for interaction within an online class (Sheridan & Kelly, 2010).

Anderson et al. (2001) defined instructor presence as "the design, facilitation, and direction of cognitive and social processes for the realization of personally meaningful and educationally worthwhile learning outcomes" (p. 5). The authors asserted that there are three components to teaching presence: design and organization, facilitating discourse, and direct instruction. Course design and organization that bolsters instructor presence is consistent and easy to navigate, has clear expectations, delivers content and activities which scaffold and support goals, and provides opportunities to practice and interact with the instructor and peers. How instructors establish and maintain a community of inquiry is reflective of their skills in facilitating discourse. The instructor is responsible for creating a safe environment for discourse, which is supportive of various points of view and enables each learner the opportunity to participate. Direct instruction encompasses the techniques used by instructors to provide learning leadership by directing class attention and diagnosing misconceptions. Instructors may provide direct instruction by presenting content, sharing personal experiences, directing specific questions at learners or groups of learners, confirming understanding, and providing specific feedback to learners on assessments.

## Proven Practices, Examples, and Results

Instructor presence in online courses begins before the start, continues during the facilitation, and carries on beyond the conclusion of the course. The following section explores these areas of instructor presence in online courses.

## Build Instructor Presence into the Course from the Start

Being present in an online course starts before learners even log in to class. Garrison, Anderson, and Archer (1999) asserted that cognitive presence and social presence are founded on thoughtful course design. Course design is also a pillar of instructor presence (Anderson et al., 2001). Creating strong instructor presence begins with the elements the instructor builds into a course's design; these elements humanize the instructor, support learning activities, and provide opportunities for interaction and collaboration.

**Build an online persona.** Learners may feel isolated or disconnected from instructors in online courses (Song, Singleton, Hill, & Koh, 2004). Instructors can help combat feelings of isolation by creating opportunities for learners to connect with and know them on a more personal level. Personal connections help establish trust within the class, which is an essential component of a healthy learning community (Garrison et al., 1999). Instructors might begin by sharing biographic information and experiences that are relevant to the course and reflective of their interests within and beyond the classroom. Instructors can share a biography along with contact and communication preferences within the course. Relevant information can be reinforced in a welcome announcement or an introductory class discussion.

When creating course communications, instructors should consider writing strategies that capture their unique personalities and speech patterns as a means of humanizing themselves that will help build their presence in the course (Garrison et al., 1999). Emoticons and popular acronyms play a role in social presence and can compensate for missing expressions and voice inflections (Cobb, 2009). However, keep in mind that learners may not be native speakers and will likely have other cultural differences, so the instructor must balance social communication strategies with thoughtful, considerate, and clear writing.

Instructors may choose to create video or audio course communications. Research has shown that thoughtfully incorporating rich media—such as podcast, video, and images—into online courses can increase learner engagement, satisfaction, and feelings of connectedness (Bolliger, Supanakorn, & Boggs, 2010; Griffiths & Graham, 2009). To be effective, incorporated media must be accessible to all learners (clear, concise, and transcribed) and should not introduce technological barriers (large downloads or proprietary software, for example).

**Make expectations clear.** Learners who participated in a survey on instructor presence in online courses at two large universities indicated that making course requirements clear had the greatest impact (Sheridan & Kelly, 2010). To make course requirements clear, instructors need to define their expectations. What is the instructor's policy on attendance, participation in activities, or "learner presence" within the course? Will the instructor accept late assignments? What communication methods should the learner use for questions or personal concerns? And when should the learner expect to hear back from the instructor?

Online courses present a great opportunity for inclusive learning where all learners get the opportunity to share their experiences with the class. However, online environments can also enable anonymity that can manifest itself in trolling or other negative behaviors that can be damaging to a learning community (Shea & Shea, 1994).

Instructors are responsible for setting the guidelines for engagement in their courses and ensuring a safe, respectful, and supportive environment for all learners. Instructors should define their course policies and share them with learners in the virtual classroom. Instructors might prompt learners to review policies before the class starts; perhaps even quiz learners on key points as part of participation requirements in the first week of class. Furthermore, instructors should model the behaviors they expect of learners in class and provide additional examples to clarify expectations.

**Support learners with effective course design.** Instructors can also make their presence known through the design of the course and the content, activities, and assessments therein. While variety in course content can help keep learners stay engaged, consistency in course navigation and organization will reduce cognitive load related to the technology used to deliver the course (Swan, 2003). Instructors should develop a consistent rhythm for the course learning units (whether weekly, thematic, or something other), orient learners to the course design approach, and stick to it. If the institution has a master organizational strategy, instructors should follow it as learners will likely be familiar with this structure.

Build in support for learners within each learning unit. Moss and Brookhart (2010) asserted that "once students understand where they are headed, they are more likely to feel that they can be successful, can actually reach the goal" (p. 30). Make learning goals transparent to learners by outlining how content, activities, and assessments align to course or program learning outcomes. Provide a learning unit checklist to empower learners to take control of time management and learning.

Content within the course units should be chunked into manageable portions that work within the limitations of the learners' working memory (Mayer, 2001). Build opportunities for learners to apply what they have learned and receive feedback on their understanding through formative assessment and collaboration or discussion with the instructor and peers.

The result of effective course design is a supportive, personalized learning environment that sets up learners and instructors for success. Instructors who prepare courses early can welcome learners to class a few days before it starts. Instructors should give learners a few pointers for getting started in a welcome message, such as visiting every page listed on the course navigation, readings to get started on, discussions to prepare for, and where to find help. This way, learners can get to know the instructor from all that is built into the course design before the course gets under way and the instructor can focus on facilitating learning after the course begins.

## Enjoy Connection to Learners throughout the Course

Many opportunities for increasing instructor presence exist during the course when the instructor has the attention of the learners. Because of transactional distance in online courses, instructor presence can be difficult; instructors may miss the immediacy behaviors of traditional face-to-face courses. The following are ways to increase instructor presence in the online classroom:

**Communication.** Communication from the instructor was found to be one of the highest contributors to learner satisfaction in courses (Sheridan & Kelly, 2010). Instructors reported that the more they made themselves available, responded quickly, and monitored learner engagement in the beginning weeks of the course, the less work they had to do later as it set the tone for the course (Casey & Kroth, 2013). In the same study, every single learner responded that "ongoing and consistent communication" (p. 107) was important to them. Another study found that learners highly appreciated when instructors made them feel like they were the priority, were interested in the learner's success, and came across as human (Hodges & McGuinness, 2014). Communication in an online course entails many components, including instructor social presence and immediacy behaviors, modeling appropriate behaviors, using media, and timely responses.

Traditional classrooms report higher learner motivation, satisfaction, and outcome achievement as a direct result of teacher immediacy behaviors, and online courses are following that trend (Schutt, Allen, & Laumakis, 2009). Immediacy behaviors refer to "actions that simultaneously communicate warmth, involvement, psychological closeness, [and] availability for communication" (Littlejohn & Foss, 2009, p. 501). These behaviors in a course context include using gestures, addressing learners by their first names, soliciting viewpoints or opinions, praising learners' comments, showing emotion, and using inclusive language ("we," "us"). Other examples include using personal stories from experience and getting into discussions based on learner questions that were not a part of the instructional plan (Schutt, Allen, & Laumakis, 2009).

Immediacy behaviors look different online and depend on the communication media, with additional behaviors available via audio and video. Synchronous communication tools are one way to communicate with students; use of a synchronous tool may help lessen the isolation some students may feel online.

E-mails from learners are like a raised hand in the traditional classroom, and learners expect an immediate response from instructors. Instructors should clearly communicate their communication policy. As part of this policy, instructors can create a question discussion forum that allows learners to post questions so that all learners can benefit from answers. This will reduce e-mail communications and the need to answer the same question repeatedly.

**Discussion boards.** An important part of instructor presence in online courses is facilitating discourse, which in many courses occurs on discussion boards (Mandernach, Gonzales, & Garrett, 2006). Discussion boards allow learners to interact with classmates and their instructor, which can increase learning if the content is relevant and the instructor has made efforts to help learners become comfortable in online discussions (Shea & Bidjerano, 2009).

Instructors should consistently participate in discussion boards by sharing their expertise and personal experience. They should also keep the discussions focused on learning goals by asking engaging questions and modeling desired behaviors. Swan and Shih (2005) found that in discussion boards with higher social presence, learners reported significant learning from their peers and instructor.

**Feedback.** Varnhagen, Wilson, Krupa, Kasprzak, and Hunting (2005) found that one of the major complaints by learners in many areas of online course evaluations was a lack of quality instructor feedback. Learners want confirmation that submitted work is on track. Learner frustration comes from insufficient in-depth feedback. Another study also found that learners wanted more detailed feedback, the type of feedback that identified specific issues to inform work on future assignments (Moore & Wallace, 2012).

There are a variety of ways to give feedback to students online. Written assignments lend themselves to in-text annotation, which allows for detailed feedback in context. LMS testing tools often provide the option to give students immediate feedback, which is valuable for formative assessment. Video or audio feedback is another option made possible in many cases. Moore and Wallace (2012) found that instructors enjoyed giving audio feedback because it was quicker to give detailed feedback than in writing. Borup, West, and Thomas (2015) found that video feedback tended to be longer and more supportive while text-based feedback was more specific and organized. Whatever approach the instructor may choose, the key is to provide detailed feedback that students can use to deepen their understanding and improve work (Sull, 2010). Give praise where it is due to motivate students to continue to apply themselves.

**Use available tools.** Many learning management systems (LMS) have built-in tools to support instructor presence. A few of the tools in Blackboard (an LMS) are surveys and announcements. Whatever the institution's LMS is, instructors should seek out the tools that are available and use them where appropriate.

Many learners believe that end-of-course evaluations are of no benefit to them, possibly because they never see the direct benefits. This could be one reason end-of-course evaluations often get low response rates. Crews and Curtis (2011) suggested that gathering in-course formative feedback will increase response rates in the end-of-course evaluations and demonstrate to learners that the instructor is engaged in the course. One of the ways to collect in-course formative feedback is through a midterm survey. Instructors can make changes or adjust courses during the term based on learner feedback.

A simple way to increase instructor presence in an online course is to use the Announcements tool. Sheridan and Kelly (2010) pointed out that part of instructor presence is posting regularly and being visible as the instructor. Posting announcements that are e-mailed to learners can do at least three things. First, it gives the learner an opportunity outside of the class to digest course content. Second, it brings the learner into the course more often. These e-mails improve learning as the more times students engage with content, the more likely they are to retain it (Roediger & Pyc, 2012). Finally, announcements show the learners that the instructor is involved in the course.

There are many ways to use announcements. At the start of the week, summarize the content to be learned, assessments to complete, or discussions to participate in. Near the end of the week, summarize content or clarify anything misunderstood or unclear. Consider using humor, images, or a personal story to break up stressful weeks and make messages more memorable. Avoid excessively long announcements and posting too often, as learners may be overwhelmed. Learners also benefit from reminders of upcoming deadlines.

**Let learners leave an imprint.** The learner's experience can influence the instructor's practice. Instructors should take time throughout the course to reflect on what's working well and what could be improved. Ko and Rossen (2010) recommended keeping a course journal with notes on the course and ideas for future improvements. At the end of the course, the journal notes can be combined with feedback from learners' end-of course evaluations to create a plan for course and instructional improvements.

## Lessons Learned, Tips for Success, and Recommendations

There are many ways to infuse instructor presence into online courses; so many, that it can be a little overwhelming. However, the methods presented in this chapter do not have to be implemented all at once. Even small efforts can make a big impact. To get started, consider the following strategies:

- **Before:** The instructors can work on developing their online persona that will help build social presence and connection with learners. For example, instructors might share a photograph along with personal experience and enthusiasm for the field of study in an instructor bio.
- **During:** Instructors should focus on learner support through prompt and meaningful feedback in discussions, on assignments, and through e-mail. Communications should acknowledge learners' experiences and interests and provide individualized feedback to support their unique learning goals.
- **After:** End-of-course evaluation feedback should be reviewed by the instructor so that necessary changes can be made to the course before it is taught again. Instructors can let learners in the

revised course know how the end-of-course feedback was used to improve the current course as a way to encourage learner feedback when the time comes.

With each new teaching experience, an instructor can incorporate another strategy to further develop teaching presence in online courses. Increased teaching presence will boost learner satisfaction and learning within online courses.

## Conclusion

Research shows that instructor presence plays a large role in the effectiveness of the online classroom. Instructor presence can be incorporated in a variety of ways. The instructor's presence should be visible to learners in the design of the course, its facilitation, and learners' direct interactions with the instructor. Hopefully, this chapter has provided accessible strategies for incorporating instructor presence in online courses.

## References

Allen, I., & Seaman, J. (2015). Grade level: Tracking online education in the United States. Babson Survey Research Group. Retrieved from http://www.onlinelearningsurvey.com/reports/gradelevel.pdf

Anderson, T., Rourke, L., Garrison, D. R., & Archer, W. (2001). Assessing teacher presence in a computer conferencing context. *Journal of Asynchronous Learning Networks, 5*(2). Retrieved from http://cde.athabascau.ca/coi_site/documents/Anderson_Rourke_Garrison_Archer_Teaching_Presence.pdf

Bolliger, D. U., Supanakorn, S., & Boggs, C. (2010). Impact of podcasting on student motivation in the online learning environment. *Computers & Education, 55*(2), 714–722.

Bolliger, D. U., & Wasilik, O. (2009). Factors influencing faculty satisfaction with online teaching and learning in higher education. *Distance Education, 30*(1), 103–116.

Borup, J., West, R. E., & Thomas, R. (2015). The impact of text versus video communication on instructor feedback in blended courses. *Educational Technology Research and Development, 63*(2), 161.

Casey, R. L., & Kroth, M. (2013). Learning to develop presence online: Experienced faculty perspectives. *Journal of Adult Education, 42*(2), 104–110.

Cobb, S. C. (2009). Social presence and online learning: A current view from a research perspective. *Journal of Interactive Online Learning, 8*(3), 241–254.

Crews, T. B., & Curtis, D. F. (2011). Online course evaluations: Faculty perspective and strategies for improved response rates. *Assessment & Evaluation in Higher Education, 36*(7), 865–878. doi:10.1080/02602938.2010.493970

Fish, W. W., & Gill, P. B. (2009). Perceptions of online instruction. *Online Submission, 8*(1). Retrieved from http://files.eric.ed.gov/fulltext/ED503903.pdf

Garrison, D. R., Anderson, T., & Archer, W. (1999). Critical inquiry in a text-based environment: Computer conferencing in higher education. *The Internet and Higher Education, 2*(2), 87–105.

Griffiths, M. E., & Graham, C. R. (2009). Using asynchronous video in online classes: Results from a pilot study. *International Journal of Instructional Technology and Distance Learning, 6*(3). Retrieved from http://www.itdl.org/journal/mar_09/article06.htm

Hodges, A. L., & McGuinness, T. (2014). Improving communication in distance-accessible advanced practice nursing courses via instructor presence. *Journal of Nursing Education, 53*(8), 479–482.

Ko, S., & Rossen, S. (2010). *Teaching online: A practical guide*. New York, NY: Routledge.

Li, Q., & Akins, M. (2004). Sixteen myths about online teaching and learning in higher education: Don't believe everything you hear. *TechTrends, 49*(4), 51–60.

Littlejohn, S. W., & Foss, K. A. (2009). *Encyclopedia of communication theory*. Los Angeles, CA: Sage.

Mayer, R. E. (2001). *Multimedia learning*. Cambridge, United Kingdom: Cambridge University Press.

Mandernach, B. J., Gonzales, R. M., & Garrett, A. L. (2006). An examination of online instructor presence via threaded discussion participation. *Journal of Online Learning and Teaching, 2*(4), 248–260.

Moore, C., & Wallace, I. P. H. (2012). Personalizing feedback for feed-forward opportunities utilizing audio feedback technologies for online students. *International Journal of e-Education, e-Business, e-Management, and e-Learning, 2*(1), 6–10.

Moss, C. M., & Brookhart, S. M. (2010). *Advancing formative assessment in every classroom: A guide for instructional leaders*. Alexandria, VA: Association for Supervision and Curriculum Development.

Roediger, H. L., & Pyc, M. A. (2012). Inexpensive techniques to improve education: Applying cognitive psychology to enhance educational practice. *Journal of Applied Research in Memory and Cognition, 1*(4), 242–248.

Schutt, M., Allen, B. S., & Laumakis, M. A. (2009). The effects of instructor immediacy behaviors in online learning environments. *Quarterly Review of Distance Education, 10*(2), 135–148.

Shea, P., & Bidjerano, T. (2009). Community of inquiry as a theoretical framework to foster "epistemic engagement" and "cognitive presence" in online education. *Computers & Education, 52*(3), 543–553.

Shea, V., & Shea, C. (1994). *Netiquette.* Albion Books. Retrieved from http://www.albion.com/netiquette/book/

Sheridan, K., & Kelly, M. A. (2010). The indicators of instructor presence that are important to students in online courses. *Journal of Online Learning and Teaching, 6*(4), 767.

Song, L., Singleton, E. S., Hill, J. R., & Koh, M. H. (2004). Improving online learning: Student perceptions of useful and challenging characteristics. *The Internet and Higher Education, 7*(1), 59–70.

Sull, E. C. (2010). Secrets of the successful online instructor revealed. *Distance Learning, 7*(4), 98–102.

Swan, K. (2003). Learning effectiveness: What the research tells us. In J. Bourne & J. Moore (Eds.), *Elements of quality online education, practice and direction* (pp. 13–45). Needham, MA: Sloan Center for Online Education.

Swan, K., & Shih, L. F. (2005). On the nature and development of social presence in online course discussions. *Online Learning Journal, 9*(3), 115–136.

Varnhagen, S., Wilson, D., Krupa, E., Kasprzak, S., & Hunting, V. (2005). Comparison of student experiences with different online graduate courses in health promotion. *Canadian Journal of Learning and Technology, 31*(1). Retrieved from https://ejournals.library.ualberta.ca/index.php/cjlt/article/view/26509/19691

# Author Biographies

Erin Noseworthy is the Director of eLearning at City University of Seattle (CityU). She oversees the administration of Blackboard, the institution's learning management system, and advises faculty on best practices in instructional design and learning technologies. She has taught educational technology courses for CityU and the University of Tennessee at Chattanooga, in addition to several faculty development courses and seminars on instructional technology. She holds a BS in education from Pennsylvania State University, an MA in instructional technology from the University of Colorado, and is working on her EdD in learning and leadership at the University of Tennessee.

Whitney Boswell is the eLearning Project Coordinator at City University of Seattle. She coordinates technology projects, delivers seminars and webinars on using technology in the online classroom, and advises faculty on best practices in instructional design and learning technologies. She has experience working as an instructional designer in secondary and higher education and in the business sector. She holds a BS in education and communication from Utah Valley University and is currently working on her MEd in adult learning at City University of Seattle.

# 5

# Engaging the Reflexive Self: The Role of Reflective Practice for Supporting Professional Identity Development in Graduate Students

**Toupey Luft and Robert Roughley**

## Abstract

Reflective practice can enhance the professional identity development (PID) of graduate students. Struggling with one's self-awareness and related academic assignments are part of a necessary process for ensuring student success as developing professionals. Yet, there are many salient barriers that can interfere with graduate students undertaking this process. Graduate students need to have the opportunity to engage in a reflective process, but they also require emotional safety to take the risks required. Appropriate faculty involvement and modeling of desired qualities is also fundamental. Strategies are suggested to address student needs.

## Overview

If professionals do not take the time to reflect upon significant moments in development, did learning take place? The reflective practices engaged in throughout the graduate career are consistent with Bolton's (2014) definition: "an in-depth review of events, either alone—say, in a journal—or with critical support with a supervisor or group" (p. 7). These practices include reflective journal assignments, papers that outline personal understanding and cultural contexts, and reviews of developing theoretical models and case conceptualization ideas with the feedback of peers and supervisors.

Bolton (2014) asserted that reflective practice, done well, can lead to a greater understanding of events and integration of theoretical knowledge with professional practice. However, these practices ask a great deal of the developing professional as part of the aim is to question previously held assumptions about oneself and to develop previously underdeveloped skills. Educators often assume that individuals know how to reflect and have the necessary self-awareness to do so, but this assumption can be problematic. Further, if some sense of group safety is not embedded into the process, reflection can feel too risky to students, and they experience resistance and can emotionally distance themselves from the learning experience (Quiros, Kay, & Montijo, 2012). The risk required in engaging in professional development reflection coupled with the lack of clear guidelines for a safe environment will not lead professionals-in-training toward success. Instead, these practices may result in students being stalled in their professional development or not engaging with the material. The outcome of this may be that a student lacks the essential bedrock for making ethical decisions that are an integral part of their professional development (Bolton, 2014).

## Literature Review

Researchers have studied how reflective practice affects students' professional identity development in the fields of medicine (Goldie, 2012; Sharpless, Baldwin, Cook, Kofman, Morley-Fletcher, Slotkin, & Wald, 2015), nursing (Bulman & Schutz, 2013), teacher education (Roffey-Barentsen & Malthouse, 2013; West, 2012), and social work (Wilson, 2013). Counsellor educators have analyzed PID's link to reflective practices, citing the importance of transformative experiences for counsellor development (Shuler & Keller-Dupree, 2015), the need for reflective learning within a counsellor training curricula (Tobin, Willow, Bastow, & Ratkowski, 2009), and the need for reflective practice to encourage self-awareness and competent practice (Rosin, 2015). Counsellor education in Canada is often underrepresented in the literature, but foundational work by Collins, Arthur, and Wong-Wylie (2010) has drawn scholar-practitioners' attention to the utility of reflective applications for training counsellors in multicultural competencies and how certain activities in graduate school can contribute to one's development as a counsellor (Chang, 2011).

Some educators have written about the necessity of including emotional growth and awareness as part of professional training programs (Pompeo & Levitt, 2014). Educators also acknowledge that encouraging emotional growth without ethical guidelines and emotional safety can be detrimental to students. In their observations about teachers-in-training, Ronfeldt and Grossman (2008) indicated that these students often felt insecure, lonely, and disillusioned about their profession before even finishing their field experiences and linked this to poor student retention. They proposed that students in certain professional fields—including teaching, the clergy, and psychology—be given opportunities to practice their skills in facilitative environments with structured feedback from both peers and instructors (Ronfeldt & Grossman, 2008).

Instructors who teach reflection must model genuineness, reflexivity, and emotional awareness in their teaching and professional practice (Matteson, Taylor, Valle, Fehr, Jacob, & Jones, 2011; Ronfeldt & Grossman, 2008). Quiros et al. (2012) highlighted the necessity of students, instructors, and field supervisors co-creating a sense of emotional safety so that students may learn the nuances of their chosen professions. Matteson et al. (2011) indicated that faculty must be willing to model the qualities they are attempting to draw out in students to enhance student retention. Lastly,

Cox, Zhu, Lynch, and Adams (2012) highlighted that mentors (who may or may not be faculty or supervisors) can provide emotional support to graduate students who are going through professional training programs and improve retention.

Educators can build safety into reflective practices with the intention to support students in making connections in the cognitive, affective, and behavioral domains, both inside and outside the classroom learning experience.

## Integration into the Student Experience

One constant remains within the scholarship of teaching and learning—the fundamental need for learners to situate their PID within their curriculum of study (Hart & Montague, 2015; Tan, Van der Molen, & Schmidt, 2016). Often absent from discussions is the fact that each student has unique narratives to bring to the inclusive classroom learning environment. Certain aspects of reflective pedagogy can be administered either in online, face-to-face, and blended graduate training formats (Langley & Brown, 2010; Murdock, Williams, Becker, Bruce, & Young, 2012). However, completing reflective assignments such as journals or self-reflective papers are not enough to enhance students' PID and are necessary but not sufficient to encourage their success as beginning professionals.

An emotionally safe classroom with well-defined guidelines (Quiros et al., 2012) and the ability to observe and absorb the professional qualities of an instructor, supervisor, or role model must also be present for students to have an enhancing learning experience (Matteson et al., 2011). These last two components are best integrated into the student experience as face-to-face components. It may be difficult to create an emotionally safe climate in online environments, as it is difficult for instructors to assess the feel or tone of a "room," particularly when asynchronous online discussions are occurring. Although emotional learning can occur online (Rowe, 2005), it may be a challenge for the instructor to judge if and when emotional "shutdowns" may be occurring.

An optimal way to create emotional safety to support reflective practice is to involve students in the creation of guidelines for the face-to-face classroom and related activities. Questions such as: *What do you as a learner, within the context of this classroom learning community, require to feel safe and respected by all members?* Students also need to develop their self-awareness and self-regulation skills so they may feel empowered to take the risks required for reflective learning. Again, in an ideal university community, the process of reflective practice is best introduced during initial coursework and encouraged throughout and beyond degree completion. By integrating these ideas into the graduate student experience, we will be able to better support student success in engaging in reflective development.

## Proven Practices, Examples, and Results

Wong-Wylie (2007) described five elements that are facilitative of reflective practices. From these five, her research indicates that three show up most often in students' recollections of critical moments in their graduate professional education: engaging in reflective tasks, having self-trust/risking, and interacting with supportive academic personnel. These can be integrated into educational programs, and as an example, they have been integrated into the Master of Counselling program at City University of Seattle in Calgary, Alberta.

## Engaging in Reflective Tasks

Students can be taught to engage in self-reflection from start to finish. In their applications, students write a personal response paper that invites them to engage actively in self-awareness and write about why they want to be in the program. Once admitted, during New Student Orientation, students create a self-care plan for the duration of their studies as graduate students. Faculty can further creatively infuse reflective practice into all domains of a curriculum by

- modeling the message—actively engage in reflective practice;
- sharing initial experiences with reflective practice—as a graduate student or beginning professional;

- identifying the cost/benefits of reflective practice to the learning experience;
- discussing the bigger picture and inform students what's in it for them;
- creating a template or an example to help students get started; and
- explaining that engaging in reflective practice is a challenging process and that faculty is there to support students.


## Having Self-Trust/Risking

Engaging in self-reflection represents an intrapersonal and vulnerable endeavor. The creation of a safe learning environment presents an essential first step in establishing a climate for engaging in collaborative sharing of learning and insights. As reflective practitioners, personal learning experiences (especially those that were lacking in safety) have offered significant insights into "better ways" of engaging in inclusive practice. The following suggested strategies should be considered:

- Actively engage each climate as a learning culture within itself
- Create and maintain community norms and agreements to support and nurture safety
- Adopt the teaching philosophy that "if uncomfortable, one is learning," taking note that there is a fundamental difference between uncomfortable and unsafe
- Encourage learners to self-monitor and manage their reflections as possible new insights and transformative opportunities for growth
- Instill a culture of confidentiality (identifying limits of confidentiality based on the requirements of regulatory bodies) where students feel safe sharing ideas with the instructor and other members of the classroom culture
- Engage in ongoing discussions surrounding self-reflection as a process orientation, rather than a completed product (i.e., journal or blog)
- Infuse an assignment that requests students to "reflect on reflecting"
- Discuss and have students summarize essential counsellor dispositions such as being aware of biases, and being open to feedback and their implications.

## Lessons Learned, Tips for Success, and Recommendations

The scholarship of teaching and learning has consistently demonstrated that learners are more engaged and easier to retain when they feel acknowledged and supported. It should be a priority to be both visible and accessible to learners via office hours, Skype, and before and after classes. It is important that educators create and maintain professional boundaries with learners, as there is always a possible danger of engaging in a duality of relationship. Students should be provided with external resources to engage in self-care. By being proactive, faculty members not only model professionalism but also demonstrate that they care about a student's well-being through the provision of external resources. Wong-Wylie's (2007) elements of supportive collegial interactions with students, in relation to reflective practice, are the basis for the following suggestions:

- Demonstrate interest in the lived experience of learners
- Create and nurture an environment of curiosity and reflection
- Share campus/community resources should a student require additional assistance based on their reflections or the process (i.e., campus counselling centre)—know when to refer students
- Foster a compassionate approach to supporting learners in their development of self-awareness as it relates to their PID, specifically acknowledging that it can be a risky endeavor and that students can be at different levels with this
- Model healthy boundaries and communication skills when resolving conflict with students or colleagues

# References

Bolton, G. (2014). *Reflective practice: Writing and professional development* (4th ed.). London, United Kingdom: Sage Publications.

Bulman, C., & Schutz, S. (2013). *Reflective practice in nursing* (5th ed.). Oxford, United Kingdom: Wiley-Blackwell.

Chang, J. (2011). An interpretive account of counsellor development. *Canadian Journal of Counselling and Psychotherapy, 45*(4), 406–429.

Collins, S., Arthur, N., & Wong-Wylie, G. (2010). Enhancing reflective practice in multicultural counseling through cultural auditing. *Journal of Counseling and Development, 88*(3), 340–347. doi:10.1002/j.1556-6678.2010.tb00031.x

Cox, M., Zhu, J., Lynch, C., & Adams, S. (2012). Aligning the Ph.D. and mentoring experiences of U.S. underrepresented minority students in engineering. In D. Myers and C. Anderson, *Dimensions in Mentoring*. Rotterdam, The Netherlands: Sense Publishers.

Goldie, J. (2012). The formation of professional identity in medical students: Considerations for educators. *Medical Teacher, 34*(9), e641–e648. doi:10.3109/0142159X.2012.687476

Hart, A., & Montague, J. (2015). The constant state of becoming: Power, identity, and discomfort on the anti-oppressive learning journey. *Journal of Psychological Issues in Organizational Culture, 5*(4), 39-52. doi:10.1002/jpoc.21159

Langley, M.E., & Brown, S.T. (2010). Perceptions of the use of reflective journals in online graduate nursing education. *Nursing Education Perspectives, 31*(1), 12-17.

Matteson, S. M., Taylor, C. M., Valle, F., Fehr, M. C., Jacob, S. A., & Jones, S. J. (2011). Re-examining academic expectations: Using self-study to promote academic justice and student retention. *Journal of Thought, 46*(1), 65–83, 116–117.

Murdock, J., Williams, A., Becker, K., Bruce, M. A., & Young, S. (2012). Online versus on-campus: A comparison study of counseling skills courses. *The Journal of Human Resource and Adult Learning, 8*(1), 105–118.

Pompeo, A. M., & Levitt, D. H. (2014). A path of counselor self-awareness. *Counseling and Values, 59*(1), 80–94. doi:10.1002/j.2161-007X.2014.00043.x

Quiros, L., Kay, L., & Montijo, A. M. (2012). Creating emotional safety in the classroom and in the field. *Reflections: Narratives of professional helping, 18*(2), 42–47.

Roffey-Barentsen, J., & Malthouse, R. (2013). *Reflective practice in education and training.* London, United Kingdom: Sage.

Ronfeldt, M., & Grossman, P. (2008). Becoming a professional: Experimenting with possible selves in professional preparation. *Teacher Education Quarterly, 35*(3), 41–60.

Rosin, J. (2015). The necessity of counselor individuation for fostering reflective practice. *Journal of Counseling & Development, 93*(1), 88–95. doi:10.1002/j.1556-6676.2015.00184.x

Rowe, J. (2005). *Since feeling is first: A narrative inquiry toward understanding emotion in online teaching and learning* (Doctoral dissertation). Available from ProQuest Dissertations & Theses Global database. (UMI No. 3200084).

Sharpless, J., Baldwin, N., Cook, R., Kofman, A., Morley-Fletcher, A., Slotkin, R., & Wald, H. S. (2015). The becoming: Students' reflections on the process of professional identity formation in medical education. *Academic Medicine: Journal of the Association of American Medical Colleges, 90*(6), 713–717. doi:10.1097?ACM.0000000000000729

Shuler, M. K., & Keller-Dupree, E. A. (2015). The impact of transformational learning experiences on personal and professional counselor-in-training identity development. *The Professional Counselor, 5*(1), 152–162. doi:10.15241/mks.5.1.152

Tan, C. P., Van der Molen, H. T., & Schmidt, H. G. (2016). To what extent does problem-based learning contribute to students' professional identity development? *Teaching and Teacher Education, 54*, 54–64. doi:10,1016/j.tate.2015.11.09

Tobin, D. J., Willow, R. A., Bastow, E. K., & Ratkowski, E. M. (2009). Reflective learning within a counselor education curriculum. *The Journal of Counselor Preparation and Supervision, 1*(1). http://dx.doi.org/10.7729/11.0104

West, C. (2012). Developing reflective practitioners: Using video-cases in music teacher education. *Journal of Music Teacher Education, 22*(2), 11–19. doi:10.1177/105708371247041

Wilson, G. (2013). Evidencing reflective practice in social work education: Theoretical uncertainties and practical challenges. *The British Journal of Social Work, 43*(1), 154–172. doi:10.1093/bjsw/brc170

Wong-Wylie, G. (2007). Barriers and facilitators of reflective practice in counsellor education: Critical incidents from doctoral graduates. *Canadian Journal of Counselling, 41*(2), 59–76.

# Author Biographies

Toupey Luft is an Associate Professor and Internship Coordinator at City University of Seattle, Calgary campus. Her scholarship has centered around human development, with a focus on adolescent girls. She holds a BA (honours) in psychology, an MSc in educational psychology, and a PhD in applied psychology, each from the University of Calgary. Dr. Luft is currently a registered psychologist in the province of Alberta.

Robert A. Roughley is a Professor and Associate Program Director for the Counselling program at City University of Seattle, Calgary campus. Dr. Roughley has been actively engaged in the scholarship of teaching and learning for fifteen years. His scholarship has focused on human sexuality, culture-infused counselling, counsellor identity development, and best practice in teaching. He holds a BA in music, a BEd and a MEd in educational studies from Queen's University, a BAEd in adult education from Brock University, and an MC and a PhD in counselling psychology from the University of Calgary. Dr. Roughley is currently a provisional registered psychologist in the province of Alberta.

# 6

# Successful Mentor Matches: What It Takes to Ensure a Positive Mentor/Mentee Pairing

**Sarah Piper-Hall**

## Abstract

This chapter is dedicated to finding the most successful strategies and tools for positive mentor-teacher/teacher-candidate matches. While the tools have remained much the same throughout the years, they have become more sophisticated and potentially virtual. The importance of mentoring in teacher preparation cannot be underscored, and the match between current and potential teacher is of the utmost importance. This chapter examines the significance of a positive and successful mentor/ mentee match and what it takes to get to that status.

# Overview

Successful mentoring matches improve both student retention and student engagement at all levels of educational endeavors. During the author's tenure with Access to Student Assistance Programs in Reach of Everyone (ASPIRE), she personally saw both successful and detrimental mentor/mentee matches and experienced firsthand the struggle and challenge that comes along with creating matches that are beneficial to both parties. Lucia (ninth grade), for example, was a young lady besieged with family problems, including a father in jail and a mother addicted to heroin. No one thought Lucia would amount to anything, and no one urged her to continue her schooling after high school or even to participate in her current scholastic situation. Lucia was matched with a connected community member who was retired and had both the time and ability to widen Lucia's world and show her that her options included anything she wanted. By the time Lucia graduated, she had raised her GPA two full points, was accepted into several prestigious universities, and was offered two full-ride scholarships to state universities. Without her mentor, Lucia would still be living at home taking care of her younger brothers and sisters, without the hope of a future any better than that which her parents experienced.

The ability to make a successful mentor match is the key to stories like Lucia's. This chapter examines several proven mentor/mentee strategies and looks ahead to innovative ideas and approaches that may provide an even stronger and more successful match. Gone are the days when mentors and mentees were matched based on availability or gender preference. At this point in time, mentor matches need to take into account much more.

# Review of the Literature

Each student's success depends on his or her role models and mentors, for without that guidance, the student is left with little to aspire to (Bell & Treleaven, 2011). A positive match between student and mentor benefits both mentor and mentee and creates an atmosphere of trust, respect, and guidance. Successful mentor/mentee matches allow both mentor and mentee to grow and learn, giving both parties the ability to mature to a new level of understanding and changing them both for the better.

Proponents of mentoring argue its merits on the basis of a paradigm Zey-Ferrell and Baker (1984) coined, the "mutual benefits model" (p. 83), which speaks to the idea that "investing some teachers with the special titles, resources, and obligations of mentorship will more readily assure various individual and institutional benefits." Individual mentors "will receive public acknowledgment of their accumulated knowledge, skill, and judgment," while "novice teachers will receive support that mediates the difficulties of the first years of teaching" (Warren, 1990, p. 299). To make the match even more beneficial, Warren (1990) mentioned the idea that "career opportunities in the occupation will be enriched. And schools, restructured to accommodate new teacher leadership roles, will expand their capacity to serve students and to adapt to societal demands" (p. 300). Other benefits for teacher candidates include "developing collegiality, networking, reflection, professional development, support and assistance, and personal satisfaction. Additional benefits for mentees can include higher rates of retention and promotion, higher success rates in receiving external research grants, higher publication rates and better perceptions" (Gardiner, Tiggemann, Kearns, & Marshall, 2007, p. 427).

So far, this chapter has been looking at positive matches and matching strategies, but there is another side to explore as well. Negative mentor matches are a real possibility and much has been written on the effects a negative mentor/mentee match has on both parties. According to Spencer (2007), six prominent factors contribute to the expiration of mentoring relationships: "(a) mentor or protégé abandonment, (b) perceived lack of protégé motivation, (c) unfulfilled expectations, (d) deficiencies in mentor relational skills, (e) family interference, and (f) inadequate agency support" (p. 331). All of these, with the exception of both (e) and (f), can be turned into positive experiences simply with a positive mentor/mentee match. Grossman (1999) found similar issues with unsuccessful matches.

## Integration into the Student Experience

The use of mentor teachers has long been viewed as a necessary and vital part of the teacher preparation experience. Goering (2013) noted the importance of mentor teachers in English, while Mcaleer and Bangert (2011) spoke to the need in the field of mathematics. Goering opted to focus on face-to-face mentoring in the classroom, also sometimes known as co-teaching, dual teaching, or pair teaching, while

Mcaleer and Bangert took the route of online mentoring to aid in teacher preparation. Both have been shown to be extremely successful, and both are valid options in the current environment. The important part is the match itself. A teacher candidate who is in a classroom with a mentor teacher who is not involved or is not actually doing much mentoring is going to be far less successful than a candidate who has a "virtual" mentor who is involved and can model appropriate teaching skills from a separate location.

The beauty of mentoring is that it can be done in a variety of ways, utilizing an assortment of mediums and in a multiplicity of settings. Mentoring student teachers is not an easy or small task, however, and both the mentor and mentee must be prepared to follow through the duration.

## Proven Practices, Examples, and Results

Following is a look at proven practices that have been successfully utilized in the past ten years. Big Brothers Big Sisters is perhaps the most well-known mentoring organization and has years of research and proven success. The Big Brothers Big Sisters of the North Bay developed the acronym "MATCHES" that succinctly summarizes the organization's theory (Park and Porter-Burns, 2014). *M* is represented by several things including motivation and mentor training. *A* includes the assessment interview. Teamwork and trust are part of *T*. *C* comprises commitment, communication, consistency, confidentiality, and compatibility. *H* is slightly more important when making mentor matches with younger children—healthy boundaries. *E* has to do with expectations of the experience, and *S* is perhaps the most important part—the continued success of the match.

Taking into account the actual personality and behavioral styles is of the utmost importance when making successful mentor matches. Daresh and Playko (1992) found that four basic styles exist which can successfully be utilized to describe individuals and then for matching purposes. The importance of this was found in Piper-Hall's (2015) research as well. All six of her research participants found that the most successful mentoring relationships occurred when personality and behavioral styles between mentor and mentee were similar.

The first style Daresh and Playko (1992) found was supportive: "This style demonstrates a high degree of respect for interpersonal relations.

Individuals who possess this style try to minimize conflict and promote the happiness of everybody. Some people see the supportive style as accommodating and friendly, while others might view it as wishy-washy." Those who are supportive tend to behave in whatever way may be needed to please others, but this may leave them frequently overcommitted. Supportive types are highly people-oriented individuals who will generally rely on others to give directions about how to get tasks done.

Next comes the directive style, which includes those who love to run things their way. These people are viewed as highly businesslike and efficient by some, and as threatening and unfeeling by others. "These people want to make sure that the job gets done, and they get impatient with lengthy descriptions about effective process."

The third style, facilitative, is composed of people who "tend to get involved with people in active, rapidly changing situations." They are seen as socially outgoing and friendly, imaginative and vigorous. Some view this style as dynamic and energetic, while others perceive the same behavior as highly egotistical. These individuals tend to be viewed as highly creative people who are also likely to generate ideas with little practical follow-through or concern for details.

The fourth and final personality/behavioral style is the scientific, which places substantial emphasis on problem solving and conceptual skills. Individuals portraying this style "tend to want much data before they make any decisions. As a result, they are viewed by others as methodical and thorough, although this behavior might frustrate some who look at their behavior as too slow."

Going back to Big Brothers Big Sisters, the organization has seven "Principles of Matching" (Park and Porter-Burns, 2014, slide 3). The first is perhaps the most important and time-tested success piece. "Invest thoughtfully in the interview process." In the North Bay chapter of Big Brothers Big Sisters, they have fifty-three interview questions for mentors and mentees, which allow them to really get a good idea of who they are dealing with (Park & Porter-Burns, 2014). For mentor teachers, the process is altered by the fact that candidates are often placed wherever there is an open location. That being said, the mentor teacher should still be invested in the match and wanting to impart wisdom and knowledge for his or her mentee.

In a perfect world, each teacher preparation program would have the following staff, dedicated to maintaining successful mentor/mentee matches in their districts (Park and Porter-Burns, 2014). First is an intake coordinator (slide 7) whose job it is to orient both mentor and mentee and take care of any background checks/fingerprinting/testing requirements that need to be completed. Next comes the match support specialist, who interviews both mentor and mentee to ensure a positive fit. Finally, a program director and staff round out the team. It is the program director's responsibility to strategize how best to make positive matches, conduct trainings, and support both teacher candidate and mentor teacher. There is often not enough time or potential locations for teacher-candidate placements. However, it is important. Weinberger, Garringer, and MacRae (2005) also noted the importance of having someone whose sole job it is to make the matches and continue ensuring the match is successful for both mentor teacher and teacher candidate.

Smith (2005) has created a checklist for both mentors and mentees, which has led to success for his students. In many teacher preparation programs, the mentee does not necessarily have the ability or opportunity to ask questions of and choose his or her mentor teacher. However, there are some basic questions that Smith proposes should be asked of all teacher candidates before each begins his or her mentoring/student teaching. "Are you committed to improving professionally? Are you open to helpful criticism? Are you willing to accept responsibility for your own professional and personal development? Are you ready to work hard and act upon the suggestions and advice of your mentor?" (p. 65). A successful match ensures that the teacher candidate is ready and willing to do the work and is open to feedback.

## Lessons Learned, Tips for Success, Recommendations

After doing an in-depth analysis of six professional women in the Pacific Northwest, Piper-Hall (2015) came to the conclusion that the most important thing in a successful mentor/mentee match is the inclusion of several tools to promote positive pairings. Tools such as personal inventories, questionnaires, online software, or the presence of a mentor director to ensure the match is successful are imperative to the overall achievement of both mentor and mentee. Her most significant recommendation is that higher education entities hire a person to take on the role of mentor director. This person should be responsible for all aspects of mentoring programs, starting with matching and continuing with follow-ups, check-ins, and possible interventions, if need be. Depending on the size of the district, institution, university, or school, this could be a full- or part-time person. Piper-Hall (2015) stringently suggested having this person focus *only* on the mentor matches. If a person is employed part-time as a mentor director and part-time in another position, the mentoring part of the equation can be quickly eaten up by the non-mentoring part. For the matches to be successful, someone needs to have his or her eye on the progression of the relationship from beginning to end.

As North and Sherk (2015) noted, there may be many people who collect information on those that enter the program, but there should be one person who assumes responsibility for making a particular match. "This is usually a match coordinator or similar position. This person's responsibility is to gather all the information you have, examine the needs" (slide 8), find a compatible mentor teacher, and monitor and guide the matchmaking process through to the end. "Obviously, this person will not be able to do this effectively if his time and energy are diverted elsewhere. . . . The last thing you want to do is make matches hastily and without proper consideration."

# Conclusion

Student retention and engagement are imperative in student success and achievement. Mentoring is a successful tool when working with students and professionals of all ages. But negative mentor/mentee matches do not provide the positivity the student needs to succeed. Programs such as Big Brothers Big Sisters have proven tools and results that have been in place for decades, but it is time to develop more innovative and advanced tools for programs/schools/organizations to use in the educational realm. There are many established strategies when creating a match, and now the mentor matching has caught up to the digital age and there is a plethora of software options on the market to ensure matches are successful. Whether via software, questionnaires, matching meetings, or other tools, the important thing to remember is that a well-thought-out and implemented teacher candidate/mentor teacher match will lead to a successful teacher in the future.

# References

Bell, A., & Treleaven, L. (2011). Looking for 'Professor Right': Mentee selection of mentors in a formal mentoring program. *Higher Education, 61*(5), 545.

Daresh, J., & Playko, M. A. (1992). *A method for matching leadership mentors and protégés.* Paper presented at the annual meeting of the Association for Supervision and Curriculum Development. New Orleans, LA. Retrieved from http://eric.ed.gov/?id=ED344315

Gardiner, M., Tiggemann, M., Kearns, H., & Marshall, K. (2007). Show me the money! An empirical analysis of mentoring outcomes for women in academia. *Higher Education Research and Development, 26*(4), 425.

Goering, C. Z. (2013). "Juggling 400 oranges": Calling all mentor teachers. *English Journal, 102*(3), 13.

Grossman, J. B. (Ed.). (1999, August). Contemporary issues in mentoring. *Public/Private Ventures Report.* Retrieved from http://eric.ed.gov/?id=ED433431

Mcaleer, D., & Bangert, A. (2011). Professional growth through online mentoring: A study of mathematics mentor teachers. *Journal of Educational Computing Research, 44*(1), 83.

North, D., & Sherk, J. (2015). *Creating and sustaining a winning match.* Folsom, CA: The EMT Group. Retrieved from http://www.emt.org/userfiles/MatchSeries2.pdf

Park, F., & Porter-Burns, A. (2014). *Demystifying matching: The keys to creating successful mentor/mentee matches.* Paper presented at the National Mentoring Summit, North Bay, CA.

Piper-Hall, S. (2015). *Creating mentoring success: Women making a difference* (Doctoral dissertation). Available from ProQuest Dissertations & Theses Global database. (UMI No. 3662832)

Smith, M. V. (2005). Modern mentoring: Ancient lessons for today. *Music Educators Journal, 92*(2), 62.

Spencer, R. (2007). It's not what I expected: A qualitative study of youth mentoring relationship failures. *Journal of Adolescent Research, 22*(4), 331.

Warren, J. (1990). The mentor phenomenon and the social organization of teaching. *Review of Research in Education, 16*, 297.

Weinberger, S., Garringer, M., & MacRae, P. (2005). *Going the distance: A guide to building lasting relationships in mentoring programs.* Folsom, CA: US Department of Education Mentoring Resource Center. Retrieved from http://educationnorthwest.org/sites/default/files/resources/going_the_distance.pdf

Zey-Ferrell, M., & Baker, P. (1984). Local and cosmopolitan orientations of faculty implications for teaching. *Teaching Sociology, 12*(1), 82.

# Author Biography

Sarah Y. Piper-Hall is an Associate Program Director for the Albright School of Education at City University of Seattle and serves as a faculty member for the Vancouver and southwestern Washington area. She has spent fifteen years in education, including seven years managing a statewide mentoring program in Oregon high schools. She holds a BS and an MBA degree from Portland State University and a PhD in leadership studies from Gonzaga University. Her focus has been on mentoring success, and she has recently published both a book on mentoring and a chapter in a collection of leading experts in their field.

# 7

# Andragogy and the Adult Learner

**Charlotte Cochran and Steve Brown**

## Abstract

Pedagogy and andragogy are two theories of learning. Pedagogy requires the students to be dependent upon the teacher for knowledge, and any experiences students may have yield little value. On the other hand, andragogy is a theory that puts the learner at the center, and it continues to be discussed as a front-runner for adult learning. According to Knowles, Holton III, and Swanson (2005), andragogy includes six assumptions: (1) the need to know, (2) the learner's self-concept, (3) the role of the learners' experiences, (4) readiness to learn, (5) orientation to learning, and (6) motivation. The theory of andragogy can be applied to the online environment, and as such, faculty members who apply the six assumptions of andragogy to their online classes will improve the learning experience for their online learners.

# Overview

Many university faculty members work with adults, a significant portion of whom are transitioning from one career to their second, third, or fourth. As such, instructional success does not necessarily result from teaching using traditional pedagogical theory, since the students have different experiences, which may influence the content and process by which they learn. Employing instruction infused by the assumptions outlined in the theory of andragogy has a greater likelihood of success. This chapter reviews the literature defining pedagogy and andragogy, while advocating for applying the assumptions outlined in andragogy to higher education, and providing examples of how andragogy can be applied to higher education classes.

# Review of the Literature

## Pedagogy

Pedagogy is the traditional method of instruction. According to Knowles et al. (2005) pedagogy means "the art and science of teaching children" (p. 61). The pedagogical theory was developed in the seventh century and it was intended for teaching children (Knowles et al., 2005). It is based on a set of beliefs which "assigns to the teacher full responsibility for making all decisions about what will be learned, how it will be learned, when it will be learned, and if it has been learned" (Knowles et al., 2005, p. 61). The assumptions of pedagogy include the learner being dependent upon the teacher who determines what and when information will be learned and how it will be learned. The experiences of the learner do not have a lot of value, and the primary methods of instruction are through lectures, assigned readings, and presentations (Taylor & Kroth, 2009a). While this method of instruction may work with young children, applying pedagogical theory with adults may not be as effective. Adult learners are different from children learners in part because adult learners have had more life experiences and they need to be viewed as being capable (Knowles et al., 2005). Thus, instruction for adults should change from a pedagogical, teacher-centered focus to an andragogical, learner-centered focus to meet the needs of an adult learner.

## Andragogy

The introduction of technology has influenced education to the point of requiring instructors to change the way they educate adults (Horsley, 2010). Simultaneously, adult learners have been required to make the adjustment from being passive students to actively participating in their learning (Turcsanyi-Szabo, 2012). This change in roles (lecturer to facilitator) is a reason to encourage faculty members to apply the assumptions of andragogy to the adult learning environment.

Andragogy focuses on the adult and is based on six assumptions (Knowles et al., 2005): "the need to know why they need to learn something, the learners' self-concept, prior experiences, readiness to learn, orientation to learning, and motivation" (p. 160). These assumptions apply to adult learners because they provide "a sound foundation for planning adult learning experiences" (Knowles et al., 2005, p. 157). Instructors who understand and are willing to apply the assumptions outlined in andragogy will have a better chance of meeting the needs of an adult learner, particularly if teaching in an online environment (Cochran, 2015).

While the theory of andragogy has been used as a guide for adult learning (Henschke, 2011) and it is a significant component of online learning (Chametzky, 2014), some scholars have argued that andragogy is not a theory at all and that the assumptions were just "principles of good practice" (Hartree, 1984, p. 205). In fact, Knowles (1989) acknowledged that andragogy is more akin to learning assumptions than a learning theory. A criticism of andragogy is the lack of an instrument that is able to measure whether the assumptions outlined in andragogy are being implemented in educational settings (Taylor & Kroth, 2009b). Nevertheless, andragogy has been applied effectively to higher education programs using face-to-face and online instruction (Harper & Ross, 2011).

The assumptions outlined in andragogy can be used as a guide by instructors (Henschke, 2011), which can enhance the experiences of students (Cochran, 2015). These assumptions can be easily applied to face-to-face classroom instruction, online instruction, or a blended learning environment (Harper & Ross, 2011; Knowles et al., 2005). When an instructor uses the andragogical model as a frame of reference when designing a class, the instructor can effectively engage the adults and facilitate a class. However, to apply andragogy effectively in an online class, technology issues need to be addressed (Chametzky, 2014).

Rather than using a teacher-centered approach, faculty members should design an online course with a learner-centered focus (De Gagne & Walters, 2009), whereby the instructors take on the role of a facilitator (Smart, Witt, & Scott, 2012). Instructors who are able to transition from a teacher-centered to learner-centered method of instruction should find that the students will be more engaged and they will take responsibility for their own learning. Faculty members who have an understanding of andragogy may have an easier time teaching in the online teaching environments. Understanding how adults learn and implementing the assumptions outlined in the theory of andragogy will help the instructor provide the necessary support and guidance to the online learners, thereby creating an environment more conducive to learning.

## Application of Andragogy in Higher Education

Each of andragogy's six assumptions can be more closely examined to see how they improve the student experience.

### Assumption 1—The learners need to know why they need to learn something

The first assumption states that "adults need to know why they need to learn something before undertaking to learn it" (Knowles et al., 2005, p.64). By explaining the purpose of the assignment and the learning outcome of the assignment prior to assigning the task, the instructor can increase the chance that the adult learner will be motivated to attempt the task. Faculty members may choose to explain or provide an outline of the learning expectations prior to beginning class or lecture, and this would be one method to implement the essential assumption in a classroom environment. Adult students are more inclined to be motivated when they understand what they are expected to learn.

Authentic case studies are useful tools to when developing class assignments for adult learners. Authentic case studies are applicable to life experiences and provide students with collaborative opportunities and time to reflect (Woo, Herrington, Agostinho, & Reeves, 2007). Assignments that connect the learner with life experiences make the class activities more relevant and, thereby, actively engross the students in their learning. Using authentic case studies, which test the learners' skill, can be an effective way to implement this assumption, especially in the online learning environment (Conlan, Grabowski, & Smith, 2011). For example, in City University of Seattle's Performance-Based Master's in Teaching Program, candidates are encouraged to use their prior work and life experiences—even if they were not in the formal K–12 educational environment—and adapt and use those experiences to demonstrate the understanding and application of course content outcomes. When adults are proactive in their learning, they will have a vested interest in learning the material.

## Assumption 2—The learner's self-concept

Knowles et al. (2005) identified adults and children as having experienced life differently to date (Harper & Ross, 2011), and the second assumption states that adults "have a self-concept of being responsible for their own decisions, for their own lives" (Knowles et al., 2005, p. 65). According to Dabbagh (2007), the online learner's self-concept is a key predictor for success, and students who have an internal locus of control tend to be more successful in the online learning environment. The online instructor must be willing to give up control of the course to allow the learners to be empowered to work on the course content together with the instructor as an equal (Conrad & Donaldson, 2004).

Faculty may consider accessing and incorporating an adult's life experiences into class activities since adult experiences are a valuable resource (Taylor & Kroth, 2009b). City University of Seattle's Teacher Certification program instructors are encouraged and, at times, required to address the learner's self-concept in a class by establishing group projects and providing opportunities for interactive discussions (face-to-face and online) to enable learners to discuss their experiences with their classmates. Faculty members and students work together to design instructional materials that are acceptable to both parties to address the learner's needs

(Chan, 2010). Activities to support and encourage online learners in this area should be activities that are collaborative in nature (Dabbagh, 2007). Adults need to be viewed as being capable (Knowles et al., 2005), and collaborative activities provide the opportunity for adults to demonstrate their capabilities. Encouraging student participation in group projects and collaborative activities also aligns with the assumptions outlined in andragogy.

## Assumption 3—The learner's prior experiences

The third andragogical assumption states that adults have different life experiences from children, thereby creating a more heterogeneous group of learners (Knowles et al., 2005). Encouraging learners to connect their learning to life experiences can help the learner gain a better understanding of the material (University of Wisconsin Whitewater, 2006). The course content "must be structured in a way that fosters sharing of experiences among learners such as through the use of group projects and interactive discussions" (Blondy, 2007, p. 121). Course content should be flexible in that it can evolve rather than follow a specific script (Conrad & Donaldson, 2004).

Suggestions for an instructor who would like to implement this assumption course would be to ask the students their opinion regarding the activities they would like to participate in to improve their learning experience (Blondy, 2007). Activities may be collaborative in nature, which allows for student interaction and conversations that may lead to mastery of course material. Students who actively participate and contribute to their learning will be more engaged and motivated to learn (Harper & Ross, 2011) and, thus, be more successful. Instructors should create a learning environment that is encouraging and conducive to learners sharing their personal experiences, ideas, and opinions (Palloff & Pratt, 2001). A useful activity for sharing past experiences involves reflections from a journal. Short writing exercises to share and reflect on learners' knowledge of a particular topic (Aragon, 2003), which may include their past experiences, can also be used as an effective assessment tool. When learners share their past experiences, the learning environment is enriched (University of Wisconsin Whitewater, 2006).

## Assumption 4—The learner's readiness to learn

The fourth assumption of andragogy is the adult learners' readiness to learn, which means aligning learning with developmental concepts (Knowles et al., 2005). The needs of the learner must be addressed quickly so as to ensure the success of the online learner (Blondy, 2007). Watkins (2005) suggests asking the learner about specific experiences with topics related to the course content and about expectations for the course. For example, an instructor could post a discussion question to the class, and the students would then be required to respond to the discussion question and to the posts made by their peers. By using an asynchronous environment, the instructor may use discussion questions to encourage student engagement with their peers. In an asynchronous environment, the students have time to reflect on the posts of others and organize their thoughts before they respond. The answers the students provide can help an instructor get a better understanding of the learners' readiness to learn the course content and it would allow the students to get a better understanding of what they are about to learn.

## Assumption 5—The learner's orientation to learning

The fifth assumption is that adult learners are motivated to learn when given authentic learning activities (Knowles et al., 2005), and as such, the curriculum "should be process based versus content based to allow learners to develop content in accordance with their specific needs" (Blondy, 2007, p. 125). It is critical to the success of learners that instructors provide adults with activities that capture their attention and keep them engaged (Conrad & Donaldson, 2004). Authentic learning activities provide "meaning beyond the learning environment" (Conrad & Donaldson, 2004, p. 84). Examples of authentic activities include case studies, team problem-solving activities, and conducting interviews (Conrad & Donaldson, 2004). Faculty members may consider focusing on creating task-based activities (Blondy, 2007). Task-based activities can be used to help learners get a sense of how to apply practice to their lives (Knowles et al., 2005).

In the first course of City University of Seattle's Performance-Based Master's in Teaching program, candidates are provided with the opportunity to demonstrate their learning using various methods such as creating an essay, a presentation, wikis and blogs, or conducting interviews. The students have the flexibility to choose the means for how they will demonstrate their mastery of the subject matter. For example, students may choose to write a traditional paper, create a PowerPoint presentation or something similar, upload alternative media, or use another approach not mentioned to provide evidence demonstrating their understanding of the outcomes outlined in the course rubric. They can also choose whether to demonstrate their mastery individually or to create a group of their choosing. Providing these types of choices can help provide motivation for adult learners, and it can help prepare them to serve as an educator in the rapidly evolving K–12 environment.

## Assumption 6—The learner's motivation

The sixth assumption is that adult learners are intrinsically motivated to learn (Knowles et al., 2005). Instructors can support the students' intrinsic motivation to learn by providing a learning environment that engages the students and encourages them to be active participants (Aragon, 2003). To create a positive learning environment for adults in an online environment, instructors must be aware of the need of learners to be appreciated, valued, and respected (Blondy, 2007). Using games in the online environment, or simulating a radio talk show to include guests, or using multimedia when appropriate—all have been used successfully to enhance student motivation (Aragon, 2003).

Implementing the learning assumptions outlined above is "invaluable in shaping the learning process to be more conducive to adults" (Knowles et al., 2005, p. 2), and it should be used as a guide for developing the adult learning environment (Blondy, 2007). Andragogy is a set of assumptions that can "apply to all adult learning situations" (Knowles et al., 2005, p. 2) to include an online environment. A benefit in applying andragogy includes the ability to adapt the assumptions to fit the needs of individual learners and to the learning situation.

Teaching adult learners, especially in an online learning environment, can be challenging. For example, online instruction requires that the instructor use a different skill set than is required in a face-to-face class (Hoekstra, 2014). Instructors who understand the assumptions of andragogy and are able to effectively apply the assumptions in the online environment may be more successful teaching in the virtual environment, and as such, the learners will also find greater success (Kenner & Weinerman, 2011).

## Conclusion

Andragogy is an adult learning theory that can be applied to various learning environments, and is particularly valuable when utilized in online courses (Harper & Ross, 2011; Knowles et al., 2005). Higher education faculty members who understand the theory of andragogy can apply the assumptions outlined by Knowles et al. (2005) when they develop courses and student assignments and activities. However, transforming theory to practice can be challenging. For example, some instructors may struggle with changing their instructional method from using a lecture format to becoming a facilitator (Bair & Bair, 2011). Online instructors who have an understanding of andragogy, along with a willingness to design an online class using the above-mentioned andragogical assumptions, will improve the learning experiences of the adult online learner (Kenner & Weinerman, 2011).

## References

Aragon, S. R. (Ed.). (2003). *Facilitating learning in online environments*. San Francisco, CA: Jossey-Bass.

Bair, D., & Bair, M. (2011). Paradoxes of online teaching. *International Journal for the Scholarship of Teaching and Learning, 5*(2), 1–15. Retrieved from http://academics.georgiasouthern.edu/ijsotl/index.htm

Blondy, L. C. (2007). Evaluation and application of andragogical assumptions to the adult online learning environment. *Journal of Interactive Online Learning, 6,* 116–130. Retrieved from http://www.ncolr.org/jiol/issues/pdf/6.2.3.pdf

Chametzky, B. (2014). Andragogy and engagement in online learning: Tenets and solutions. *Creative Education, 5,* 813–821. http://dx.doi.org/10.4236/ce.2014.510095

Chan, S. (2010). Applications of andragogy in multi-disciplined teaching and learning. *Journal of Adult Education, 39*(2), 25-36. Retrieved from http://www.cait.org/Journal_of_Adult_Education_Vol_39_No2.pdf

Cochran, C. (2015). *Faculty transitions to online instruction: A qualitative case study* (Doctoral dissertation). Retrieved from http://gradworks.umi.com/37/14/3714737.html

Conlan, J., Grabowski, S., & Smith, K. (2011). *Adult learning.* Retrieved, from http://projects.coe.uga.edu/epltt/index.php?title=Adult_Learning

Conrad, R., & Donaldson, J. A. (2004). *Engaging the online learner*. San Francisco, CA: Jossey-Bass.

Dabbagh, N. (2007). The online learner: Characteristics and pedagogical implications. *Contemporary Issues in Technology and Teacher Education, 7*(3). Retrieved from http://www.citejournal.org/vol7/iss3/general/article1.cfm

De Gagne, J. C., & Walters, K. (2009). Online teaching experience: A qualitative metasynthesis (QMS). *MERLOT Journal of Online Learning and Teaching, 5*(4), 577–589. Retrieved from http://jolt.merlot.org/vol-5no4/degagne_1209.pdf

Harper, L., & Ross, J. (2011). An application of Knowles' theories of adult education to an undergraduate interdisciplinary studies degree program. *The Journal of Continuing Higher Education, 59*, 161–166. Retrieved from http://www.tandfonline.com.proxy1.ncu.edu/loi/ujch20

Hartree, A. (1984). Malcolm Knowles' theory of andragogy: A critique. *International Journal of Lifelong Education, 3*, 203-210. doi:10.1080/0260137840030304

Henschke, J. A. (2011). Considerations regarding the future of andragogy. *Adult Learning, 22*(1), 34–37. Retrieved from http://www.aaace.org/adult-learning-quarterly

Hoekstra, B. (2014). Relating training to job satisfaction: A survey of online faculty members. *Journal of Adult Education, 43*(1), 1-10. Retrieved from https://www.mpaea.org

Horsley, T. L. (2010). Syllabus selection: Innovative learning activity. *Journal of Nursing Education, 49(6)*, 363–364. doi:10.3928/01484834-20090521-02

Kenner, C., & Weinerman, J. (2011). Adult learning theory: Applications to non-traditional college students. *Journal of College Reading and Learning, 41*(2), 87-96. Retrieved from http://www.crla.net/journal.htm

Knowles, M. S. (1989). *The making of an adult educator: An autobiographical journey*. San Francisco, CA: Jossey-Bass.

Knowles, M. S., Holton III, E. F., & Swanson, R. A. (2005). *The adult learner: The definitive classic in adult education and human resource development* (6th ed.). San Diego, CA: Elsevier.

Palloff, R. M., & Pratt, K. (2001). *Lessons from the cyberspace classroom: The realities of on-line teaching*. San Francisco, CA: Jossey-Bass.

Smart, K. L., Witt, C., & Scott, J. P. (2012). Toward learner-centered teaching: An inductive approach. *Business Communication Quarterly, 75*(4), 392–403. http://dx.doi.org/10.1177/1080569912459752

Taylor, B., & Kroth, M. (2009a). A single conversation with a wise man is better than ten years of study: A model for testing methodologies for pedagogy or andragogy. *Journal of the Scholarship of Teaching and Learning. 9*(2), 42–56. Retrieved from http://josotl.indiana.edu/article/view/1725/1723

Taylor, B., & Kroth, M. (2009b). Andragogy's transition into the future: Meta-analysis of andragogy and its search for a measureable instrument. *Journal of Adult Education, 38*(1), 1–11. Retrieved from https://www.questia.com/library/p436763/journal-of-adult-education/i2508034/vol-38-no-1-2009

Turcsanyi-Szabo, M. (2012). Aiming at sustainable innovation in teacher education—from theory to practice. *Informatics in Education, 11*(1), 115–130. Retrieved from http://www.mii.lt/informatics_in_education/

University of Wisconsin Whitewater. (2006). *The online course experience.* Retrieved from http://www.uww.edu/icit/olr/stu/learningonline/olr_asset_layout_1_19517_20356.htm l

Watkins, R. (2005). *75 e-Learning activities.* San Francisco, CA: Pfeiffer.

Woo, Y., Herrington, J., Agostinho, S., & Reeves, T. C. (2007). Implementing authentic tasks in web-based learning environments. *Educause Quarterly, 30*(3), 36–43. Retrieved from http://net.educause.edu/ir/library/pdf/eqm0735.pdf

# Author Biographies

Charlotte Cochran is an Associate Program Director at City University of Seattle (CityU) and has served as an Associate Professor for the Albright School of Education since 2007. She holds a PhD in education technology and e-learning from Northcentral University, an MEd in special education from Grand Canyon University, a BEd in education from Lakehead University (Canada), and a BPhEd in physical education from Brock University (Canada).

Steve Brown is an Associate Program Director at City University of Seattle, supervising the Tacoma region's Teacher Certification program and directing the Performance-Based Master's in Teaching program. He has taught courses for CityU for over a decade. Prior to coming to CityU, Steve served as a school administrator, high school teacher, school board member, creator and founder of an educational business, and trial lawyer in Seattle. He holds a BA in political science from the University of Chicago and a JD from the University of Michigan.

# Insider Knowledge–
# Influenced Pedagogy

**Arden Henley**

## Abstract

This article summarizes an approach that enhances adult student engagement and success by consciously incorporating student experiences that relate to topics covered in class. A specific form of didactic exercise is used to incorporate student experience. This approach also provides an opportunity for exploration and discussion of less formal kinds of knowledge that may nevertheless be of value and significance to students and contribute to their engagement in learning. Some implications for the epistemology of learning are discussed.

## Overview

In his account of Cezanne's genius, the French philosopher Merleau-Ponty (1964) made the following assertion:

It is not enough for a painter like Cezanne, an artist, or a philosopher, to create and express an idea; they must also awaken the experiences which will make their idea take root in the consciousness of others. (p. 19)

To the artist and philosopher, the teacher should be added. In the context of preparing students for professional practice, including simulated practice experiences has the benefit of giving students a taste of the world they are about to face (or, in the case of adult learners, are already facing), and an opportunity to further find their footing. Ideally, this approach has the virtue of "epistemological correctness" because it embodies an allegiance to the source of ideas in human experience and a recognition of competencies in navigating particular worlds such as the classroom, in the case of education, and the therapy room, in the case of counselling.

"Epistemological correctness" is a term used by Lave and Wenger (1990) to suggest that learning as it normally occurs is embedded in the activity, context, and culture in which it occurs (i.e., it is situated) in contrast with most classroom learning activities that involve knowledge, which is abstract and out of context. This emphasis on the connection to professional practice is also in accord with a broader focus in *continuing professional education* on experiential education (Coady, 2015) and, more specifically, on incorporating narrative approaches to instruction (Walsh, 2011). Variations of this approach to teaching have been described in previous publications (Henley, 2011; 2013).

## Engaging the Life Experience and Preexisting Knowledge of Adult Learners

Focusing on adult education in particular, adult learners typically bring a richness of life experience and knowledge with them when they resume postsecondary studies. A key to student success in adult learning is to engage, integrate, and make use of this richness. Engaging the life experience and preexisting knowledge of adult learners builds on an existing foundation, while, at the same time, demonstrating an appreciation for the often hard-won life experience of the mature learner. Insider knowledge–influenced pedagogy is an approach that directly addresses this key success factor.

Akin to Polanyi's concept of *tacit knowledge,* "insider knowledge" is specific, localized, and storied knowledge directly flowing from individuals' and the community's interpretations of their life experience and the stratagems that emerge from these interpretations. In addition to affirming the value of adult learners' accounts of their life experiences, recognizing insider knowledge takes into account that more formal knowledge originates in particular human experiences and that initial description, interpretation, and dialogue with others about these experiences constitutes a link to more formal and evidence-based levels of abstraction. This vital and engaging connection is frequently overlooked in the translation of this more colloquial knowledge into the language of the professions and, more formally, in its reification in academic contexts.

In the following account, Epston (2011) spelled out the tentative and poignant features of insider knowledge:

> I would describe an "insider knowledge" as innocent as a newborn child; as delicate as a sprouting seed that has just broken through the soil, as shy and apprehensive as children arriving at what will be their school for their very first day. When we try to speak about them, we can seem as awkward as a fish out of water. "Insider knowledges" are often before or without words, and for that reason, when inside knowers try to speak about their skills/knowledges/theories, they can appear either foolish or to be making unjustifiable claims. (p. 5)

It is this awkwardness and vulnerability that often results in insider knowledge failing to make the grade and being excluded from professional dialogue and learning.

Counselling can be described as a refinement of daily conversation rather than a separate and arcane expert domain. As such, both students and instructors are already familiar with helping conversations, so what is helpful (and what is not) is not entirely a mystery. For example, the common experience of overhearing a conversation in the next booth in a restaurant in which one participant is in some kind of trouble and the other listens well, empathizes, asks a couple of questions, and makes a couple of astute and helpful observations, all within the framework of ordinary daily life. The complainant then says something like, "Oh, I never thought to look at it like that before. I think I'll try telling her I don't understand rather than arguing. Thanks so much; you were really there for me." Framing counselling in this way invites students to relax, step up with accounts of their own experience, and bring forward preexisting know-how. It stimulates interaction and participation, key elements in learning, and overcomes the initial tendency of adult learners to feel that they are starting from behind. In short, it contributes to student engagement and success by creating an aura of confidence and curiosity from the outset. On this foundation, bridging techniques that conjoin this insider knowledge to common counselling practices can be added. For example, enhancing deep listening can be used as a basis for developing the therapeutic relationship.

## Integrating "Underexpressed" Knowledge

Based on a rich life experience, we "know" a great deal about many things, though what we know remains "underexpressed knowledge" *until* someone asks. For example, asking students to "represent" their possible thoughts, feelings, awareness, and dilemmas of themselves as elders in a conversation with a partner (and vice versa) is a means of evoking underexpressed knowledge about aging. "Represent" in this context means to speak on behalf of or give voice to oneself as an elder. "Representation" does not include an imperative to play or act out with gestures and feelings as in role-play, but a direction to convey an intimate and particular knowledge. The "representational" element here is important in freeing participants from the self-consciousness of role-play on behalf of uncovering, accessing, and intuiting the underexpressed. Including an observer to the exercise assigned to follow up the dialogue with a question based on what she or he became curious about while listening (and not on a critique of the conversation) adds another layer to the learning experience. The use of curiosity as a basis for responding invites observers to engage with and give expression to their own experience and accounts and contributes to an emotionally safe environment in which the personal and professional can be integrated.

As an example, a student, representing a dilemma from her "elder self" talked about an opportunity she had turned away from, blinded by the desires and social expectations of the moment, and now saw as a missed opportunity for fulfillment. The participants witnessed an instance of the impact of nostalgia and regret, common experiences of aging. This approach also offered the person listening and asking questions an opportunity to see what kinds of questions and observations work well under such circumstances. It evoked what David Epston has referred to as "ethnographic imagination," which engenders empathy on the part of the listener, an important skill for both therapists and educators to cultivate (Epston, 2014; Kasl & Yorks, 2016). Group discussion combined with student expression of experience and reflection incorporates a pedagogical approach that is an extension of Karl Thom's development of "internalized other" interviewing (Tomm, Hoyt, & Madigan, 1998). This form of interviewing is based on the premise that we all have centers of knowing built around our understanding of others with whom we are or have been in relationship. We "know" to some extent (depending on our perceptual clarity and insight and the depth of the relationship) what others think and feel. An extension of this approach in the context of pedagogy presumes that we also have a relationship with ourselves and, therefore, a capacity to speak about what we have experienced in the past and will experience in the future.

In this form of instruction, learning and knowledge production access and enhance "insider knowledge" based on dialogue that uses the language of the initial experience and with fidelity to that experience as a value. Then, in the context of further dialogue and reflection, the templates of current and past theorizing and contemporary research can be brought to bear on the phenomenon, activating a link to the learner's own experience and existing knowledge. In this way, more formal kinds of knowledge can be viewed and critiqued as evolutions of the "already known" rather than standing aloof as esoteric domains in and of themselves. With antecedents in Vygotsky, this form of pedagogy understands learning as first "performance" and, subsequently, dialogue, reflection, and abstraction (Brown, Collins & Duguid, 1988).

Insider knowledge–influenced pedagogy also introduces an alternative epistemology; a different way of knowing that exposes the constructed and culturally shaped natures of knowledge by engaging students in knowledge creation as a process rather than a given, a process that relates intimately to their experience of daily life and how they account for these experiences. It provides an opportunity for previously underexpressed or, in some instances, subjugated knowledge to emerge, circulate, and coexist with more established and formally recognized forms of knowledge. These less socially countenanced forms of knowledge are nevertheless cherished by various individuals and communities, especially minorities, and are often in use as significant means of living well (Webster-Wright, 2009). From a student-learning point of view, the evocation of these forms of knowledge creates an inclusive and enlivening learning environment in which what matters personally and culturally, and professionally, is explored (Dirkx, 2008; 2013). This point is much in evidence where life stories and associated knowledge of Canada's indigenous minority is explicitly incorporated.

## From a Curriculum Perspective

From a curriculum point of view, the inclusion of stories that illuminate personal, interpersonal, and social phenomena relevant to course objectives is a further reflection of this pedagogy. For example, at CityU in Canada modules about Canada's Truth and Reconciliation Commission explicitly incorporate stories told by indigenous people about their residential school experience. These touching and, at times painful, accounts directly access the impact of over one hundred years of racism and colonization in Canada during which aboriginal children were removed from their families and sent to institutions called residential schools. These government-funded, church-run schools were located across Canada and established with the purpose of eliminating parental involvement in the spiritual, cultural, and intellectual development of aboriginal children (Truth and Reconciliation Commission, 2015). An indigenous scholar designed and instructed these instructional modules, which are, in turn, embedded in ethics courses in the CityU Canada Master of Education and Master of Counselling programs. These modules incorporate an understanding of colonization from an indigenous perspective and a call to action to which students are asked to respond with specific commitments.

## Conclusion

Insider knowledge–influenced pedagogy is especially suited to instructing adult learners, most of whom have some degree or another experience with the phenomena under discussion and many ideas of different origins as well. This form of pedagogy activates this storehouse of knowledge and respects its significance to learners while offering an opportunity to further refine the "already known" and relate it to more formal, text-based knowledge. The net effect is an experience of learning in which the intellectual schemata and related competencies of the professions are complemented with a sense of personal meaning and authenticity.

In summary, insider knowledge–influenced pedagogy:

- Enhances student success by engaging students' prior experience and knowledge
- Inspires confidence by evoking students' preexisting knowledge and establishing a link between this foundational, experiential knowledge and current evidence-based research and academic theory
- Makes use of students' experience and knowledge as a readily accessible resource for practice-focused exercises and discussion
- Provides a useful complement to courses in which competency or performance-based outcomes are emphasized
- Promotes student success by evoking engagement and interaction; demonstrating the connection between personal experience, "local" knowledge, and evidence-based research and academic theory; and facilitating practice-focused exercises and demonstrations that enhance course-related competencies
- Enhances interpersonal competencies such as empathy and adds a sense of authenticity to the learning process

# References

Brown, J. S., Collins, A., & Duguid, P. (1988). Situated cognition and the culture of learning. *Educational Researcher, 18*(1), 32–42.

Coady, M. J. (2015). From Houle to Dirkx: Continuing professional education (CPE), a critical state-of-the-field review. *Canadian Journal for the Study of Adult Education, 27*(3), 27–41.

Dirkx, J. (2008). Care of the self: Mythopoetic dimensions of professional preparation and development. In T. Leonard & P. Willis (Eds.),

*Pedagogies of the imagination: Mythopoetic curriculum in educational practice* (pp. 65–83). New York, NY: Springer.

Dirkx, J. (2013). Leaning in and leaning back at the same time: Toward spirituality of work-related learning. *Advances in Developing Human Resources, 15*(4), 356–369.

Epston, D. (2011). More travels with Herodotus: Tripping over borders lightly or "psychiatric imperialism." *Journal of Systemic Therapies, 30*(3), 1–11.

Epston, D. (2014). Ethnography, co-research, and insider knowledge. *The International Journal of Narrative Therapy and Community Work, 1,* 65–68.

Henley, A. (2011). *Social architecture: Notes & essays.* Vancouver, BC: The Write Room Press.

Henley, A. (2013). *Legitimate peripheral participation: Learning reconceived as a transformation of social identity.* In K. D. Kirstein, C. E. Schieber, K. A. Flores, & S. G. Olswang (Eds.) *Innovations in teaching adults: Proven practices in higher education* (pp. 175–184). North Charleston, SC: CreateSpace.

Kasl, E., & Yorks, L. (2016). Do I really know you? Do you really know me? Empathy amid diversity in differing learning contexts. *Adult Education Quarterly, 66,* 1 3–20.

Lave, J., & Wenger, E. (1990). *Situated learning: Legitimate peripheral participation.* Cambridge, United Kingdom: Cambridge University Press.

Merleau-Ponty, M. (1964). *Sense and non-sense* (H. L. Dreyfus & P. A. Dreyfus, Trans.). Chicago, IL: Northwestern University Press.

Tomm, K., Hoyt, M., & Madigan, S. (1998). Honoring our internalized others and the ethics of caring: A conversation with Karl Tomm. In M. Hoyt (Ed.), *The handbook of constructive therapies* (pp. 198–218). San Francisco, CA: Jossey-Bass.

Truth and Reconciliation Commission of Canada. (2015). *TRC Findings.* Retrieved from http://www.trc.ca/websites/trcinstitution/index.php?p=890

Walsh, M. (2011). Narrative pedagogy and simulation: Future directions for nursing education. *Nurse Education in Practice, 11*(3), 216–219.

Webster-Wright, A. (2009). Reframing professional development through understanding authentic professional learning. *Review of Educational Research, 79*(2), 702–739.

## Author Biography

Arden Henley is the Vice President and Principal of Canadian programs at City University of Seattle. Previously he was the director of White Rock Family Therapy Institute, the director of Clinical Services at Peach Arch Community Services, and the executive director of the South Okanagan Children's Services Society. He has a BA from McMaster University, an MA from Duquesne University, and an EdD in leadership from Simon Fraser University. Dr. Henley has practiced organization development and family therapy for over forty years and consulted broadly with community and government agencies.

# 9

# When West Meets East: Decoding Chinese Culture and How Intercultural Communication Is Applied in Classrooms

**HongYing Douglas**

## Abstract

This chapter reviews Hofstede's cultural dimension model, the Lewis model, and Trompenaars's cultural universalism versus particularism to provide intercultural communication tools to educators who are confronted with the challenge of how to effectively teach foreign students, particularly from China. This chapter also investigates how cultures are exhibited and intertwined in students' use of the English language. Techniques on how to navigate a class mostly made up of Chinese students and strategies for how to help students succeed in their graduate studies are provided.

## Overview

In 1995, the author came to the United States to pursue her master's degree in teaching English. Her university in Virginia was relatively small, and she was the only international student in the graduate program. Being foreign to every aspect of the States, she quickly realized her desperate need to learn to adjust. While attaining her degree, the author came across a variety of professors: professors who thought highly of her simply because she fought through endless cutthroat competitions to win her place in a college in China, professors who were kindhearted and fascinated about the Asian culture but couldn't quite figure out how to offer academic support, professors who felt sorry for her because she was a lonely "poor thing" and decided to give her high grades that she probably didn't earn, and professors who challenged her the same way they did her American peers. These professors refused to lower the university's academic standards just to preserve her "self-esteem." They assumed strength and challenged her and helped her grow.

After one year of being silent in class, learning to adapt to linear thinking and apply it in writing, and all the tears, self-doubts, and fatigues later, the author started to think and act like a graduate student. She came to realize her journey could be of great value to the professors who teach those excited, but often feeling lost, newcomers from China. That became the genesis of this chapter: an insider's view.

## Review of the Literature

As the world is becoming increasingly globalized, so is education. To many Chinese, an educational experience in the United States is the key to becoming a global citizen and, most importantly, a ticket for a better job, hence a better life. China's GDP in 2014 was an estimated $13,200 per capita, and China has always been a saving society with the gross national saving rate close to 49 percent (Central Intelligence Agency, n.d.). Chinese parents save to sponsor their only child to learn innovation and creativity in the United States. As China's middle class is expanding, sending children to the West is no longer an impossible dream. Data from the Institute of International Education (n.d.) indicates that as of 2013/2014, 274,439 Chinese students were studying in American universities or colleges, which comprised 31 percent of the total international student population in the United States.

As the number of students from China pursuing higher degrees in the United States increases, many professors find themselves in uncharted territory teaching a class where the majority of students are from the Far East, or particularly China. To prevent cultural communication breakdowns from happening while helping students grow academically, professors need to quickly learn and understand students' cultures and effectively apply cultural communication skills in classroom instruction.

## Hofstede's Cultural Dimension Model

Hofstede's cultural dimension model illustrates how a certain national culture is scored in relation to other cultures. Of the six dimensions, power distance, individualism/collectivism, and uncertainty avoidance are particularly applicable in promoting understanding between Western instructors and Eastern students in an increasingly globalized classroom setting. The following chart shows how the United States and China score on Hofstede's power distance, individualism/collectivism, and uncertainty avoidance dimensions.

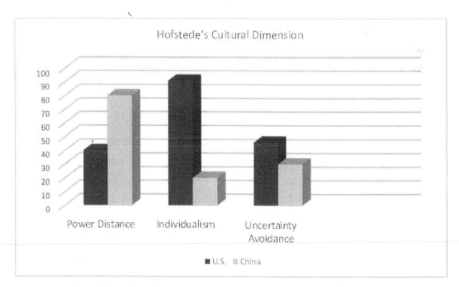

*Source: Hofstede (n.d.), China in Comparison with United States*

**Power distance.** Power distance explains how equal a society is, how people in this society see equality and authority, whether they accept inequality, how much they are willing to defend themselves when confronted with power, and how much fear authority can provoke. Compared with the United States' score of 40, China's 80 points indicate that power disparity is accepted, fearing authority is the norm, superiors hold most of the power, going beyond ranking and questioning authority is unacceptable, and punishment for those who do is well justified (Hofstede, n.d., China in Comparison with United States). In the States, democracy is the foundation, and achieving equality is the end goal. In a society as such, people are encouraged to break barriers, and challenging authority is greatly admired.

The power distance dimension is a useful tool in analyzing interactions between instructors and students. When instructors from a low-power distance society meet students from a high-power distance society, misunderstandings will likely occur. Seeing instructors as authority figures who can't be challenged, Chinese students are reluctant to voice their opinions or express their disagreement because in China asking questions and voicing disagreement are seen as disrespectful and will be penalized or publicly shamed. In the States, educators are facilitators; they are not seen as know-it-alls. They encourage students to participate, interact, and approach them with questions and concerns. The flip side of this democratic, nonauthoritative Western approach is that it may confuse foreign students. To put it simply, Chinese students prefer to see their professors as authority figures. Otherwise, they will quickly lose respect for their instructors and question the value of the education they are receiving if they see their instructors as their equals.

**Individualism vs. collectivism.** Hofstede's individualism dimension measures "the degree of interdependence a society maintains among its members" (The Hofstede Centre, n.d., What about China, para. 4). China scores a 20 as opposed to a 91 for the United States in individualism. In the States individualism is a mindset and way of life; individuals are responsible for their own achievements. Whereas in China, the translation of individualism is "GeRenZhuYi," which connotes selfishness. Although it might be overgeneralizing to define China as a "we" society and the United States as an "I" society, this wide gap does explain why Chinese students frequently struggle to establish an individual identity in the States. They likely form in-groups among their Chinese peers, and within the group they will help each other, trade favors quid pro quo, and live a comfortable Chinese life in the United States. The positive side of this cultural bondage is they are less lonely; the negative side is that they fail to gain new experiences, take risks, and take advantage of what the United States offers.

**Uncertainty avoidance.** Hofstede defines uncertainty avoidance as "the extent to which the members of a culture feel threatened by ambiguous or unknown situations and have created beliefs and institutions that try to avoid these" (Hofstede, n.d., What about China? para. 9). China scores a 30 in this dimension, whereas the United States a 46 (Hofstede, n.d., "China in Comparison with United States"). Hofstede's interpretation of the States' relatively low score lies in its willingness to tolerate the unknowns, welcome new and different ideas, and underscore technological innovation and creativity. As Hofstede puts it, the American society is less likely to be threatened by the unknown and will play an innovative force to influence other cultures (n.d., What about the USA?). China's low score in this dimension can be highlighted by "pragmatism" and "ambiguity" (n.d., What about China? para. 10). Although social norms are strictly conformed to and anyone who violates them will be crucified, laws and rules are seen as bendable. The "go with the flow" mentality is exhibited by Chinese students in both academic and nonacademic lives, where they occasionally fail to comply with the schools' rules and policies, and laws in general.

## The Lewis Model

The Lewis model divides cultures into multi-active, linear-active, and reactive. "Reactive or listening cultures rarely initiate action or discussion, preferring first to listen to and establish the other's position, then react to it and formulate their own" (CrossCulture, n.d., Cultural Classification: Reactive, para. 1). Lewis (n.d.) describes Chinese culture as reactive, where people are "courteous, amiable, accommodating, compromising, and good listener(s)." In a reactive world, people tend to be polite to the extent of hiding true feelings, and losing face can lead to communication breakdown or even contractual rejection. The Chinese are good listeners and compromisers who are eager to accommodate. Voicing opinions is not encouraged, and if they feel compelled to express themselves, they will express something nice and complementary. The Lewis Model explains why Chinese students in the US universities are seen as passive participants in teamwork, whose opinions are indirect and sometimes hard to comprehend. On the bright side, they are pleasing and polite and nonconfrontational.

## Trompenaars and Hampden-Turner's Model of National Culture Differences

One of the seven dimensions developed by Trompenaars and Hampden-Turner is universalism versus particularism. Universalists believe that rules are equally applied, and they tend to trust the legal systems and not to rely on personal connections, whereas particularists believe that connections and personal relationships trump rules and laws (2012). "GuanXi," a Chinese term meaning important ties or connections, is the number-one priority if people want to achieve their goals. With people, rules are flexible; "GuanXi" can bend laws. Chinese students in the States tend to carry over this type of mentality and try to manipulate rules. They may cheat on tests or commit plagiarism and expect not to be caught or not to be penalized. This behavior is not typical of Chinese as long as a society rewards those who bend rules.

## Integration into the Student Experience

Cultural communication skills can be used in all aspects of instruction. Professors can teach students to accept their responsibilities for learning, which is quite the opposite of what they were taught in their home country. Professors can help students understand that syllabi and schedules are academic contracts, and deadlines should be respected. Professors can create a learning environment where risk taking is rewarded, and students can actively participate in discussions and voice their opinions without worrying about "losing face" or being punished. Professors can teach students to be resourceful and help them develop the needed confidence to navigate university services without fear of being judged. Professors can help prevent cheating and plagiarism by enforcing the scholastic honesty policy and making students understand that no one is above the "law" of the school, even though he/she is from a culture where power and influence can bend rules.

## Proven Practices, Examples, and Results

Channeling culture and putting intercultural communication skills in use are vital to instructional success in a globalized classroom. Instructors need not feel like they're walking on eggshells for fear of offending foreign students or hurting their feelings. As much as they need instructional support, foreign students are rather resilient, so by being firm and resourceful and not lowering the school's academic integrity, instructors will likely provide the support that students desperately need.

# Multisensory Instruction

International students learn two things: content and language skill. Fulfilling the requirements of the test of English as a foreign language (TOEFL) and graduate record exam (GRE) can get a foreign student admitted to an institute in the United States, but to succeed and grow academically requires far more than high scores on the two tests. Information retention in a second language is low. International students often complain they heard everything their instructors said but could not recall a thing, or they read the text material a few times but still couldn't recall what they just read a few minutes ago. Almost all international students have had this type of almost "out-of-body" experience to various degrees. To help students retain knowledge in their second language, instructors need to employ a multisensory instructional strategy. For example, instructors may need to give students a variety of instructional choices such as breaking down texts into small pieces, using PowerPoint, videos, and study groups, and meeting with students in person.

# Structured and Explicit Instruction

Foreign students' daily life is filled with surprises. They interact with confusion and ambiguity, constantly guessing, negotiating meaning, and making sense of their academic and nonacademic environments, and none of these interactions is natural for them. To reduce students' confusion and stress caused by confusion, instructors need to better structure their course materials and instruction. Structured and explicit teaching helps students understand and follow instructions more effectively.

## Silence and Face

"The bird that sticks its head up will get shot first"—a Chinese proverb

"The squeaky wheel gets the grease"—an American proverb

The two proverbs show a sharp contrast between the two cultures; one emphasizes standing out, one blending in. The American culture encourages people to voice their ideas, to get noticed, to be heard, while Chinese people choose to be silent for fear of punishment for speaking out or being wrong. China is a high-context culture where what is said is not as important as what is not said, and face has become a complex concept that many non-Chinese find extremely challenging to interpret. Worrying about losing face, Chinese students tend to be quiet because they don't want to feel embarrassed with their ideas in addition to their relatively low English-speaking skills. Sometimes students will say yes or lie to protect their instructor's face. So one lesson to instructors is when students say yes, it may not mean that they agree, but if they say maybe, it most likely means no. Instructors from a low context culture as the United States may need great exposure to be able to interpret these types of behaviors.

## Lessons Learned, Tips for Success, and Recommendations

The SCORE communication principle by Berardo (2012, p. 225) is of great value to instructors who teach students having cultural, academic, and language challenges in the United States.

## S—Simplify and Specify

When instructors' language use is not simple and information is not specific, misunderstandings will likely occur particularly for foreign students. Instructors need simple, direct language with clear details; the use of idioms and slang needs to be avoided.

## C—Clarify and Confirm

For foreign students, misunderstanding is common, so it is important for both instructors and students to apply this principle and check understanding regularly. To minimize misunderstanding, they both need to use expressions such as "what I meant was . . . ," "just to clarify . . . ," "so what you are saying . . ."

## O—Organize and Outline

When instructors present course materials in a well-organized manner and outline the key points, students are likely to be able to understand and follow the instruction effectively. Numbering key ideas and using headings and subheadings are helpful.

## R—Rephrase and Reframe

Instructors need to use a variety of ways to communicate ideas. When one way doesn't work, instructors need to try another way to be understood, and to check students' understanding, instructors need to ask students to rephrase what they just heard.

## E—Explain with Examples

Using examples is an effective way to help students understand instructions and course materials. However, instructors need to be mindful when choosing examples. Examples need to be generational and less culturally rich because students may get confused and miss the point.

## Conclusion

International students will likely succeed when they have professors who "get them." Professors with higher cultural intelligence will likely challenge students and help them grow. They will not simply pass students on to become someone else's problem, or coddle and patronize them because they feel sorry for "these poor kids" and don't want to hurt their feelings. Cultural communication skills will help American professors properly challenge and sufficiently support international students. In doing so, they maximize students' learning outcomes and experiences.

# References

Berardo, K. (2012). Framework: The SCORE communication principles. In K. Berardo, D. K. Deardorff, & F. Trompenaars (Eds.), *Building cultural competence: Innovative activities and models* (pp. 225–230). Sterling, VA: Stylus Publishing.

Central Intelligence Agency. (n.d.). The world factbook: East & Southeast Asia: China. Retrieved from https://www.cia.gov/library/publications/the-world-factbook/geos/ch.html

CrossCulture. (n.d.). Cultural classification: Reactive. Retrieved from http://www.crossculture.com/about-us/the-model/reactive/

The Hofstede Centre. (n.d.). What about China? Retrieved from http://geert-hofstede.com/china.html

The Hofstede Centre. (n.d.). What about the USA? Retrieved from http://geert-hofstede.com/united-states.html

Trompenaars, F., & Hampden-Turner, C. (2012). *Riding the waves of culture: Understanding diversity in global business* (3rd ed.). London, United Kingdom: Nicholas Brealey Publishing.

# Author Biography

HongYing Douglas received her MA in education with a focus on language and literacy from Christopher Newport University. She taught

English for several years at the University of Arizona before returning to school to earn her MBA at the University of Colorado. Her teaching career spans more than twenty years. She has taught in the English Language program, Teacher Education program, and language-assisted MBA and MBA programs at City University of Seattle.

# Part II

# Proven Practices for Motivating and Engaging Adult Students

# 10

# Student Motivation in Online Courses

**Gregory Price**

## Abstract

Student achievement in online education shows no significant difference from traditional face-to-face learning (Hawkins, Barbour, & Graham, 2012; Lewis, Whiteside, & Dikkers, 2014). With this as a backdrop, online education has been given a remarkable boost in consumer confidence, credibility, and growth (Lewis et al., 2014). Yet understanding student motivation in online education has shown this medium is still in its developmental infancy. Administrators are quickly making adjustments, as motivation factors heavily into student retention rates. Curriculum design, quality assignments, faculty communication, and student feedback all affect student engagement, satisfaction, and motivation. The online environment favors students who have basic technology capabilities, can manage time well, and desire independence. Administrators that support these features positively affect student success (Kranzow, 2013). This chapter will look into successful pedagogical strategies for administrators, curriculum designers, and faculty for the online environment.

## Overview

In today's changing labor markets, adults are finding it necessary to maintain currency and improve workplace skills. Often this means returning to the classroom as adult learners. However, much has changed in education over the years. Courses are now online and, generally speaking, adult learners who are new to the online environment are unaccustomed to this style of learning. Consequently, this affects the experience they have as they navigate today's online courses. In this environment students are expected to possess some basic technical skills, be adept at time management, and desire independence. These factors enhance a student's online success. Though these factors enable students to perform, students expect the environment to also function in a way that supports these success factors.

The educator's job is to create a learning environment that takes these factors into account. In this way, students function better and become adept learners. This translates into a motivating learner environment. Educators can create this motivating environment by designing quality courses. Thus, incorporating a supportive learner environment with these student success factors can have a positive impact in motivating the learner (Ilgaz & Gülbahar, 2015).

Knowing what motivates adult online learners serves to increase the quality of the learning process. Course design, instructor communication strategies, learner expectations, and student-centered independence all influence student motivation. Collectively, these factors contribute to adult self-efficacy, a critical component to online success and retention rates. Though adult learners take ownership of self-motivation, demotivation is perceived as a "teacher-owned problem" (Petty & Thomas, 2014, p. 475). Therefore, the way to retain adult learners is to create an environment that overcomes barriers to classroom participation. Wise (2003) created a formula that can be applied to today's online courses. The formula is "challenging tasks + good instructors + success + recognition = motivation" (Wise, 2003, p. 42). This formula offers a simple model to deliver the best in online adult education.

## Review of the Literature

Learning in the online environment is different. Students are aware that they are in control of their environment, and they take responsibility for and invest in their own learning (Ilgaz & Gülbahar, 2015). For this scenario to manifest success, students need to come equipped with basic technical skills to overcome the demands of the learning management systems (LMS) used in online courses. But to increase the odds of success, administrators must ensure course design is aligned with the learning goals, and instructors should incorporate a positive presence in the course while responding to students quickly and effectively (Lewis et al., 2014).

Aside from the technological challenges learners may experience, it has been found that administrators, curriculum designers, and faculty are also struggling to adapt to changing technology (Ilgaz & Gülbahar, 2015). Key findings in the literature suggest that educators are presently comfortable delivering face-to-face instruction. The challenge is that in-class methods of instruction do not always translate well to online pedagogy. On the upside, researchers are helping to identify new supportive and adaptive mechanisms to engage and instruct today's online student (Alijani, Kwun, & Yu, 2014).

Lewis et al. (2014) found that adult students have a need to be in control, take responsibility for, and invest in their learning, but the classroom must also have student support mechanisms in place. Should these support mechanisms not be incorporated in the delivery of the course, student motivation may wane, leading to hurdles students may find difficult to overcome, leading to reduced retention. However, applying the model Wise (2003) derived, and using the ideas appropriately and consistently, can motivate students. These learner-centered approaches where "individual learner characteristics, preferences, motivations, and goals" are addressed can motivate students to achieve their desired educational outcomes (Cornelius, Gordon, & Ackland, 2011, p. 381).

## The Student-Learner Perspective

The online learning environment is different for the adult learner. Students are faced with making their own schedules, working at their own pace, completing assignments within a flexible environment, and studying independently. Though the tactical avenues to this style of education may sound appealing, students have found the single most challenging aspect of online learning is being responsible for completing their own work on time (Alijani et al., 2014; Plummer, 2012).

Consequently, best practices in online delivery contain assignments where students become reflective in their learning and connect the content to personal experience (Alijani et al., 2014; Roehl, Reddy, & Shannon, 2013; Quek Choon, 2010). These activities support active engagement and are learner centered. Though students have found reflective learning satisfying, this single approach to learning does not solve all the motivational challenges students face. Further studies in student social engagement may be necessary as a critical aspect to further student-centered learning.

## Advancing Online Engagement

The Internet has advanced opportunities across the business landscape by bringing individuals, communities, and organizations closer together. Web 2.0 has further advanced this bridge by giving these same groups the ability to interact socially. Understanding this two-way social interaction and integrating the idea into an online pedagogical model can be quite different. Integrating these ideas into the online classroom has proved challenging as many instructors perceive the environment as a mechanism to deliver content in a unidirectional manner.

The challenges can be more difficult when trying to integrate social interactions in a virtual environment as there are significant differences in teaching practices between face-to-face instruction and the virtual classroom. To fully understand these differences, instructors may need a paradigm shift to understand their "roles, responsibilities, and instructional strategies" in the online classroom (Hawkins et al., 2012, p. 124). The upside is that instructors are experimenting with different integrative teaching approaches. One such approach that is gaining traction is where instructors are integrating blogs, wikis, journals, and video technologies as ways to integrate social interaction that can act as a virtual replacement for face-to-face instruction.

Within the online educational environment, Lewis et al. (2014) showed that by delivering a consistently engaging student-centered experience, students can be motivated. Engagement is key. Plummer (2012) stated that quality and engaging content, along with instructional support, often delivers the highest student-centered success rates. This active-learning pedagogy delivers the necessary competencies students need today: critical thinking, self-reflection, creativity, communication, independence, and collaboration (Quek Choon, 2010). The active-learning pedagogy has been found to unlock gains in student performance by significant margins (Alijani et al., 2014; Prince, 2004).

## Integrating a High-Quality Student Experience

Students with no previous experience in online education can often feel as if they are unable to master the required set of new rules. Much of this is the result of students missing the connection they had in the face-to-face classroom. Thus, course developers in the online environment will want to replicate, as much as possible, the face-to-face feel in an online classroom.

Students can develop a similar connection in the online environment, but it can take time to nurture. For students just starting out in online education, there are some helpful characteristics to be aware of, such as (1) have an open mind, (2) be capable of building self-efficacy, and (3) regulate learning. By knowing these outcomes, students can support higher levels of confidence and increase their morale, both of which can lead to higher academic accomplishment (Alijani et al., 2014; Moore, 2014).

Additionally, instructors who integrate a variety of active-learning pedagogic strategies can support this student-centered academic success. By keeping the educational environment simple and the learning flexible, the approach suits "learner characteristics, preferences, motivations and goals" (Cornelius et al., 2011, p. 381).

Taking these characteristics and incorporating them into the classroom supports a constructivist model where learners take responsibility for their own learning. For students, this creates a dynamic relationship between course assignments, personal knowledge, and experience. Learners take the discussion from concrete examples found in self-reflection and they begin to conceptualize deeper meaning by engaging with members of the learning community.

For some instructors, doing this may be unfamiliar to their teaching style. For them to engage online students successfully, it is advised they experiment with various instructional strategies until they find teaching techniques that incorporate their own voice, deliver the course content in an engaging manner, and develop supportive relationships. Once instructors achieve this, the classroom has a comfortable, independent feel and supportive atmosphere—additional key factors that support student motivation (Moore, 2014).

Faculty who incorporate self-reflection assessments help the learning community develop critical thinking skills. By keeping the learning flexible and including resources that support the learning activities, students approach the content by exploring ideas within their personal and professional interest. The method encourages peer interaction, self-discovery, and motivation to further engage in their learning goals. To further student-centered learning and instruction, faculty can apply the community of inquiry as a natural integration to student-centered instruction.

## Community of Inquiry

Furthering instructional success, one of the better-known models is the community of inquiry (CIO) framework as shown in Figure 1 (Hawkins et al., 2012; Johnston, Greer, & Smith, 2014). This framework incorporates three distinct student-centered constructs: "teacher presence, cognitive presence, and social presence" (Hawkins et al., 2012, p. 125). Combined, these three elements of instructional presence create a powerful online learning experience. This framework forms a distinctive student-centered engagement that develops active discussions, acknowledges and understands perspectives from others in the classroom, and challenges student assumptions (Johnston et al., 2014).

*Figure 1. Hawkins, Barbour, & Graham, 2012; Johnston, Greer, & Smith, 2014*

By including all three elements of presence in the classroom, the intersection delivers a consistent online presence that builds self-efficacy through motivating pedagogic practices. The following descriptions help breakdown and define this success:

**Teacher Presence**. Instructor presence creates meaningful outcomes: curriculum design, active instructor facilitation, and integrating multiple pathways for both the cognitive and social aspects of the educational process. As students enter the depths of the course, instructors are engaged, present, active, and provide meaningful feedback (Hawkins et al., 2012).

**Cognitive Presence**. Cognitive presence engages students in the course content. By incorporating engaging assignments, students become enveloped into the reflective process where meaning takes shape based on experiences presented outside of the classroom (Hawkins et al., 2012).

**Social Presence**. Social presence links the student's sense of community by seeing people as individuals with whom they can establish a sense of trust and connection through informal communication tactics such as humor and self-disclosure. This construct takes form in the online environment through engaged stimulation of student-to-student interaction through enhanced understanding of others' thoughts, feelings, and motivations (Hawkins et al., 2012; Johnston et al., 2014).

Taken as a whole, community of inquiry supports an active-learning environment that focuses on student-centered learning. To achieve such an outcome, administrators will need to commit to supporting instructors through ongoing professional development (Alijani et al., 2014; Hawkins et al., 2012; Johnston et al., 2014).

# Training, Feedback, and Support

Of the many roles the program administrator is tasked with, ensuring faculty are instructing courses in a manner congruent with the rules and policies of the institution, the school or department, and the program is a core function. Faculty work hard to improve their craft, to provide quality instruction, and to adapt to new standards. As online education continues to evolve at a rapid pace, faculty members look to the administrator to provide these necessary tools, updates, feedback, instruction, and training to keep them current. Faculty who are competent in course instruction, have good technological capabilities, and are familiar with instructional tools in the LMS transfer a positive emotional component that is visible to student learners. Administrators are responsible for improving faculty teaching competencies, and by doing so will have more engaged faculty. Research has shown a positive correlation between faculty engagement and learner motivation (Ilgaz & Gülbahar, 2015).

## Conclusion

Staying current in any industry falls within a continuum. In the educational industry, learning and adapting to new instructional pedagogy is a requirement to maintain and enhance one's career. This directly affects students in the classroom.

As the transition from face-to-face to online classrooms continues, developing effective online instructional pedagogy is becoming paramount to student success, the instructor, and the institution. Knowing and understanding the needs of the student entering an online program while also delivering effective instructional methodologies within the classroom becomes a formula for success. Simply stated, "Challenging tasks + good instructors + success + recognition = motivation" (Wise, 2003, p. 42).

## References

Alijani, G. S., Kwun, O., & Yu, Y. (2014). Effectiveness of blended learning in KIPP New Orlean's schools. *Academy of Educational Leadership Journal, 18*(2), 125–141.

Cornelius, S., Gordon, C., & Ackland, A. (2011). Towards flexible learning for adult learners in professional contexts: An activity-focused course design. *Interactive Learning Environments, 19*(4), 381–393.

Hawkins, A., Barbour, M. K., & Graham, C. R. (2012). Everybody is their own island: Teacher disconnection in a virtual school. *International Review* of *Research in Open and Distance Learning, 13*(2). Retrieved from http://www.irrodl.org/index.php/irrodl/article/view/967/2143

Ilgaz, H., & Gülbahar, Y. (2015). A snapshot of online learners: E-readiness, e-satisfaction and expectations. *International Review of Research in Open & Distance Learning, 16*(2), 171–187.

Johnston, S. C., Greer, D., & Smith, S. J. (2014). Peer learning in virtual schools. *Journal of Distance Education (Online), 28*(1), 1–31. http://dx.doi.org/10.4135/9781483325361.n8

Kranzow, J. (2013). Faculty leadership in online education: Structuring courses to impact student satisfaction and persistence. *Journal of Online Learning & Teaching, 9*(1), 131–139.

Lewis, S., Whiteside, A., & Dikkers, A. G. (2014). Autonomy and responsibility: Online learning as a solution for at-risk high school students. *Journal of Distance Education (Online), 29*(2), 1–11.

Moore, R. (2014). Importance of developing community in distance education courses. *TechTrends: Linking Research & Practice to Improve Learning, 58*(2), 20–24. doi:10.1007/s11528-014-0733-x

Petty, T., & Thomas, C. C. (2014). Approaches to a successful adult education program. *College Student Journal, 48*(3), 473.

Plummer, L. (2012). Assuring a virtual second chance. *T H E Journal, 39*(2), 20–22.

Prince, M. (2004). Does active learning work? A review of the research. *Journal of Engineering Education—Washington, 93*(3), 223–232.

Roehl, A., Reddy, S. L., & Shannon, G. J. (2013). The flipped classroom: An opportunity to engage millennial students through active learning. *Journal of Family and Consumer Sciences, 105*(2), 44-49.

Quek Choon, L. (2010). Analysing high school students' participation and interaction in an asynchronous online project-based learning environment. *Australasian Journal of Educational Technology, 26(3),* 327–340.

Wise, B. J. (2003). Motivate at-risk students with meaningful work. *Education Digest, 69(4),* 39–42.

## Author Biography

Greg Price is the Academic Program Director for the Master of Arts in Leadership and Human Resource Management programs at City University of Seattle. He is also an Associate Professor teaching courses in leadership and business. In private industry, he served as a director for a training organization in Tokyo, Japan, and as publisher and vice president for a regional publishing company. He earned a BA in economics from the University of Washington, an MBA from the University of Phoenix and is presently a doctoral candidate earning an EdD in leadership at City University of Seattle.

# 11

# Motivating Unmotivated Adult English Language Learners in an Advanced Reading-Writing Course

**Rachel Peterson and Christine Knorr**

## Abstract

Adult English learners in advanced ESL courses often lose their motivation to deepen their language skills once a functional level of fluency has been achieved. Applying a holistic, dynamic, literature-based curriculum based on the principles of experiential learning to enhance the skills of these students has been a proven success strategy in the design of City University of Seattle's (CityU) Advanced Communications I: Intro to Composition and Literature Course. The proven practices behind this course design can substantially motivate the advanced second language student toward deeper fluency and academic success while remedying the factors that cause second-language error fossilization.

## Overview

English as a second language (ESL) instructors experience a discrepancy in classroom learning environments between low-intermediate-level adult learners and advanced-level adult learners. While there is engagement in class activities, an eagerness to find and correct errors, and a joy in discovering new vocabulary in lower-level students, advanced students often exhibit bad attitudes, bemoaning even minimal amounts of homework and exhibiting marked ambivalence toward self-editing habitual mistakes—mistakes that can be easily resolved by students when prompted. These advanced second-language students can be hard to engage if they are grouped with peers who also display this behavior. In advanced ESL courses, the classroom dynamic can become oppressive, with little student engagement in course content or group activities. The reasons behind this lack of motivation are complex, but two factors in particular contribute simultaneously to a marked malaise toward even the highest-quality educational experience: adequate fluency for daily life in an English immersion environment and a loss of motivation that leads to error fossilization.

These factors are not separate issues. They are woven together by students' conflicting life experiences, inside and outside the classroom. As international students study abroad and gain higher functional fluency, their individual quirks of language (grammar, pronunciation, word choice errors) can become masked in English-speaking environments. In large, international cities where native English speakers are used to hearing international students' accents, or on campuses where international students from the same country communicate only with each other (avoiding native English-speaking peers), using similar broken English and similar accents, international students may not realize that their language progress has stagnated. This creates an illusion of high functional fluency in the mind of an international student, who believes that if his or her English is sufficient for Starbucks orders, apartment rentals, and the Department of Licensing, then he or she must be speaking articulately and no longer needs to monitor his or her mistakes. To add to this illusion, native English speakers—such as classmates, waiters, or bank tellers—may feel it is rude to provide corrections, instead attempting to bridge communication gaps in whatever polite way possible. Repeated mistakes do not hamper daily communication, so these functionally fluent second-language (L2) adult students lose vigilance toward catching and correcting errors.

A marked loss of motivation occurs when this functional fluency is challenged by instructors in academic settings. Without fellow international students to communicate exclusively with, or when forced to partner in projects with native English speakers, L2 adults' faith in their language skills inside of class plummets. This challenge becomes amplified whenever the adult L2 student is in a university or community college setting where he or she is competing academically with native speakers who seem to complete assignments and hear details in lectures effortlessly. This failure of academic language fluency also happens in advanced ESL classes. Some teachers criticize simple mistakes and language usage failures, which can result in L2 students' damaged confidence and vexation. Loss of self-confidence inhibits motivation; the student feels so inadequate in the classroom that he or she wants to give up because it is too herculean a task to improve (Qian & Xiao, 2010). Academic demands in English are more challenging than the demands of life outside campus, so the advanced L2 student feels like a learning barrier has been created in the classroom. This L2 student's perception of plateauing and never reaching higher fluency, combined with sufficient fluency outside of class, leads to a decline in motivation.

Academic depression alongside arbitrary language errors is known as fossilization, and may become a serious barrier toward academic language fluency. Although some research suggests that fossilization is permanent, other research shows that stagnation of learning and weakened confidence can be reversed by applying a dynamic, literature-based curriculum centered around experiential learning theory. Experiential learning stimulates L2 students, immersing them in the culture of the language they are learning and offering them a holistic learning approach, while broadening and refining their fluency through effective instructor and peer feedback. Utilizing curriculum that propels advanced English learners through experiential learning is a proven strategy in the design of City University of Seattle's Advanced Communications I: Intro to Composition and Literature Course.

# Review of the Literature

Experiential learning theory (ELT) is a collaboration of works by John Dewey, Kurt Lewin, Jean Piaget, William James, Carl Jung, Paulo Freire, and Carl Rogers. These scholars devised six propositions that make up ELT: (1) learning should be measured as a process rather than measured in outcomes, (2) learning is characterized by relearning, (3) being able to learn is to resolve all conflict with what blocks you from adapting to the world, (4) learning is holistic and about adaptation to the world, (5) synergy in transactions between a person and his environment will result in learning, and (6) learning is defined as creating knowledge (Mohammadzadeh, 2012, p. 124). ELT is highly motivating for students; as they fully interact with the course materials, the knowledge gained from those materials ceases to be an abstraction in a textbook, and instead becomes a tool to overcome challenges inside and outside the classroom.

In coursework designed with ELT, each student participates in the process of active, individual learning. Individual learning focused on gaining skills in advanced English means students are trained to see language learning as a process—one in which mistakes are inevitable. The objective "is to make better and more sophisticated mistakes" as L2 students progress in the language; reframing mistakes as "taking risks" means embracing their learning process as a positive and natural flow toward a goal (Schwarzer, 2009, p. 29). Seeing mistakes as part of the learning process rather than as threats to success helps L2 learners prevent recoil inside and outside the classroom, even when tasks are daunting and unfamiliar, such as reading a full-length novel in the acquired language. City University of Seattle's Advanced Communications I is designed around ELT. The course uses a historical fiction novel, Jamie Ford's *Hotel on the Corner of Bitter and Sweet*, as the text at the centerpiece of other authentic materials.

Using historical fiction in language classrooms is a proven technique to engage students. Well-chosen narratives bring emotion and vibrancy to history that can appear abstract and dry in textbooks. Historical fiction's narrative power allows readers to share a character's perspective and kindles the desire to share their own perspectives on presented themes. High engagement with a text improves reading comprehension; when students read historical fiction, they see history through the perspective of the characters, and this process represents deep comprehension (McTigue, Thornton, & Wiese, 2013). For many L2 students, enrollment in

CityU's Advanced Communications I will mean being asked for the first time to read an unabridged novel in a second language. Students are also expected to respond to each chapter through a daily writing journal, answering reflection and comprehension questions. These responses, alongside academic writing/research tasks and professionally guided historical tours of Seattle—all of which are based on the historical and thematic contexts in the novel—create a balanced course that integrates and invigorates all language skills (reading, writing, vocabulary, grammar, listening, and speaking).

## Integration into the Student Experience: Holistic Exposure to the Text Creates Relevance, Critical Thinking, and Global Perspectives

Some of the specific factors that contribute to the reading motivation of L2 students are curiosity, a desire to be challenged, a need to share learning experiences with peers, and consistent achievement of satisfactory scores on tasks. Of these, being curious about a topic and then being challenged to explore it through a variety of experiential learning techniques especially generates the desire to learn. It is therefore important to choose materials that are engaging and relevant. To prevent resistance to extensive reading, it is necessary to assign interesting reading topics and activities that support collaboration among peers (Komiyama, 2013).

When Advanced Communications I students begin to read Ford's novel, even the most reluctant, disengaged learners find themselves immersed in the characters' lives. The novel has several vital features—authenticity, relatability, and a regional setting—that increase students' desire to become involved in the story. Because the novel is well researched and accurate, its historical world appears vibrant and alive. The characters in the novel live between two worlds; living up to the cultural views and expectations that each character inherited from their immigrant parents and grandparents, and struggling to assimilate as American children coming of age in the World War II era. In both situations, the characters face racial prejudices and hardships that make them question their identities. These challenges mirror those that L2 students themselves face while studying abroad, and the ideas presented by the text are applicable to international students' political and social media environments. Accessibility of the text connects students to the new culture in which they live and to the second language they use in ways more enthralling than reading a textbook. Finally, because the novel is set locally, students can visit the locations they read about such as Jackson Street, Maynard Alley, Kobe Park Terrace, and the Panama Hotel Cafe; this transports them physically into the text's setting and compels them to think critically about history. Finally, supplemental media and a professional, guided historical tour of Seattle's Chinatown/International District makes gained knowledge more memorable than simply reading alone. The classroom experience is created by the students processing their emotions regarding topics broached by the novel. "By reflecting on the experience and incorporating the experience into their existing schema, the individual gains and grows" (Tyler & Guth, 1999, p. 157). Choosing the right materials is therefore the first step in applying the principles of experiential learning to any curriculum.

Immersion in advanced English language curriculum through historical fiction narrative and visits to the real-world locations in that narrative are highly engaging. But in ELT, this is only part of the learning process. The next steps are overcoming obstacles in learning, adapting holistically to learning material, and then sharing this process with others to gain recognition and internalize accumulated knowledge. Responding to the curriculum through writing and discussion with peers helps students to overcome personal obstacles and think globally. That is why reflective journaling adds holistic dimension for adult L2 learners: by writing answers to reflection questions every day—questions following reading, media viewing, or a field trip—students discover that the themes presented by the text are not abstract, but deeply personal and relevant to their lives.

Reflection on learning material provides "a mechanism for understanding how their experiences have contributed to who they are, for managing positive and negative forces in their lives, and for reconstructing their images through language" (Zacharakis, Steichen, de Sabates, & Glass, 2011, p. 85). This provides adult L2 learners a unique opportunity to reframe their life in a second language, which gives them "a perception of personal power and motivation" that has a strong impact (Zacharakis et al., 2011, p. 93). This perception of empowerment is crucial; adult L2 learners who believe their English studies are beneficial to life outside the classroom invest more effort and "approach their out-of-class lives as a language learning laboratory" (Schwarzer, 2009, p. 27). When L2 students do not believe they can overcome challenges, they will not find meaning in what they learn and their motivation atrophies. But when they internalize learning, their self-image increases, promoting motivation and proficiency in language development (Kim, 2013).

Once students have begun to process their reading experiences, sharing those experiences with peers builds synergy between what is being learned and how it is communicated. Sharing the insight gained from reading, wanting to show excellence, and achieving recognition from peers and instructors for this insight has been found to be the second most motivational factor in stimulating adult L2 learners to read extensively (Komiyama, 2013). Class discussions are believed to be more authentic to adult learners when there is demonstrated active listening and participation (McDougall, 2015, p. 102). Active listening and sharing increases the ability of adult L2 students to develop understanding of multiple perspectives and to engage in critical thinking. When there is authenticity in the course materials, it generates a positive effect on adult learners; they become autonomous and self-directed and feel the prior life experience they bring to coursework is valued. They "become ready to learn when life circumstances lead them to this point, and they need to see that knowledge and skills have immediate application and relevance to a real-life context" (McDougall, 2015, p. 96). Shared experience with others regarding gained knowledge and deepened skills has been seen "as a key factor in promoting peer relations and group development in the classroom" (Dörnyei & Csizér, 1998, p. 217).

## Strategies for Application of Historical Fiction to Curriculum

Seattle is fortunate that author Jamie Ford set *Hotel on the Corner of Bitter and Sweet* in the International District/Chinatown neighborhood, and that this neighborhood's community, led by the Wing Luke Museum and the Panama Hotel, is dedicated to preserving the area's history and providing any reader of Ford's novel with an authentic experience. Of course, not every city can boast a local, engaging historical fiction novel supported by historical tours and museums. However, this does not mean accessible and authentic historical fiction cannot be used in other cities and towns. It is possible to find any number of writers across the United States and abroad who are publishing quality historical fiction. Creativity and research may be necessary for instructors who want to include experiential learning theory in their courses, but it is a worthwhile investment toward the motivation of adult L2 students. This curriculum is also adaptable to other classrooms and students outside the scope of ESL. Using historical fiction and applying ELT to supplementary learning activities is a proven practice that also applies to history, literature, culture, and media studies courses. The motivation gained through ELT and the comprehension heightened by historical fiction narratives have been demonstrated in more traditional educational settings.

It is also necessary to specifically address how ELT can slow the process of one of the most common obstacles adult L2 students face: fossilization. Fossilization is defined as an "absence of progression toward the target in spite of conditions conducive to learning" (Han, 2013, p. 137). Adult English learners who reach advanced ESL courses—and even undergraduate or graduate college programs—will often suffer from fossilization of errors and loss of incentive to overcome mistakes and deepen their language acquisition. It has been suggested that this process occurs when students mistakenly believe they have already learned something presented by a text or instructor, and consequently avoid correction when mistakes are made (Nakuma, 1998). Through self-awareness and acknowledgment that learning is a process instead of a checklist, the principles behind ELT guide adult L2 students back toward an attitude of open-mindedness that can overcome the personal habits blocking fluency. Instead of a classroom of students who make individualized, lackadaisical, repetitive errors, a classroom where experiential learning has been applied can better address the complicated factors stagnating learning. A dynamic learning environment instills in L2 learners a habit of self-correction. This immersive experience with both the course materials and their peers helps students to bridge the gap between functional fluency and academic fluency. The stimulation found in the process of reinvigorating language learning through ELT halts language stagnation and slows and reverses fossilization.

## Defining Motivation through Regular Communication and Feedback

Motivating students through ELT curriculum as a strategy to prevent malaise, increase growth, and slow the process of fossilization is a worthy endeavor. Nevertheless, attention must be paid to what ways students are motivated, rather than only focusing on how motivated they are (Komiyama, 2013). To find out what actually motivates students requires both open and frequent dialogue. It's imperative to communicate with each student at the beginning of a course to target four key areas: (1) which specific areas in language that learners hope to improve, (2) what they feel blocks them or challenges them, (3) what they are expecting the instructor to do for them, and (4) what areas of learning they expect to be responsible for themselves. To address these areas and get feedback from students, surveys can be created, and class discussions or message board postings during the first few days of class.

But to be an effective tool, getting feedback and applying it once is not enough. In the middle of the course, students should be offered a summary of what specific tools and skills the instructor has presented so far, and ask students to reflect on this and rate the progress they have made. This is also a great time to ask students if there are any obstacles they need additional help or review for overcoming. Finally, at the end of the course, open a final opportunity for discussion and reflection. Ask students to reflect on the four areas they shared during the first week and compare how they feel about these areas now: be sure to address each student's goals, challenges, expectations, and accountability when giving final instructor feedback. This process of ongoing and open dialogue is indispensable for both the instructor and the student, as it keeps communication open and addresses unmet needs. It also provides the framework for quality feedback between the student and instructor, which can be more positive, personal, and meaningful than the survey-style tools used by most universities at the end of a course.

## Conclusion

City University of Seattle's Advanced Communications I: Intro to Composition and Literature Course is supported by the theory of experiential learning and coincides with using authentic source materials and historical fiction to increase student motivation. Historical fiction, supplemental media, museum visits, guided tours, journal writing, and research opportunities reinforce concepts, allowing students to learn and relearn as they identify and overcome challenges. Through this, students yield valuable global perspectives and broaden critical thinking. They are also able to break through and overcome fears of risk taking and injured self-confidence, which are factors that erode motivation and create fossilization errors. Employing experiential learning in the ESL classroom is a both a holistic and personal approach that develops language skills and overcomes many learning plateaus.

# References

Dörnyei, Z., & Csizér, K. (1998). Ten commandments for motivating language learners: Results of an empirical study. *Language Teaching Research, 2*(3), 203–229.

Han, Z. (2013). Forty years later: Updating the fossilization hypothesis. *Language Teaching, 46*(2), 133–171. http://dx.doi.org/10.1017/S0261444812000511

Kim, T. (2013). An activity theory analysis of second language motivational self-system: Two Korean immigrants' ESL learning. *Asia-Pacific Education Researcher, 22*(4), 459–471. doi:10.1007/s40299-012-0045-x

Komiyama, R. (2013). Factors underlying second language reading motivation of adult EAP students. *Reading in a Foreign Language, 25*(2), 149-169.

McDougall, J. (2015). The quest for authenticity: A study of an online discussion forum and the needs of adult learners. *Australian Journal of Adult Learning, 55*(1), 94–113.

McTigue, E., Thorton, E., & Wiese, P. (2013). Authentication projects for historical fiction: Do you believe it? *Reading Teacher, 66*(6), 495–505. doi:10.1002/TRTR.1132

Mohammadzadeh, A. (2012). The relationship between experiential learning styles and the immediate and delayed retention of English collocations among EFL learners. *English Language Teaching, 5*(12), 121–130.

Nakuma, C. K. (1998). A new theoretical account of "fossilization": Implications for L2 attrition research. *International Review of Applied Linguistics in Language Teaching, 36*(3), 247.

Qian, M., & Xiao, Z. (2010). Strategies for preventing and resolving temporary fossilization in second language acquisition. *English Language Teaching, 3*(1), 180–183.

Schwarzer, D. (2009). Best practices for teaching the "whole" adult ESL learner. *New Directions for Adult & Continuing Education, 121*, 25–33. doi:10.1002/ace.322

Tyler, J. M., & Guth, L. J. (1999). Using media to create experiential learning in multicultural and diversity issues. *Journal of Multicultural Counseling & Development, 27*(3), 153.

Zacharakis, J., Steichen, M., de Sabates, G. D., & Glass, D. (2011). Understanding the experiences of adult learners: Content analysis of focus group data. *Adult Basic Education & Literacy Journal, 5*(2), 84–95.

## Author Biographies

Rachel Peterson is a senior faculty member for the English Language programs in the Washington Academy of Languages. Throughout her twelve years of experience in teaching academic English and test preparation to international students, she has also led classes and workshops in creative writing for domestic students. Prior to earning TESOL certification, she received an MTOM degree from San Diego's Pacific College of Traditional Oriental Medicine and spent her first ten postgraduate years as a practitioner in the field of complementary medicine. She is currently enrolled in City University of Seattle's BA in Applied Psychology program.

Christine Knorr is the Academic Director for the English Language programs. As a binational and native speaker of French and English, Ms. Knorr was exposed to both US and French culture and has a deep appreciation for both. For over twenty years, Christine has taught both French and English to a broad range of students: business professionals, refugees and immigrants, international students, and children. Christine has developed curriculum and has managed and directed several language schools: American Cultural Exchange, French-American School of Puget Sound, and more recently, the School of Management's English Language programs at City University of Seattle.

# 12

# The Use of Media in the Undergraduate-level Social Science Courses

**Anna Cholewinska**

## Abstract

Using social and popular media and current news in the classroom can engage students and allow them to connect theory and practice. In addition, these tools can help students master critical thinking and media literacy skills. While using media and current news is not a new concept in K–12 education, it seems uncommon at the college level. This chapter will discuss some examples of how to incorporate social and popular media and current news in undergraduate-level social science courses in a meaningful way that corresponds with Bloom's taxonomy. It will also discuss some of the possible strategies and potential benefits of that educational approach. Finally, some observations and lessons learned from the classes will be shared.

# Overview

Professor: First, I love the articles you present to read, which make you think, of course. Because there's never a chance to let the instructors know what we think past the survey, I want you to know that I've really enjoyed this class and learning so much more than I ever knew about the interactions between medical entities, professionals, and policies with society. So often all we humans do is grumble about lousy service. Medicine and its many aspects are varied and complex. I believe, fully, that it is the power of the consumer that must make a solid and immovable stand for excellent healthcare and take action to ensure that medicalization and society complement rather than conflict. (Anonymous student, personal communication, June 21, 2015)

This comment, sent to a college professor in a sociology class, is evidence that students come to classes to learn practical applications, not only theoretical models and frameworks, terms, and concepts. Students immediately want to see how theory applies to what they would do as professionals. While in some classes, such as practicum or internship courses, it is possible to do activities that show students applications of the theoretical concepts to specific situations; in others, it is more challenging and requires not only a lot more planning, preparation, and creativity from instructors. However, in most classes, instructors could use news stories and real-life examples to illustrate concepts and theories that they teach. This chapter will discuss some examples of how to incorporate social and popular media and current news into undergraduate classes to enhance students' learning of course concepts and skills.

# Review of the Literature

While using media, popular magazine articles, and news in the classroom is not a new concept, it is mostly utilized in the K–12 system (Tisdell, 2007). In higher education, current news, social media, or motion pictures appear to be used primarily in communication or journalism courses (Lopez & Aguaded, 2015; Considine, Horton, & Moorman, 2009; Fleming, 2014). The purpose of using this content in these courses is mainly to analyze the quality of the professional writing and presentation of the issue or topic and to illustrate course concepts. The idea of using current news or popular and social media, such as motion pictures or blogs, to enrich college-level classes and allow students to learn from them does not seem to resonate among instructors, even though it offers a huge variety of opportunities for the instructors and students. For example, bringing news to college-level courses allows instructors to promote critical thinking skills, media literacy, and information literacy in general (Tisdell, 2007). Additionally, Vossen-Callens (2014) argued that it also allows instructors to incorporate Bloom's taxonomy with the help of popular and social media. She showed how students are not only able to learn and understand course concepts but also to master higher-level learning skills, such as analysis and evaluation.

Depending on the field and students' proficiency, various activities could be used in the classroom to promote interaction with others, engagement in the discussions and other class activities, and mastery of critical thinking skills. Furthermore, even though there is already some evidence that a hands-on, collaborative approach enhances reflexivity and advances conceptual thinking, using popular media in graduate-level classes is almost unheard of (Creamer, Ghoston, Drape, Ruff, & Mukuni, 2012). In this study, motion pictures were successfully used in a doctoral-level research methods class. As they concluded, students were challenged to see that knowledge is rarely produced in isolation or through sudden, unaccountable bursts of revelatory insight, but rather is more generally produced through a slow and meticulous process of trial and error and substantive interactions with others equally invested in a thoughtful and meaningful scientific inquiry (Creamer et al., 2012, p. 419).

## Integration into the Student Experience

Social and popular media, and current news, can be incorporated into the student experience in multiple ways. As Vossen-Callens (2014) noted, students who are disengaged will not learn much in their classes. Lectures are rarely engaging enough to keep students interested. Real-life examples, offered by instructors from their own experience and practice or from the experience of others, not only keep students interested but also help them understand what they are learning. Moreover, lectures typically require students to take notes and memorize or simply understand course concepts. These are necessary as a starting point for any learning, but analyzing, synthesizing, and evaluating would be the natural next steps that students would need to take.

In particular, current news offers a great opportunity for instructors and students to master those skills. Through a series of projects, students can learn how to work with different sources and information gathered from them. Learning how to determine which sources of information are reliable and which are not could serve as an initial activity for the students in their learning of information literacy. Additionally, the analysis of the sources could lead to other activities—summarizing articles, differentiating between facts and opinions, supporting opinions with facts, learning how to identify cause and effect, or comparing and contrasting topics and issues in the news. These are basic critical thinking and information-literacy skills taught in many college-level classes. They are also typically required by professional organizations creating guidelines or accrediting college programs.

The American Psychological Association (2013), for example, listed information literacy as one of the learning goals and outcomes for undergraduate psychology students (APA, 2013). Learning these skills in hands-on, practical activities would be a significant experience for students. It is important to note that, while in college, students typically have access to their school library and selected scholarly databases. Furthermore, students could ask for the librarians' help to locate appropriate and applicable resources. After they graduate, students will need to do all that work themselves as they may not have access to scholarly databases. For this reason, information literacy and critical thinking skills are essential for them and, therefore, should be mastered in various courses.

Current news, and personal blogs, could be incorporated into teaching in a form of case analysis. Using the most current examples would allow instructors to see how students learned that process and how they analyze specific cases on their own. More advanced students might also be tasked with identifying additional cases for the analysis and sharing them with their classmates for a collaborative analysis. In this process, they will also learn how to search for information and select appropriate cases and work collaboratively with others. Similarly, books, motion pictures, and documentaries could serve as cases for analysis with the use of course concepts and theories. Using those will offer students an experience of observing certain social issues, similar to what they could see in the society.

Social media—such as Facebook, Twitter, LinkedIn, and blogs—also offers valuable opportunities for instructors or their students and could be used to promote social networking and intellectual growth. As Chou (2012) noted, there is already research that shows benefits of self-reflection about learning and professional activities. Therefore, encouraging students to create personalized blogs about their own learning, course content, or course-related activities is a valuable learning experience. Additionally, it also supports collaborative learning and trains students in peer reviewing as they should also submit commentary posts to their classmates. YouTube, Flicker, and Khan Academy are rarely viewed as social media tools, even though they are widely used for personal, professional, and teaching purposes (Seaman & Tinti-Kane, 2013).

Photos, documentaries, and movies from YouTube and Flicker are often incorporated into courses. In their recent versions, learning management systems such as Blackboard allow seamless embedding of video clips and pictures from YouTube. It is also worth noting that YouTube allows instructors to record their own lectures and other instructional materials to share with students directly from learning management systems. These videos are not available to the public as they are hidden on the private channels. They could be personalized and directly address specific students or groups. Since the process of creating and embedding such instructional resources can be done without any special skills or equipment, it is easy for instructors to use these options. Finally, educational organizations, such as Khan Academy, offer databases of instructional resources for various classes, including math, science, medicine, art, and history. Videos with micro-lectures in more than thirty subjects, created for Khan Academy, are widely used by educators at all levels. According to the Khan Academy website, there are more than thirty-seven million learners using its instructional materials.

## Proven Practices, Examples, and Results

While all instructors teaching in the Bachelor of Arts in Applied Psychology program at City University of Seattle use real-life examples in their classes, some are proficient in incorporating current news and popular social media into their classes. Those instructors are typically perceived by their students as highly engaged and their classes as interesting. In end-of-course evaluations, such as the one quoted at the beginning of this chapter, students have expressed their appreciation for additional materials from the popular media and current news. Students do realize that these real-life stories not only help them truly comprehend the course concepts but also allow them to master their practical skills, and see how these cases, presented by their instructors, apply to specific situations.

Discussion activities gain a lot of depth when they begin with short videos presenting specific content. For example, in the Sociology of the Family course, short documentaries created by *National Geographic* are presented to students to discuss various marital and nonmarital arrangements, such as polyandry, polygyny, or free love. Students, instead of just reading about these arrangements in the text or in the lecture notes provided by the instructor, are able to see a family of each type and understand the benefits and challenges of such families. Therefore, students are not limited to just memorizing definitions, but they make a connection between a definition and a real family they've observed. Similarly, the instructor can share various articles found in the popular media to illustrate concepts taught in the class. Some of those articles generate rich discussions with a significant number of posts. For example, a supplementary discussion of a child abuse case, based on a video and article from the news, generated nineteen additional posts in the class of thirteen students, even though it was not mandatory to comment in that particular thread. It is important to note that there were also several additional threads that week, initiated by the instructor who posted supplementary materials for students. Altogether, thirty-five extra posts were generated in all additional threads that included ancillary resources.

Moreover, as mentioned above, popular media could be brought into courses in the form of books or motion pictures. The Applied Psychology program has utilized these sources in several courses as major assessments in which students were tasked to analyze them from the social perspective. For example, in the Abnormal Psychology class, students analyzed the main characters of an assigned movie in the context of the presenting circumstances and symptomology relevant to abnormal and maladaptive behavior. Students were to clearly indicate comprehensive provisional diagnoses of the characters by summarizing interpretations and perceptions of the characters' experiences based on course learning. In this paper, students were expected to demonstrate their ability to synthesize learning into an analytical essay that covered an overview of abnormal psychology and the study of maladaptive behavior.

Finally, posting popular magazine articles and current news can motivate students to actively participate in the discussions. Posting articles also models behavior that allows students to find articles to enrich discussions and other course activities. It can empower students to be active learners by seeking and sharing information with others and consequently contributing to various course and collaborative activities. For example, it was observed in several sociology courses in which the instructor shared supplemental articles from the news and popular magazines that, within about two sessions, students started sharing similar resources as well. By the end of the course, most students shared at least one additional article with the rest of the group.

## Lessons Learned, Tips for Success, and Recommendations

Incorporating social and popular media and current news into teaching is not difficult, yet it requires reflection and caution. As Fleming (2014) noted, there are several strategies that help with incorporating articles and current news into courses. It is important not only to start with the students' interests but to also clearly discuss why certain articles or cases were shared with them. Therefore, instructors should ask thought-provoking questions about the shared information and establish a connection between the class and the community (Fleming, 2014). Additionally, educators need to introduce ancillary articles or information by elaborating why they were important to share and their relation to the course concepts. That could model similar actions by students, who could not only offer information to the class but also explain why it was worth sharing with others.

It is important to avoid overwhelming students with too many supplemental materials. Often, educators create their own bank of articles or information that they want to share with students. They must be careful about what to share with a particular group of students as the composition of the group and class dynamics might affect how specific information or cases are received and perceived by students. Additionally, sharing too many cases or articles with students might lead to students' fatigue and, in fact, decreased participation in the activities. Moreover, timing of the addition of supplementary information is important. Ideally, those additional resources should be shared in the middle of the session as students are the most attentive at that time. For example, in the Sociology of the

Family class, materials shared on the second, third, fourth, and fifth day of a weeklong session were more often viewed and commented on than those shared on days six and seven. A closer look at the patterns of participation in the activities revealed that while students were active on these days, they seemed to be more concerned with fulfilling activity requirements as prescribed by the syllabus and thus responding to fellow students and to additional questions posed by their instructor.

## Conclusion

Using social and popular media, and current news, could enrich courses and students' learning experiences. They offer multiple opportunities for various practical activities for students, such as critical thinking exercises, case analysis, and case studies. Finally, they also contribute to establishing connections between theory and practice, and class and the community. It is important, however, to remember that they are only supplemental resources and should never replace scholarly resources that students need to use to create their work.

## References

American Psychological Association (2013). *Learning goals and outcomes: APA guidelines for the undergraduate psychology major.* Retrieved from www.apa.orgede/precollege/about/psymajor-guidelines. aspx

Chou, P.N. (2012). Teaching strategies in online discussion boards: A framework in higher education. *Higher Education Studies, 2(2),* 25–30.

Considine, D., Horton, J., & Moorman, G. (2009). Teaching and reading the millennial generation through media literacy. *Journal of Adolescent and Adult Literacy 52(6),* 471–481.

Creamer, E. G., Ghoston, M. R., Drape, T., Ruff, C., & Mukuni, J. (2012). Using popular media and a collaborative approach to teaching grounded theory research methods. *International Journal of Teaching & Learning in Higher Education, 24*(3), 415–420.

Fleming, J. (2014). Media literacy, news literacy, or news appreciation? A case study of the news literacy program at Stony Brook University. *Journalism & Mass Communication Educator, 69*(2), 146–165.

Khan Academy. (2016). You can learn anything. Retrieved from https://www.khanacademy.org/youcanlearnanything

Lopez, L., & Aguaded, M.C. (2015). Teaching media literacy in colleges of education and communication. *Media Education Research Journal, 22*(44), 187–195.

Seaman, J., & Tinti-Kane, H. (2013). *Social media for teaching and learning.* Boston, MA: Pearsons Learning Solutions.

Tisdell, E. J. (2007). Popular culture and critical media literacy in adult education: Theory and practice. *New Directions for Adult & Continuing Education, 2007*(115), 5–13. doi:10.1002/ace.262

Vossen-Callens, M. (2014). Using Bloom's taxonomy to teach course content and improve social medial literacy. *Journal of Interdisciplinary Studies in Education, 3*(1), 17–26.

# Author Biography

Anna Cholewinska is an Associate Professor and Academic Program Director at City University of Seattle. She has spent more than twenty years teaching students in undergraduate and graduate programs. She has also trained teams in multiculturalism. She earned an MA in sociology from the University of Warsaw, Poland.

# 13

# Learning Communities as a Vehicle for Improved Teaching and Learning

**Rachel Osborn**

## Abstract

Learning communities are widely recognized as an effective tool for improved teaching and learning. To improve teaching and learning, intentional planning and implementation are required. Learning communities that are implemented intentionally and supported by scheduling, budgeting, materials, and institutional leadership can be a powerful tool for improved teaching and learning. There are specific steps and practices that school systems can follow to build and implement learning communities that increase institutional capacity for sustained improvements in teaching and learning.

# Overview

What is a learning community? What conditions and design elements are necessary to have learning communities that result in changes in instructional practice and increased student achievement? As universities and school systems strive to increase student success rates, it is more important than ever to plan for, and provide, a vehicle for achieving this goal. This chapter will present professional learning communities (PLCs) as a vehicle for improving the quality of both instruction and learning. Learning communities will be discussed within the context of adult learning principles, building instructor capacity, building a culture of collaboration, mentoring for both new and experienced instructors, distributed leadership, and social media and technology. Various practical examples for implementation and tips for success will also be included.

# Review of the Literature

## What Is a PLC?

According to Fenning (2004), "learning organizations must not rely only on previous achievements they have made, but must also be visionary and perceptual in building learning communities" because this increases student success and retention. DuFour and Mattos (2013) asserted that PLCs are one of the most powerful strategies for improving both teaching and learning. The reason for this is that PLCs create collaborative culture and collective responsibility for improving teaching and learning. Instructors in PLC schools

- take collective responsibility for student learning and have higher levels of professional satisfaction;
- share teaching practices that work;
- improve both student achievement and professional practice; and
- are more likely to remain in the profession.

Caine and Caine (2010) described PLCs as a learning group that collaborates to improve teaching practice. This collaboration can take the form of study groups, action research teams, communities of practices, conversation circles, and online communication. Caine and Caine (2010) emphasized the social nature of learning and the underutilization of educators' colleagues as resources for learning and professional development. Caine and Caine (2010) also recognized the importance of school culture as a critical piece in creating the necessary conditions for successful learning communities. They asserted that:

- Life is a process; successful relationships and communities are a process; and they need to be built, nurtured, and sustained.
- The goal of these communities is successful and effective professional development that increases real-world or classroom teaching competence.
- To become more expert at anything, the community needs to encourage and support the brain/mind principle of relaxed alertness. Fear can hinder the intake and processing of information. Positive affect supports higher-order brain functions.
- Learning communities need opportunities to research information, link it to what they know, and plan for how to apply the material to their classroom.
- Types of learning communities include study groups, action research teams, communities of practice, conversation circles, and online learning groups. These each have different purposes, routines, and procedures.

## Adult Learning Principles and PLCs

In our quest for effective professional development, attention to adult learning principles and conditions that support effective professional development is critical. Wei, Darling-Hammond, and Adamson (2010) and Killion and Hirsh (2013) recommended the following conditions for successful professional development:

- Professional development days embedded into the workday
- Schedules that allow for periodic collaboration meetings of three to four hours
- Support for technology and the necessary infrastructure
- Differentiated staffing and compensation

- Funding for consultants, technical assistance, conferences, professional books, and journals

Wei et al. (2010) provided detailed recommendations about what needs to happen during the professional development time to support increased teaching effectiveness and student achievement. Wei et al. (2010) defined effective professional development as comprehensive, sustained, and intensive activities that improve instructor and leader effectiveness in raising student achievement. According to Wei et al. (2010) and Killion and Hirsh (2013), effective professional development

- helps develop a collective responsibility for student achievement and is aligned with rigorous standards and school improvement goals;
- is conducted at the institution/school level (job embedded) and led by institution leaders or practitioner leaders;
- is a continuing cycle of determining learning needs based on data analysis;
- includes strategies such as lesson studies and the development of formative assessments;
- includes job-embedded coaching to support the transfer of skills/ knowledge into the teaching of courses; and
- is assessed on the effectiveness of the professional development, and this helps to guide ongoing improvements.

The PLC groups described by Caine and Caine (2010) meet the guidelines for effective professional development as described by Wei et al. (2010) and Killian and Hirsh (2013). Study groups, action research teams, and communities of practice involve ongoing, intensive, job-embedded activities that support instructors in changing their practice. The collaboration that changes instructor practice is also most likely to have a positive effect on student achievement and success.

## Building Capacity for PLCs

Penuel, Fishman, Yamaguchi, and Gallagher (2007) studied the professional development (PD) practices of 454 instructors. This examination included the duration and time span of PD, the focus of PD and how active learning was incorporated into the PD, and instructor perceptions of how PD aligned with their own goals, how the PD efforts were supported, and what barriers existed. The study concluded that the initial PD activities did affect overall program implementation and that it was effective to engage instructors in aligning PD activities with standards and in planning how to implement the PD information in the classroom. Effective PD was critical to building instructor capacity.

Penuel et al. (2007) acknowledged that curricular reforms and changes are highly demanding on instructors. They emphasized the need for interactive PD that allows for cycles of learning, and practice is critical in building the capacity necessary for instructors to successfully navigate and implement these numerous reforms. The learning cycles are similar to the PLCs discussed by Caine and Caine (2010) and DuFour and Marzano (2011). Collaboration, which is also part of a PLC, was specified by Penuel et al. (2007) and DuFour and Marzano (2011) as promoting successful instructor implementation of reforms. Implementation was also influenced by instructor perception. Instructors needed to perceive that the change was necessary and that is was also embraced by their peers (Penuel et al., 2007). According to Caine and Caine (2010), DuFour and Marzano (2011), and Penuel et al. (2007), time spent on PD, using university partners, and data reporting, analysis, and collaboration are important for successful implementation of PD and for building instructor capacity.

## Distributed Leadership, Shared Culture, and Vision for PLCs

DuFour (1997) emphasized that institutions cannot produce students who are continuous learners and collaborators if the instructors in the institution do not act out these characteristics. Traditionally, instructors have worked in isolation. When PD occurred, there was no follow up or support for implementation. The training was not assessed, and there was no relationship to school or district goals. There was an assumption that adult learning only happened outside of the school. In a learning organization, the following would be present, according to DuFour (1997):

- New staff would be oriented and would have a mentor, support groups, regular observations and supportive, constructive feedback.
- Curricular or department teams would meet regularly to review and agree on standards, pacing, materials, and assessments.

- Peer observations would be common with the giving and receiving of feedback as standard practice for all instructors.
- Instructors would participate in study groups and action research.
- All instructors would serve on improvement task forces at some point in their career.
- Professional sharing at meetings would be expected.
- These collaborative support structures would be supported by time and schedules.

According to DuFour (1997), these conditions will build instructor leadership, and also support a shared mission and vision in an institution. These conditions are also necessary for successful PLCs as described by Caine and Caine (2010) and DuFour (1997). DuFour (1999) also described actions that leaders can take to build a shared mission and vision in their institution and to support successful PLCs. According to DuFour (1997; 1999) and DuFour and Mattos (2013), successful leaders:

- lead through shared vision and values, not rules and procedures;
- enlist faculty members in decision making and empower individuals to act;
- provide staff with information, training, and parameters to make good decisions;
- are results oriented; and
- ask the right questions instead of presenting solutions.

DuFour (1999) emphasized that effective leadership is vital in planning any change initiative or PD program. Because PLCs rely on the effective communication and functioning of small teams, a leader who builds staff capacity and a shared mission and vision is important for PLCs to be effective. If PLCs are to maintain reflective inquiry, they must be given the power to act and make decisions that support the shared mission and vision (DuFour, 1997; DeFour, 1999).

## A Culture of Collaboration and PLCs

An understanding of change in institutions and how instructors and staff respond to change initiatives is critical when attempting to build a collaborative culture that will support successful PLCs. Evans (2000) discussed some important differences between business change models and how change occurs in schools. Instructors can be more sensitive to change than their corporate peers, and they can value stability and tradition over change and innovation. Therefore, business or corporate change models may not succeed because school life is different from the corporate world. In a school, relationships can be more powerful than change initiatives. If change in instructional practice is a goal of any PD model or PLC, the model must account for instructor preparedness and reaction to change.

DuFour and Marzano (2011) provided specific steps that leaders can take to build a culture of collaboration and implement effective PLCs to improve teaching and learning in their institutions. Important points included:

- Effective implementation of PLCs increases that capacity in adults.
- Learning communities must have norms, protected time to collaborate together, and leaders should carefully monitor their work.
- It is important to celebrate PLC team achievement and address situations of nonparticipation.
- The purpose and goal of the PLC must be revisited, articulated, and celebrated on a regular basis.

## Mentoring New and Experienced Instructors

Gagen and Bowie (2005) presented a case for formal training of mentor instructors. Mid-career instructors have expertise and skills that can be of benefit to new instructors. Mentor training can support these mid-career instructors in providing an important service to new instructors. The PLC model described by Caine and Caine (2010), DuFour (1997; 1999), DuFour and Marzano (2011), and DuFour and Mattos (2013) can also provide mentoring for instructors. When instructors meet in collaborative groups to do PLC work, the conversations and exchange of information that occur are a natural vehicle for mentoring and transmitting valuable expertise to one another.

## PLCs and Minority Instructors and Students

Abilock, Harada, and Fontichiaro (2013) and Smith and Ingersoll (2004) highlighted the shortage of minority instructors and the need for minority instructors. The discussion also addressed the low numbers of minority instructor candidates. Minority instructors are needed because the subgroups that are often labeled as "not meeting adequate progress" by some federal laws include groups of minority students, and special education and English language learners. According to Abilock et al. (2013) and Smith and Ingersoll (2004), mentoring programs are needed to recruit minority students into fields such as teaching because research indicates that the results of minority instructors include:

- positive gains by minority students;
- fewer minority students in special education;
- a decrease in the absenteeism of minority students; and
- more minority students in extracurricular activities.

PLCs are a natural vehicle for supporting minority instructors and minority students. The relationships that are built in a PLC support a safe exchange of ideas around culture and strategies that can be important for changing instructor practice and supporting minority students. The discussions around student data that occur in a PLC help to ensure that students are considered as individuals and that their progress is carefully and continually monitored.

## Technology and PLCs

Borko (2004), McConnell, Parker, Eberhardt, Koehler, and Lundeberg (2013), and Schrum and Levin (2013) provided information about the elements of effective professional development and a comparison of face-to-face and virtual PLCs. They highlight how technology can be used to support PD that is differentiated for the goals and needs of individuals. By carefully choosing and planning for technology that is part of a larger comprehensive system, the following aspects of PD and PLCs can be supported and successful via online PD:

- personalization,
- collaboration,
- access,
- efficiency, and
- learning design.

The use and success of technology for PD and PLCs is limited when it is not planned as part of a larger vision, if there is no tech support, and if there is inadequate support for learners. Virtual professional learning communities have the same function and goals and face-to-face PLCs, except that they utilize technology to meet and communicate. Both face-to-face and virtual PLCs require the same key components for success:

- supportive and shared leadership,
- shared values and vision,
- collective learning and application of learning,
- supportive conditions, and
- shared practice.

DuFour (1997; 1999) put forth three "big ideas" for successful PLCs:

1. Emphasis on learning
2. Development of a culture of collaboration
3. Focus on results

McConnell et al. (2013) reported on a study that compared face-to-face PLCs with virtual PLCs. Both groups demonstrated equal time on task, the same types of discourse, and addressed the same types of issues. Both groups reported the following uses of their PLC:

1. Sharing articles and information
2. New perspectives from group members about evidence
3. Hearing practical solutions from others
4. Accountability to the group
5. Focus on professional discourse
6. Developing professional friendships

McConnell et al. (2013) concluded that virtual PLCs are an effective mode for PLC meetings when time, driving, or remoteness of location prevent face-to-face meetings.

## Integration into the Student Experience

There are various best practices that can be implemented in the classroom that ensure the PLC is an effective, supportive structure. These practices are easily implemented but require consistency over time:

- Provide explicit explanations to the students at the beginning of the course about the purpose and importance of a learning community.
- Illustrate specific examples that show how collaborating in a learning community will support both their success in the course, and also how it specifically relates to a career they are preparing for.
- When possible, allow for flexibility in the course syllabus so that students may discuss as a group possibilities for due dates, the best types of groupings for projects, and input on scoring rubrics.
- During discussions, take a step back and allow students the time to arrive at decisions as a group. This will cement their perception of themselves as a successful learning community.
- As often as possible, ask students for feedback about the course, projects, and learning, wait for responses, and be prepared to adjust instruction and projects after collaborative discussions.
- Ensure that students know the value of collaborating in a professional learning community. Their ability to collaborate with others can have more impact on their future career than their intellectual ability.
- Commit to facilitating the growth of a learning community mindset in their courses and share successes and challenges across an academic program.

Integrating the learning community mindset into the student experience can be done with a high rate of success when the instructor provides the time, flexibility, and facilitation of conversations that allow the learning community to grow. A school- or department-wide commitment to this mindset will have a significant effect on its success.

## Proven Practices, Examples, and Results

The strategy of building a strong learning community cohort is best used by planning for the group to address essential questions and develop shared group norms. Goss (2007) provided specific discussion questions for facilitating the development of the students from a group to an intentional learning community. According to Goss (2007), questions for the cohort members to discuss during an orientation may include:

1. How will we schedule our time, what will we give up, to commit to the work of this cohort?
2. What common investments will we all make consistently?
3. What are our shared norms for attitudes and behaviors that will not be part of our community?
4. How will we promote harmony in our cohort and growth for every member?
5. What does it mean to be a member of this cohort?
6. Why are we in this together?

Establishing a quality cohort model will promote student success. More students will complete the program. The quality of learning and achievement will be higher. Students will be more confident and become effective leaders as a result of participating in a quality cohort.

## Lessons Learned, Tips for Success, and Recommendations

Advertising a "cohort model" or stating a support of "learning communities" does not equate to increased student success. These models require intentional planning and an understanding of the practices needed to ensure success. The literature provides us with many examples of best practices for cohorts and learning communities, and specific steps to follow in establishing a successful cohort or learning community. A program or department that commits to both an awareness of best practices and intentional implementation will see the most impact in student successes.

## Conclusion

This chapter has presented and explained PLCs as a vehicle for improving teaching and learning. Various practical examples for implementation, and tips for success, have also been included. PLCs have been presented in the context of building instructor capacity and distributed leadership, shared mission and vision, adult learning principles, building a culture of collaboration, instructor mentoring, and the use of technology for PLCs. The research cited demonstrates that effectively implemented PLCs support improved instructor practice and increased student achievement.

## References

Abilock, D., Harada, V., & Fontichiaro, K. (2013). Growing schools: Effective professional development. *Instructor Librarian, 41*(1), 8–13.

Borko, H. (2004). Professional development and instructor learning: Mapping the terrain. *American Educational Research Association, 33*(8), 3–15.

Caine, G., & Caine, R. (2010). *Strengthening and enriching your professional learning community: The art of learning together.* Alexandria, VA: Association for Supervision and Curriculum Development.

DuFour, R. P. (1997). The school as a learning organization: Recommendations for school improvement. *NASSP Bulletin, 81*(588), 81–87. doi:10.1177/019263659708158813

DuFour, R. P. (1999). Help wanted: Principals who can lead professional learning communities. *NASSP Bulletin, 83*(604), 12–17. doi:10.1177/019263659908360403

DuFour, R., & Marzano, R. J. (2011). *Leaders of learning: How district, school, and classroom leaders improve student achievement*. Bloomington, IN: Solution Tree.

DuFour, R., & Mattos, M. (2013). How do leaders really improve schools? *Educational Leadership, 70*(7), 34–40.

Evans, R. (2000, Spring). Why a school doesn't run or change like a business. *Independent School Magazine, 59*(3), 42–46. Retrieved from http://www.nais.org/Magazines-Newsletters/ISMagazine/Pages/Why-a-School-Doesn%27t-Run-or-Change-Like-a-Business.aspx

Fenning, K. (2004). Cohort-based learning: Application to learning organizations and student academic success. *College Quarterly, 7*(1). Retrieved from http://www.senecacollege.ca/quarterly/2004-vol07-num01-winter/fenning.html

Gagen, L., & Bowie, S. (2005). Effective mentoring: A case for training mentors for novice instructors. *Journal of Physical Education, Recreation & Dance, 76*(7), 40–45.

Goss, J. (2007). Cohort programs in higher education: Learning communities or convenience groupings. Paper presented at the annual meeting of the American Educational Research Association. Chicago, IL. Retrieved from http://su.academia.edu/JohnRGoss/Papers

Killion, J., & Hirsh, S. (2013). Investments in professional learning must change. *Journal of Staff Development, 34*(4), 10–20.

McConnell, T. J., Parker, J. M., Eberhardt, J., Koehler, M. J., & Lundeberg, M. A. (2013). Virtual professional learning communities: Instructors' perceptions of virtual versus face-to-face professional development. *Journal of Science Education and Technology, 22*(3), 267–277.

Penuel, W. R., Fishman, B. J., Yamaguchi, R., & Gallagher, L. P. (2007). What makes professional development effective? Strategies that foster curriculum implementation. *American Educational Research Journal, 44*(4), 921–959.

Schrum, L., & Levin, B. (2013). Instructors' technology professional development: Lessons learned from exemplary schools. *TechTrends, 57*(1), 38–42.

Smith, T. M., & Ingersoll, R. (2004). What are the effects of induction and mentoring on beginning instructor turnover? *American Educational Research Journal, 41*(3), 705.

Wei, R. C., Darling-Hammond, L., & Adamson, F. (2010). *Professional development in the United States: Trends and challenges.* Dallas, TX: National Staff Development Council.

## Author Biography

Rachel L. Osborn is a faculty member at City University of Seattle and has served twenty years as a school principal, program coordinator, instructional coach, and classroom instructor in the K–12 school system. She holds a BA in elementary and special education from Central Washington University, an MA in bilingual education and English as a second language from Heritage University, a principal certificate and a program administrator's certificate from City University of Seattle, and an EdD in school improvement from the University of West Georgia.

# 14

# Embedded Library Instruction: Improving Student Success on 21st Century Learning Outcomes

**Carolyne Begin and Tammy Salman**

## Abstract

This chapter will consider academic library contributions to increasing student success in terms of academic research, which is an essential skill to master in higher education programs. This chapter includes a review of the literature and a sharing of successful practices that have been adapted to reflect the twenty-first-century's complex information environment and the need for more highly skilled and knowledge-based workers.

# Overview

Academic research and writing is often difficult for students to master, particularly for adult learners who may be new to higher education or returning after a prolonged absence. In the twenty-first century, academic research looks different than it did when many adult learners first encountered higher education. While the steadfast academic library remains an institution devoted to procurement and dissemination of information, it has evolved over the last few decades. Academic libraries are intertwined with innovative technology, open-access advocacy, and the teaching missions of their institutions. They have been transformed into learning hubs, research commons, and resource centers dedicated to instruction and outreach focused on teaching students best practices for finding, analyzing, evaluating, and synthesizing information in a digital context.

This transformation has prompted changes in expectations for academic libraries inside and outside higher education institutions. Increasingly, accreditors have put pressure on colleges and universities to "ensure that the use of library and information resources is integrated into the learning process" (Northwest Commission on Colleges and Universities [NWCCU] 2.C.6) and to provide evidence that library instruction will "enhance [students'] efficiency and effectiveness in obtaining, evaluating, and using" information sources (NWCCU 2.E.3).

# Review of the Literature

In modern education, there is a need for increased attention to the foundational skills adults need to access resources and services, attain higher levels of education, stay viable in the workplace, and participate fully in their communities. Results of the Survey of Adult Skills, administered by the Programme for International Student Assessment (PISA) and reported by the OECD (2013), link higher literacy proficiency with improved employment outcomes and life satisfaction. However, the survey also unearthed disparities among nations in terms of educational opportunities and support for citizens' growth.

Key indicators used to define success in the twenty-first century include proficiency in literacy, numeracy, and problem solving using technology (OECD, 2013), and broader indicators such as the American Association of Colleges and Universities' liberal-education-based Essential Learning Outcomes (AAC&U, 2008). These indicators emphasize the need for educational institutions to produce citizens capable of meeting twenty-first-century challenges, such as employers' desire for college graduates to have better cultural awareness, greater science and technology competencies, and deeper analytical skills when they enter the workforce (AAC&U, 2008).

Globally, the need for high-skilled knowledge workers has increased as the service sector and high-technology manufacturing continue to grow and traditional manufacturing declines. Such shifting has highlighted the need for more educational opportunities that focus on digital literacy; information, communication and technology (ICT) literacy; and computer proficiency (OECD, 2013). Additionally, education experts such as Strucker (2013) and Rotherham and Willingham (2010) have pointed to a knowledge gap among adults. These experts discussed societal recognition that basic education is not enough; educational attainment must reach beyond high school to meet new labor demands. Higher education, particularly at the community college and career/technical levels, has sought means to address the knowledge gap through development of college readiness programs, transition courses, and pathways programs that teach students what it means to succeed as a college student.

Additional discussions about adult-learner populations have emphasized the various challenges and barriers adults—particularly working adults in a family care role—face when they enter higher education for the first time or reenter higher education. Falasca (2011) reviewed the literature on barriers to adult learning, categorizing these barriers as external (aging, health issues, family roles, job circumstances) and internal (narrow perspectives about what constitutes education, reliance on previous notions, anxiety, and negative perceptions) (pp. 586–587). In addition, English-language proficiency and cultural background may also pose barriers to knowledge acquisition (Lange, Canuel, & Fitzgibbons, 2011). Such internal and external barriers may challenge students' motivation and persistence in higher education. While the motivation to start an academic program may be strong (O'Neill & Thomson, 2013), students' persistence and desire to continue or finish may wane based on a combination of these factors. According to O'Neill and Thomson (2013), more attention must be paid to improving self-efficacy outcomes for adult learners by emphasizing the relevance of educational experiences, and through quality interactions with instructors.

# Integration into the Student Experience

## Embedded Information Literacy

Within higher education institutions, academic libraries are in a position to help address the knowledge gap and help adult learners overcome some of the barriers to learning, particularly in terms of navigating expectations for academic research skills. To successfully complete many course assignments and academic programs, students must be able to effectively locate, analyze, and synthesize information. Importance has been placed on determining students' individual knowledge and skill level with regard to academic research. Where some students may have a solid understanding of what academic research is, others may have limited experience (Lange et al., 2011).

Information literacy is not a new concept, but one that is often used in education to describe the process of identifying a need for information and successfully locating, evaluating, and using a variety of sources to adequately respond to the information need or question. Information literacy is at the heart of academic research, but it is also a concept with broader applications and implications for society. Birdsong and Freitas (2012) noted various adult populations who benefit from scaffolded, just-in-time information-literacy instruction, including business employees, older adults, consumers of health information, and global populations struggling to catch up with information and technology advances in the developing world.

In efforts to meet twenty-first-century learning demands, academic librarians have reframed what information literacy encompasses. The Association of College and Research Libraries (ACRL) developed a framework consisting of the following six frames: (1) authority is constructed and contextual, (2) information creation as a process, (3) information has value, (4) research as inquiry, (5) scholarship as conversation, and (6) searching as strategic exploration. Each concept includes related learning outcomes called "knowledge practices" and "dispositions" (2015, p. 2) that show how each frame might be demonstrated by learners. Use of the new framework is in its infancy, and higher education institutions are just beginning to infuse curricula with this updated information-literacy language.

## Faculty-Librarian Collaboration

Collaborative efforts between faculty and librarians have been well documented in the literature. Often, such collaborations focus on courses, such as composition, that are required for incoming students to build foundational research and writing skills. Examples include Burgoyne and Chuppa-Cornell's (2015) experience collaborating with faculty to run an information-literacy course alongside a composition course, an effort which resulted in higher completion rates and GPAs. In another example, Jacobs and Jacobs (2009) discussed their collaborations with composition faculty, which led to a shift in thinking and, ultimately, improved the way research and writing assignments were written.

Examples can also be found in disciplines such as business. Students in business programs must effectively evaluate, select, analyze, and synthesize information and data to develop accurate business plans and create innovative, competitive strategies for solving complex problems. A small-scale study suggests improved outcomes and perceptions for students who experience library-integrated business research instruction. Students were able to apply strategies learned in one course effectively in later courses (Kelly, Williams, Matthies, & Orris, 2011).

## Proven Practices, Examples, and Results

The following practices and examples are based on the experiences of librarians at City University of Seattle (CityU). CityU is an institution that enables students to complete their education in various teaching modes. Curriculum is centralized and offered in many geographic locations. While in-person classes are available, most courses are offered online, as hybrid courses, or in person with a minimum online element. This model encourages collaboration between departments that fosters a unique relationship between the library and academic departments. CityU's environment makes it possible to collaborate with faculty to embed information-literacy instruction into the classroom. The online environment makes the courses flexible and adaptable to new techniques that enable integration. As a result of this relationship, the CityU library has developed three possible options for integration into an online class, and the options are classified into three levels depending on how integrated the library's instruction is.

This is facilitated by Blackboard, the learning management system (LMS), and could be adapted to any LMS used by an institution.

## Tiered Information-Literacy Instruction

**Level 1 instruction.** The first level constitutes an access point for students to contact their liaison librarian. All contact information for the librarian for the class is added to the faculty information section of the Blackboard shell.

**Level 2 instruction.** Level two includes a more involved interaction with the class content. Materials, such as course modules related to the course content or research elements, are added to the course for students to use at their convenience.

**Level 3 instruction.** The third level is the focus of the faculty-librarian collaboration for this chapter as it involves students, the instructor, and the librarian working together to prepare and scaffold information-literacy learning. The focus of this level is to embed librarians into courses at the beginning of student learning. This would constitute embedding a librarian into the fundamental courses for a program. Collaboration with course managers is crucial in identifying these courses and ensuring that instruction is sufficient to learn the skills needed throughout the program. The third level involves an activity or class session moderated by the librarian in collaboration with the instructor. Students will learn a skill that is needed for an assignment in the class and receive the support needed to complete the assignment. The following section will demonstrate examples of level 3 instruction that have been implemented at CityU.

## Instruction Practices and Examples

**BEAM method.** Bizup's (2008) BEAM framework is a new way of thinking about the resources that students use when conducting research for their assignments. It encourages students to focus their attention not on what their sources and other materials are, but on what they might do with them (Bizup, 2008, p. 75). Typically, when librarians teach research skills to students, they focus on the discovery of the items and the evaluation of the item itself. "BEAM presents a lexicon that moves away from the description of sources by type or provenance" (Rubick, 2014, pp. 99–100). Beyond these skills, students lack the knowledge to incorporate resources effectively into their work. By teaching limited skills, students also lose the way in which the item needs to be used effectively in academic research and writing. While BEAM is typically used in general studies, this method seemed suited for assignments in the CityU's School of Management, particularly in the writing of business plans and marketing plans where the assignment is composed of parts that need to be researched individually. This research skill is needed to produce a final product that is conducive to the work done in the workplace. The library launched a new activity using BEAM in an entry-level marketing class to increase student awareness of the library resources and to improve students' critical analysis abilities. This student support encourages students to interact with the librarian and enables them to become familiar with the resources available to them at the library early in their academic career.

The BEAM framework for research is composed of four parts: background, exhibits, arguments, and methods. Each part signifies an area of research that students are expected to fill by participating in the library activity. By collaborating with the course manager and instructors that teach the entry-level marketing class, the liaison librarian for the class was able to embed an activity to guide students through this process and to teach them research skills. In this class, each element has been incorporated into a secondary discussion board monitored and graded by the librarian. Each week, the students select a resource from the library or from the web and post it in the discussion boards with justification. This helps the students in placing the resource within the context of their assignment and supports the students in starting the plan early. By working on one element of BEAM per week, they learn that each area of the marketing plan needs to be backed up with a resource. When the BEAM framework is applied to specific courses within a program, the students can also learn what materials are required in the field when doing research (in this case, a marketing plan). The resources are shared with the class and a discussion about each resource takes place in the discussion boards.

**Topic triangle.** The Topic Triangle (often referred to as the Inverted Triangle) is a technique that librarians have put in practice in many CityU classes. The triangle enables students to think about their topic in a way that helps them research in the library.

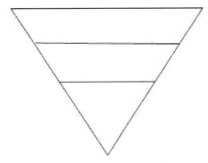

*Figure 1: Topic Triangle*

Using this inverted triangle, students are encouraged to place a broad topic in the first line. As they think about their topic, the triangle helps students narrow their topic. The following areas of the triangle can be filled in with narrower topics to help decide on the focus and to narrow the subject enough for library research. Each topic is entered in the library databases or catalog to get resources for the assignment.

This activity is most often conducted in library class sessions but can also be integrated into Blackboard shells or given to students as a handout when needed. This activity spans across all programs and is often the first step in deciding on a topic. This can be used for small papers or a thesis. The facilitation from the librarian enables students to learn what topics are too broad and which are too narrow. It also starts a discussion on keywords and research at the library.

# Results

Results for these activities have been primarily qualitative with comments from faculty and students. The benefits to the marketing plan have shown a better use of the library and a better use of resources that are typically involved in a marketing plan. Students learn a combination of skills that are fundamental in writing and research. Since the example entry-level marketing course is one of the first courses taken at CityU, these skills can be carried forward to other classes. The scaffolding aspect is important to consider when embedding activities.

Instructors have seen progress in students' ability to research and a better use of resources in the final assignment for MK300. A marketing instructor stated:

> My experience has been that the quality of the work submitted by students after incorporating the library discussions/activities has been quite apparent.... They are able to substantiate themselves in a powerful way with appropriate resources thanks to these activities. The result is students who have a *much* stronger grasp of how to gather and use resources. I highly recommend incorporating this concept into other courses. (personal communication, November 17, 2015)

Another marketing instructor has seen significant improvement in the final product (marketing plan assignment) for the course as a result of sharing the detail the librarians have incorporated into this course.... [she] would like to see this process incorporated into all undergraduate courses that are taken early in a student's university learning. This would ensure or, at best, give them (the students) a better foundation when thinking critically and writing appropriately. (personal communication, November 15, 2015)

These results have led to lasting collaboration between the library, the marketing course manager, and the faculty.

The topic triangle has also generated good feedback from instructors who have seen the results of the activity. Topics are more succinct and the research associated with them is better as a result.

In addition to qualitative feedback, library associations are encouraging libraries to find new ways to assess the work they are doing. As an ongoing project, the library is working with data to quantify the impact that projects like BEAM and other forms of embedded librarianship have on student engagement and success.

## Lessons Learned, Tips for Success, and Recommendations

Library student support is contingent on collaboration with faculty and embedding librarians into classes where the students can benefit from the support. Student support is one of the core elements of the library as a department.

## Lessons Learned

As new twenty-first-century students, many are learning information-literacy skills for the first time. BEAM and other activities embedded in class have exemplified this observation. With these activities and collaboration with faculty, the library can ensure that students get this instruction early and frequently. One of the most important lessons the library has learned is that students respond best to library instruction when it is related to assignments in the class. Repetition not only encourages students to participate but also builds on the skills that they already have. It also enables the students to make the connection to the work they did in other classes. The library has the benefit of being able to be involved in many classes and being able to help the students with these connections.

## Tips for Success and Recommendations

**Work on a shared goal.** In the collaborative spirit of CityU, different departments can work together to achieve necessary results. By determining what these goals are and working with others to gets results, faculty can share the workload and emphasize the expertise of the variety of people that work at CityU.

**Collaborate early.** Talk to your librarian early and make decisions regarding embedded instruction in classes. Classes taken early in their academic career are better for faculty and for students.

**Build a relationship**. Having a relationship between departments at CityU will make the student experience unique and engaging. By setting an example, students will learn that the librarians are there to help with their academic career.

**Embed instruction into the class.** Having information-literacy instruction embedded into the class helps students learn the context in which it can be useful. Designing activities and presentations with the assignments or tasks in mind helps the students be more successful and learn from the experience.

# Conclusion

The twenty-first-century student is encountering challenges that are unique to this new learning environment. Just as the academic institution has changed, libraries have also seen the need to adapt. Online learning has created opportunities that librarians have used to make these changes. Through collaboration with faculty, librarians can now be embedded into the classrooms where need is determined. By using these new methods, the CityU librarians have experimented with activities that teach information literacy to increase student support. The success of these programs has encouraged the CityU librarians to explore new ways to teach information literacy in unique environments.

# References

Association of American Colleges and Universities (AAC&U). (2008). College learning for the new global century. Retrieved from https://secure.aacu.org/AACU/PDF/GlobalCentury_ExecSum_3.pdf

Association of College and Research Libraries (ACRL). (2015). Framework for information literacy in higher education. Retrieved from http://www.ala.org/acrl/standards/ilframework

Birdsong, L., & Freitas, J. (2012). Helping the non-scholar scholar: Information literacy for lifelong learners. *Library Trends, 60*(3), 588–610.

Bizup, J. (2008). BEAM: A rhetorical vocabulary for teaching research-based writing. *Rhetoric Review,* 27(1), 72–86.

Burgoyne, M. B., & Chuppa-Cornell, K. (2015). Beyond embedded: Creating an online-learning community integrating information literacy and composition courses. *The Journal of Academic Librarianship, 41,* 416–421. http://dx.doi.org/10.1016/j.acalib.2015.05.005

Falasca, M. (2011). Barriers to adult learning: Bridging the gap. *Australian Journal of Adult Learning 51*, 3. Retrieved from http://files.eric.ed.gov/fulltext/EJ954482.pdf

Jacobs, H. L. M., & Jacobs, D. (2009). Transforming the one-shot library session into pedagogical collaboration: Information literacy and the English composition class. *Reference & User Services Quarterly, 49*(1), 72–82.

Kelly, A. S., Williams, T. D., Matthies, B., & Orris, J. B. (2011). Course-integrated information literacy instruction in Introduction to Accounting. *Journal of Business & Finance Librarianship, 16*(4), 326–347. doi:10.1 080/08963568.2011.605651

Lange, J., Canuel, R., & Fitzgibbons, M. (2011). Tailoring information literacy instruction and library services for continuing education. *Journal of Information Literacy, 5*(2), 66–80. http://dx.doi.org/10.11645/5.2.1606

Northwest Commission on Colleges and Universities (NWCCU). Standards for Accreditation. Retrieved from http://nwccu.org/Pubs%20 Forms%20and%20Updates/Publications/Standards%20for%20 Accreditation.pdf

Organization for Economic Co-operation and Development (OECD). (2013). OECD skills outlook 2013: First results from the survey of adult skills. Paris, France: Author. http://dx.doi. org/10.1787/9789264204256-en

O'Neill, S., & Thomson, M. M. (2013). Supporting academic persistence in low-skilled adult learners. *Support for Learning, 28*(4), 162–172. doi:10.1111/1467-9604.12038

Rotherham, A. J., & Willingham, D. T. (2010). "21st-century" skills: Not new, but a worthy challenge. *American Educator, 34*(1), 17–20. Retrieved from http://www.aft.org/sites/default/files/periodicals/ RotherhamWillingham.pdf

Rubick, K. (2015). Flashlight: Using Bizup's BEAM to illuminate the rhetoric of research. *Reference Services Review, 43*(1), 98–111.

Strucker, J. (2013). The knowledge gap and adult learners. *Perspectives on Language and Literacy, 39*(2), 25–28.

# Author Biographies

Carolyne Begin is the Associate Director of Instruction at the City University of Seattle Library and Learning Resource Center. She holds a BA in sociology from the University of Victoria and an MA of library science from Emporia State University. She has experience developing and teaching information literacy to diverse groups of adults and ESL learners in higher education.

Tammy B. Salman is a former librarian and Associate Director of Instruction at the City University of Seattle Library and Learning Resource Center. Currently, she is coordinator of student learning assessment and curriculum development at Lane Community College in Eugene, Oregon, and has experience with information-literacy instruction and teaching adult learners in graduate programs. She holds a BA in journalism from the University of Oregon and an MA of library and information science from the University of Washington.

# 15

# Attachment Security in the Classroom: A Proposed Professional Development Framework for Teachers

**Jill Taggart**

## Abstract

An attachment theory lens is used to explore the models that teachers carry into their personal and professional relationships. Attachment insecurity affects a teacher's ability to effectively collaborate with teaching peers and administration. It also affects teachers' sensitivity, consistency, and empathy toward students in their charge, particularly if the students themselves are relationally insecure (Ahnert, Pinquart, & Lamb, 2006). Several scholars (Cohen, 2015; Gergen, 2009; McNamee & Moscheta, 2015) stress the importance of self-reflective practice in creating relational engagement in education as it results in better student outcomes. The ability of those to engage in relational self-reflective practice, often the cornerstone of education and counsellor training, would not reach the required depths to effect meaningful behavioral change in those with attachment insecurity. An alternative professional development concept using guided book study is discussed.

## Overview

Teachers at all levels of instruction are required to balance the academic requirements of the coursework with group process. Increasingly, there is a requirement in education to build competencies in social/emotional learning. This course content has the potential of eliciting emotional triggers for both students and instructors. This can result in the need to put aside curriculum to focus on process. The degree to which teachers are effective in first noticing and then acting on emotional processes is intrinsic to good pedagogy. However, if teachers are working through their own histories of loss, trauma, abuse, or relational insecurity and find themselves similarly triggered by the course content, this might affect their ability to remain psychologically present for students. This chapter discusses how educators might engage teachers in a process of professional development that indirectly encourages self-reflective pedagogy, particularly if these teachers are resistant to self-reflective practice. The goal will be to enable them to be more relationally engaged in the classroom.

A review of the history of problems educators witness in the classroom when instructors themselves are relationally unavailable and the relationship of this problem with attachment research and the teacher/student relationship are discussed. A model of teacher professional development to engage teachers in self-reflective practice is presented.

## Review of the Literature

Since Bowlby (1969/1982) developed his theory of attachment security, numerous studies have suggested that individuals carry attachment styles into many types of relationships, including the classroom as both students and teachers (Ahnert, Harwardt-Heinecke, Kappler,

Eckstein-Madry, & Milatz, 2012; Cassidy, 2008; Castro, Cohen, Gilad, & Kluger, 2013; Verschueren & Koomen, 2012). Attachment theorists describe *attachment style* as a particular way in which we perceive ourselves in relationships. If we receive sensitive, consistent, and responsive caregiving during the sensitive phases in our infancy (birth up to roughly three years of age), we develop a positive model of self and others (*attachment security*) based on our success in consistently eliciting the care we need. Conversely, if our caregiving is inconsistent, less sensitive, or inappropriate, we develop negative models of others as being unresponsive or overly responsive and a negative sense of self as we have not been successful in eliciting the care we need. Those with *attachment avoidance* aim to keep their attachment needs inactivated or dormant because in the past the caregiver had not been present for them. Those with *attachment resistance/ambivalence* cannot control their attachment system activation and become preoccupied with their relationship needs (Ainsworth, 1989; Bowlby, 1969/1982; Main & Goldwin, 1998).

As this model of ourselves in relation to important caregivers is formed during pre-language stages of development, it stays largely in our unconscious. This *working model* is responsible for a particular line of movement or schema of our perception of the world and ourselves in it. We then internalize experiences with primary attachment figures and carry these internal models into future relationships. Hence, if individuals were insecure in their caregiver/child relationships, they might be insecure in their romantic relationships (Castellano, Velotti, Crowell, & Zavattini, 2014). There is evidence to suggest that this insecurity is transmitted to children (Fearon, Shmueli-Goetz, Viding, Fonagy, & Plomin, 2014) and to professional relationships (Richards & Schat, 2011) including the classroom.

## Attachment Security in the Classroom

Many adult caregivers, including teachers, act as attachment figures for young children. Children in school will seek out their teacher as a secure base for exploration or a safe haven when frightened (Koomen & Hoeksma, 2003; Pianta, 1992), or for comfort seeking when otherwise distressed (Howes & Ritchie, 1999). There are also similar behavioural reactions in the patterns of separation-reunion behaviours between teachers/children and parents/children suggesting that the teacher/student relationship in children under the age of twelve mirrors a primary caregiver attachment relationship (Pianta, 1992).

However, the degree to which a child feels comfortable approaching a teacher when frightened or anxious is determined by the teacher's approachability. Ahnert et al. (2006) found that teacher sensitivity was instrumental in communicating approachability. Other dynamics such as the affective quality of the teacher-child relationship, in terms of closeness, lack of conflict, and low dependency (Pianta, 2001), and teacher responsiveness to students (Bakermans-Kranenberg, van Ijzendoorn, & Juffer, 2003) predict relationship quality. A higher-quality relationship then predicts measurable outcomes in students' academics, social, emotional, and behavioural competencies. A sensitive and responsive teacher will serve as a secure base that enables students to succeed (Ripski, LoCasale-Crouche, & Decker, 2011).

## Attachment Insecurity in the Classroom

The insecurely attached child (either resistant/ambivalent or avoidant) arrives at school with risks for academic, developmental, and socioemotional difficulties (Sabol & Pianta, 2012). In kindergarten, attachment insecurity predicts an increase in peer conflict, externalising and internalising behaviours (O'Connor, Collins, & Supplee, 2012). Moreover, children with attachment insecurity–avoidant behaviours are more likely to engage in conflict-loaded relationships, and those with attachment insecurity–resistant/ambivalence behaviors are more dependent and anxious. Ahnert et al. (2012) found that both attachment insecurity models were related to higher cortisol profiles, indicative of higher stress response activation, which affects students' ability to absorb information. In adolescence, insecure internal models are linked to risky sexualized behaviours (Kobak, Herres, & Laurenceau 2012), behavioural reactivity (Ahnert et al., 2012), peer difficulties, and low academic achievement (Verschueren, Doumen, & Buyse, 2012).

The problem is exacerbated when insecure children are paired with an insecurely attached teacher. Buyse, Verschueren and Doumen (2011) found that teachers with an underlying insecure attachment–dismissive style are less sensitive, less responsive, and less likely to recognize the child's attachment needs, therefore less likely to provide a secure base. They did not form close alliances, and this lack of attachment affected student success. Table 1 provides an alignment of adult and child attachment categories.

## Table 1.

*Categories of attachment style for adults and children* (Ainsworth, 1989; Bowlby, 1969/1982; Main & Goldwin, 1998).

| Adult Attachment Classifications | Child Attachment Classifications |
|---|---|
| **Autonomous/Secure** Values attachment relationships; has compassion and understanding of parental behaviour, compassion for self, and ability to self-reflect on the effects of their own behaviours | **Secure** Shows a balance of secure base and safe haven behaviour; separations don't decrease exploration; clear safe haven behaviour in reunion |
| **Dismissive** Distances themselves from early experiences to keep attachment system inert by claiming lack of memory; presenting an idealized image of early experiences; presenting derogatory views of parents without compassion | **Avoidant** Little outward response to separations from parent; little or no safe haven behaviour (e.g., no greeting, no acceptance of parents' reunion attempts) |
| **Preoccupied** Overactivation of attachment needs; emotionally overinvolved with parents, little compassion or understanding of parents; evidence or role reversal (child acts as parent); little self-reflective ability | **Resistant/Ambivalent** Child is fearful of exploration when parent is absent and clearly distressed. When parent returns, their attachment system does not deactivate: parental comfort is not effective |

| Unresolved/Disoriented | Disorganized |
|---|---|
| Lapses in monitoring discourse about traumatic experiences of death of an attachment figure or in recounting incidences of abuse or trauma (dissociation; overprovision of details; magical thinking) | Disoriented behaviour such as moving away from parent when upset; mix of approach and avoidant behaviour; freezing or stilling; signs of fear of parent |

## Attachment Insecurity in Professional Contexts

A person's underlying model of self and relationships is reflected in school classroom relationships. Gillath, Sesko, Shaver, and Chun (2010) found that this explanation also extends to collegial relationships. Testing scenarios from corporations in a laboratory, they found higher levels of inauthenticity and dishonesty in individuals with attachment insecurity. The components of authenticity include an accurate awareness of one's motives, feelings, desires, strengths, and weaknesses; unbiased processing or not denying, distorting, exaggerating, or ignoring private knowledge or internal experiences; behaving in relation to one's values; and having a relational orientation in which one is genuine in relationships with others. Those with attachment-dismissiveness and attachment-preoccupation were both found to score higher on measures of inauthenticity and lying (tendency, frequency, and reasons). Similarly Richards and Schat (2011) found that individuals with attachment-dismissiveness were self-reliant and less likely to form affiliations with colleagues, suppressed negative emotion, and did not seek support for work-related difficulties. Castro et al. (2013) also found that such individuals avoided deeper conversation. Those with attachment-preoccupation displayed dysfunctional interaction patterns, less affiliative behaviour, and were more likely to want to quit their jobs. They were ineffective listeners because they were concerned with ensuring conflict avoidance throughout their interactions. Their underlying attachment style had a direct effect on their professional life. These studies suggest that an underlying dismissive or preoccupied attachment style hinders the expression of authentic, honest, and collaborative interactions at work.

Although Bowlby's (1969/1982) original research suggested that attachment models were trait based and therefore set for life, there is more recent evidence from neuroscience that attachment insecurity is reversible should the insecure individual encounter future relationships with secure individuals, such as a romantic partner, therapists, or teachers. In these cases, the negative model of self and others shifts to a more secure trajectory (Roisman, Padrón, Sroufe, & Egeland, 2002). The resolution of negative models through later secure attachments is known as *attachment earned security*.

## A New Approach to Teacher Professional Development

Many scholars suggest that educators would benefit from reflective processes to create a deeper understanding of their relational intelligence. Cohen (2015), Gergen (2009), and McNamee and Moscheta (2015) argued the importance of teacher relational engagement with students and colleagues. To be relationally engaged, educators must engage in "a reflective exploration of one's own values and taken-for-granted ideas about education, learning and knowledge generation" (McNamee & Moscheta, 2015, p. 26). In this model, the teaching relationship takes prominence over the content of interactions (e.g., dialogue). In other words, knowledge is generated from the "embodiment of people relating with each other" (p. 27) and not to what is being said.

To be fully attuned to this process of deeper self-reflection, an individual would have to want to and see the benefit from *inner work* (Cohen, 2015). Those with attachment insecurity models are less likely to see the benefit of this work or not able to access deeper reflective processes as they are still caught up in their unfulfilled attachment needs: fear of activating their dormant attachment needs (dismissive); or obsessing over their attachment fears and anxieties (preoccupied). Hazan and Shaver (1990) found that those with dismissive relational strategies are less likely to share reflective processes. In addition, although they are open to exploring new ideas, they are generally less likely to collaborate on projects with peers. The research therefore suggests that self-reflective inner work would not be successful for the insecurely attached.

The creation of a safe place for students in the classroom begins with the teacher's ability to build a safe community. A teacher's ability to do this would be compromised if he or she lacked secure relational strategies due to attachment insecurity. Self-reflective practices that feature *inner work* (Cohen, 2015) alone would not achieve the goal of deeper reflection to effect positive relational change. However, approaching the self-reflective process as a professional development opportunity instead of inner work or personal growth might be perceived as less emotionally threatening. Those with dismissiveness could be encouraged to use the collaborative process when there is a set work plan involved that has a set curriculum with established goals or competencies. One such example is the use of book study groups in teacher education.

Early developmental theories such as Vygotsky's (1997) often cite the usefulness of collaborative learning opportunities in education, such as study groups. Vygotsky's (1997) zones of proximal development (ZPD) is an example of communicating learning and culture through collaborative peer efforts. Learning communities are either "formal or informal learning communities [that] can act as powerful mechanisms for [teacher] growth and development" (Desimone, 2011, p. 69).

The proposed method would consist of a book study, in which a text would be chosen to meet professional development goals. It is based on the assumption that the expertise lies with the community not the individual, and that collaboration will ensure that all have ownership in the goals attained (Hirsh & Killion, 2009; Moore & Whitfield, 2008). Teachers would meet weekly to discuss the book contents and also reflect on their own personal growth. The chosen book should pertain to some aspect of relational or collaborative learning or to the application of attachment security in the classroom. For example, Kirke Olson's (2014) *The Invisible Classroom* applies attachment theory and neuroscience to the creation of safe learning communities in schools. As the focus of the book study is on achieving student success instead of personal exploration, it should encourage a deeper discussion of reflective practices.

As in any type of group collaboration, there is a balance required between content and process. Stanley (2011) suggested five important considerations for study groups: (1) establishment of group rules (number of sessions, absences), (2) group norms (role of facilitator or member), (3) conflict resolution between pedagogy and content, (4) assignments, and (5) the applications of findings to the classroom. While these considerations are often found in group counseling (Yalom, 2005), the aim of these groups will be educational even though the material may uncover deeper reflective processes seen in counseling psychology groups.

The most important aspect of the study group is the technique of the leader as the group's norms are shaped and then modeled through the leader. According to Yalom (2005), "the posture of the [leader] must be one of concern, acceptance, genuineness, empathy" (p. 117). The group itself is the "agent of change." While the group leader will establish the norms of interaction, all members will be tasked to collaborate, accept, and support all members; encourage interpersonal learning; act in an altruistic manner; and provide hope and encouragement (Yalom, 2005).

An experienced educator and attuned group leader will mold content with process while creating a safe place to explore new ideas and deeper reflection. The modeling of a deeper reflective process by the group leader along with the presence of relationally secure group members may encourage the less secure to take a step toward self-reflection. This would only occur if the book study does not explicitly discuss the self-reflective content.

The explicit benefit and attraction of the book study for teachers will be the application of the book contents to specific classroom practice. For example, Olson's (2014) *The Invisible Classroom* provides a thorough discussion of the neurobiology of classroom safety, attachment in the classroom, the impact of implicit and explicit memory on learning, and finally, interventions to build a strengths-based collaborative classroom and school culture. Book study participants would read a portion per week and discuss their experiences of implementing the suggested strategies. The implicit benefit would be the subsequent discussion of book content to student success, the teachers' teaching strategies, and its effects on their own personal relational strategies both inside and outside the classroom.

## Limitations and Recommendations

As with any collaborative enterprise, the consistent attendance of participants is required to gain the most benefit. As it is less likely that those with attachment-dismissiveness would see benefit from the collaborative process, the school administration or group facilitator may have to identify those individuals who might benefit from the group and employ counseling-informed *person-centered strategies* to build *unconditional positive regard* (Rogers, 1980) with these individuals. The alternative would be to mandate participation. However, as Lopez, Osterberg, Jensen-Doss, and Rae (2011) pointed out, mandated participants may initially adopt new learning, but this learning is not maintained in the long term.

The recommendation would be to build a book study series into teachers' schedules using different content to appeal to a broad group of educators. For example, novels or biographies might be initially selected. The book study might then discuss strategies for student success, such as reading instruction or critical analyses. Subsequent books chosen in the series would begin to explore psychological and emotional processes, balancing content and process throughout. The aim would be to have a coherent group membership with set norms and rules before more sensitive texts were chosen. In other words, attachment security between the facilitator and members would have already been modeled and a space of safety created to now delve into more emotive content. The attachment-dismissive teacher would be on the road to attachment security as trust, safety, and empathy are routinely modeled in the book study group.

# Conclusion

While there are many factors that affect the teacher/student relationship, an attachment theory lens to discuss the effects of teacher attachment insecurity in the classroom and its impact on learning outcomes for students and professional relationships is proposed. The primary aim was to present one model of professional development that would encourage participation by those teachers with insecure relational strategies, particularly those attached-dismissive. Approaches used in counseling psychology and education that employ self-reflective practice might not be most effective for those teachers with a dismissive strategy as they would be less likely to participate in a collaborate process that delves into insecure models of self.

Professional development based on a featured book would instead focus teachers on the intellectual exercise of applying content. A skilled group facilitator would model self-reflective practice; secure group members would do the same. If the content of the book relates to social emotional learning, there would be an opportunity to reflect on one's own attachment history in the process of the book study. The implicit result would be that those teachers with attachment insecurity would be more likely to reflect on the impact of their attachment insecurity in the context of the book study; then, they could consider inner work in a more explicit way. The ultimate aim would be that this attachment security experience would then be more effectively modeled in classrooms.

A lack of connection with secure, empathic teachers and administrators has increasingly negative outcomes for a child progressing through school. There is a pressing need for all educators to address their personal barriers to building real connection in the classroom and school community, whether through inner work or a more structured professional development book study model.

# References

Ahnert, L., Harwardt-Heinecke, E., Kappler, G., Eckstein-Madry, T., & Milatz, A. (2012). Student-teacher relationships and classroom climate in first grade: How do they relate to students' stress regulation? *Attachment & Human Development, 14*(3), 249–263.

Ahnert, L., Pinquart, M., & Lamb, M. E. (2006). Security of children's relationships with non-parental care providers: A meta-analysis. *Child Development, 77*(3), 664–679.

Ainsworth, M.D.S. (1989). Attachments beyond infancy. *American Psychologist, 44*(4), 709–716.

Bakermans-Kranenburg, M. G., van Ijzendoorn, M. H., & Juffer, F. (2003). Less is more: Meta-analyses of sensitivity and attachment interventions in early childhood. *Psychological Bulletin, 129*(2), 195–215.

Bowlby, J. (1969/1982). *Attachment and loss: Vol. 1 attachments* (2nd ed.). New York, NY: Basic Books.

Buyse, E., Verschueren K., & Doumen, S. (2011). Preschoolers' attachment to mother and risk for adjustment problems in kindergarten: Can teachers make a difference? *Social Development, 20*(1), 33–50.

Cassidy, J. (2008). The nature of the child's ties. In J. Cassidy & P. R. Shaver (Eds.). *Handbook of attachment: Theory, research and clinical applications* (pp. 3–22). New York, NY: Guilford.

Castellano, R., Velotti, P., Crowell, J., & Zavattini, G. (2014). The role of parents' attachment configurations at childbirth on marital satisfaction and conflict strategies. *Journal of Child & Family Studies, 23*(6), 1011–1026.

Castro, D. R., Cohen, A., Gilad, T., & Kluger, A. N. (2013). The role of active listening in teacher-parent relations and the moderating role of attachment style. *The International Journal of Listening, 27*(3), 136–145.

Cohen, A. (2015). *Becoming fully human within educational environments.* Burnaby, British Columbia: The Write Room Press.

Desimone, L. M. (2011). A primer on effective professional development. *Phi Delta Kappan, 92*(6), 68-71.

Fearon, P., Shmueli-Goetz, Y., Viding, E., Fonagy, P., & Plomin, R. (2014). Genetic and environmental influences on adolescent attachment. *Journal of Child Psychology & Psychiatry, 55*(9), 1033–1041.

Gergen, K. J. (2009). *Relational being: Beyond self and community.* Oxford, United Kingdom: Oxford University Press.

Gillath, O., Sesko, A. K., Shaver, P. R., & Chun, D. S. (2010). Attachment, authenticity and honesty: Dispositional and experimentally induced security can reduce self and other deception. *Journal of Personality and Social Psychology, 98*(5), 841–855.

Hazan, C., & Shaver, P. R. (1990). Love and work: An attachment-theoretical perspective. *Journal of Personality and Social Psychology, 59*(2), 270-280.

Hirsh, S., & Killion, J. (2009). When educators learn, students learn: Eight principles of professional learning. *Phi Delta Kappan, 90*(7).

Howes, C., & Ritchie, S. (1999). Attachment organization in children with difficult life circumstances. *Development & Psychopathology, 11*(2), 251–268.

Kobak, R., Herres, J. & Laurenceau, J. P. (2012). Teacher-student interactions and attachment states of mind as predictors of early romantic involvement and risky sexual behaviours. *Attachment & Human Development, 14*(3), 289–303.

Koomen, H. M. Y. & Hoeksma, J. V. (2003). Regulation of emotional security by children after entry to special and regular kindergarten classes. *Psychological Reports, 93,* 1319–1334.

Lopez, M. A., Osterberg, L. D., Jensen-Doss, A., & Rae, W.A. (2011). Effects of workshop training for providers under mandated use of an evidence-based practice. *Administration and Policy in Mental Health and Mental Health Services Research, 38*(4), 301–312.

Main, M., & Goldwin, R. (1998). *Adult attachment scoring and classification system*. Unpublished manuscript. University of California at Berkeley.

McNamee, S., & Moscheta, M. (2015). Relational intelligence and collaborative learning. *New Directions for Teaching and Learning, 143,* 25–40.

Moore, J., & Whitfield, V. F. (2008). Musing: A way to inform and inspire pedagogy through self-reflection. *The Reading Teacher, 61*(7), 586–588.

O'Connor, E. E., Collins, B. A., & Supplee, L. (2012). Behaviour problems in late childhood: The roles of early maternal attachment and teacher-child relationships trajectories. *Attachment & Human Development, 14*(3), 265–288.

Olson, K. (2014). *The invisible classroom: Relationships, neuroscience and mindfulness in school*. New York, NY: Norton.

Pianta, R. C. (Ed.) (1992). Beyond the parent: The role of other adults in children's lives. *New directions for child development, 57,* 1–144.

Pianta, R. C. (2001). *STRS: Student-Teacher Relationship Scale: Professional manual.* Odessa, FL: Psychological Assessment Resources.

Richards, D. A., & Schat, A. C. H. (2011). Attachment at (not to) work: Applying attachment theory to explain individual behaviour in organizations. *Journal of Applied Psychology, 96*(1), 169–182.

Ripski, M. B., LoCasale-Crouche, J., & Decker, L. (2011). Preservice teachers: Dispositional traits, emotional states and quality of teacher-student interactions. *Teacher Education Quarterly, 38*(2), 77–96.

Rogers, C. (1980). *A way of being.* New York, NY: Houghton Mifflin.

Roisman, G., Padrón, E., Sroufe, L., & Egeland, B. (2002). Earned secure attachment status in retrospect and prospect. *Child Development, 73*(4), 1204–1219.

Sabol, T. J., & Pianta, R. C. (2012). Recent trends in research on teacher-child relationships. *Attachment & Human Development, 14*(3), 213–231.

Stanley, A. M. (2011). Professional development within collaborative teacher study groups: Pitfalls and promises. *Arts Education Policy Review, 112*(2), 71–78.

Verschueren, K., Doumen, S., & Buyse, E. (2012). Relationships with mother, teacher and peers: Unique and joint effects of young children's self-concept. *Attachment & Human Development, 14*(3), 233–248.

Verschueren, K., & Koomen, H. M. Y. (2012). Teacher-child relationships from an attachment perspective. *Attachment & Human Development, 14*(3), 205–211.

Vygotsky, L. S. (1997). *Educational psychology.* Boca Raton, FL: St. Lucie Press.

Yalom, I. (2005). *The theory and practice of group psychotherapy* (5th ed.). New York, NY: Basic Books.

## Author Biography

Jill Taggart is the Director of Canadian Education programs and Professor at City University of Seattle in Canada. She was formerly adjunct faculty at Laurentian University in Ontario and at the University of Southampton in the United Kingdom. She holds a BA from University of Toronto, an MS in animal behaviour, an MS in research methods and statistics, and a PhD in developmental and social psychology from the University of Southampton. She has been teaching at City University of Seattle since 2011. She is also a registered clinical counsellor and operates a counselling clinic in Vancouver, Canada.

# 16

# The Presence of the Teacher: Theory into Practice

**Charles Scott**

## Abstract

The concept of presence of the teacher augments the "social presence" and "teacher presence" components of the community of inquiry (COI) theory and points to the significance of the being-ness of the teacher in pedagogy. This chapter presents various theoretical framings of the presence of the teacher, along with research that supports its value in achieving student success and enhancing student learning outcomes in online and face-to-face learning. The chapter ends with suggestions for implementation and an argument for the importance of the presence of the teacher in higher education.

# Overview

> [It] doesn't really matter what the teacher talks about. You remember all those classes you took in college? It doesn't matter what was said. What we remember are a few presences. What was being taught was the presence of a few people, and there was a connection between the presence and us. But we sat there and took notes and thought we were studying the French Revolution or duck embryos or something, when what we were really learning about was coming through the teacher. (C. Barks, personal communication to T. Coburn, December 21, 2011, in Coburn, 2013, p. 7)

These are telling words from Coleman Barks, eminent translator of the works of Jalāl ad-Dīn Rumi, to Thomas Coburn, former president of Naropa University. They echo Palmer's (2007) famous line from the first page of his classic *The Courage to Teach*: "We teach who we are" (p. 1).

Online, distance education modalities are becoming more commonplace every year (Allen & Seaman, 2014). In the past twenty years, there has been a considerable amount of scholarship centered on the development of effective and meaningful learning communities as a means of enhancing student learning, particularly within online, distance-education settings in postsecondary education. The work of Anderson, Garrison, and other scholars (Anderson, Rourke, Garrison, & Archer, 2001; Garrison & Arbaugh, 2007; Garrision, 2009; Garrison, Anderson, & Archer, 1999) in developing "communities of inquiry" (COI) through "social presence," "teacher presence," and "cognitive presence" has been central to advancing effective online learning and is based on the sociocultural perspectives of Vygotsky (1978). The core argument for these perspectives is that learning is socially influenced and situated and that we need to pay attention to the social dynamics of learning.

The ontological conceptions of the presence of the teacher can add richness to the formulations of teacher presence and/or social presence in the models of communities of inquiry in online or face-to-face settings. The current formulations of communities of inquiry are reviewed, outlining the ontological models of teacher presence in the works of a number of scholars, and discussing the implications of and offering specific recommendations for the teacher's presence with respect to pedagogical practice and teacher training.

# Review of the Literature

## The Community of Inquiry Model

A major milestone in distance and online education occurred with the development of the community of inquiry (COI) model developed by Garrison, Anderson, and Archer (1999). A community of inquiry is composed of teachers and students in any educational setting, where learning occurs as a result of three necessary elements: cognitive presence, social presence, and teaching presence (see Akyol & Garrison, 2008, 2011, 2014; Archibald, 2010; Chakraborty & Nafukho, 2015; Garrison & Arbaugh, 2007; Lin, Hung, & Lee, 2015).

*Cognitive presence* is "the extent to which the participants in any particular configuration of a community of inquiry are able to construct meaning through sustained communication" (p. 89). It is the foundation of critical thinking and engagement. *Social presence* is "the ability of participants in the Community of Inquiry to project their personal characteristics into the community, thereby presenting themselves to the other participants as "real people" (p. 89). It is about generating authenticity in learning (Sung & Mayer, 2012), covering the affective and relational dimensions of learning (Savvidou, 2013). Social presence supports the development of cognitive presence. *Teaching presence* consists of, first, the design, organization, and presentation of both the curriculum and the pedagogy. Second is the facilitation of learning by the teacher. Teaching presence supports both social and cognitive presence.

The COI model began as a social constructivist design of teaching and learning. Annand (2011) argued that it has become an empirically based objectivist paradigm that surrounds higher education. Rourke and Kanuka (2009) concluded that students reported more superficial learning in COIs: an "uncritical acceptance of new facts and ideas" in contrast to that which was "deep and meaningful" (p. 24). The authors concluded that the COI model in practice had deficiencies in allowing critically informed, deep, and meaningful learning. Annand (2011) also questioned whether social and teacher presence had any significant impact on student learning and concluded that they needed to be re-conceptualized. However, recent research does support the significance of social presence

(Cobb, 2009; Cui, Lockee & Meng, 2013; Garrison & Arbaugh, 2007); Brooks and Young (2015) discovered that meaningful teacher communication was significant in enhancing a positive emotional experience of students. Finally, Bentley, Secret, and Cummings (2015) pointed to the evolution in defining social presence, pointing, again, to the significance of the affective dimensions in learning.

The theory surrounding the presence of the teacher is meant as a response to this call for the continuing evolution of social presence. Tsiotakis and Jimoyiannis (2016) asserted that we need a more complete understanding of teachers' performance, interactions and collaborations, and learning impact within online communities. A more expansive, ontologically based conception of teacher and social presence that can significantly contribute to a deeper cognitive engagement and enhanced learning outcomes should also be considered. A few approaches are cited below.

## Martin Buber: Presence as Dialogical Being

Buber's (1958/2000) concept of presence is part of his dialogical philosophy and the formation of the *I-Thou* relationship. Each person in the relationship is fully present to the other. Individuals place themselves squarely in the here and now in meeting the other. The meeting is "continually present and enduring" (p. 27). Participants advance themselves into the relationship with the "whole being," even in the face of the uncertainty of the encounter, being open to what emerges in the encounter.

The individual also represents convictions, beliefs, and values. The dialogical teacher offers an "answer from the depths, where a breath of what has been breathed in still hovers" (Buber, 1947/2002, p. 77). This is the person who thinks "existentially," who "stakes his life in his thinking . . . standing his test" (p. 95) with conviction and a sense of self and place. Out of a personal experience of his, when a young man came to him in crisis, Buber (1947/2002) wrote:

> He had come to me, he had come in this hour. What do we expect when we are in despair and yet go to a man? Surely a presence by means of which we are told that nevertheless there is meaning. (p. 16)

## Cohen and Bai: Enlightened, Exceptional Teachers; Enlightened Teaching

Cohen and Bai (2008) used Daoist principles in creating an "enlighten-ment field" in the classroom. "I don't believe I can know what is meaningful to students unless and until I make a connection with those students and find out something about who they are and their individual needs" (p. 4). They advocated for a "heuristic" process of developing self-awareness and teaching from that state of awareness.

> You can learn to trust that you and your students are in the midst of the infinitely creative and complex *dao-field*, and there, practice being in a Zen state, at any moment. Focus now, not just now, but every now that you are able to notice. You can notice your physical self, your breath, your heart's beat, your thoughts, sounds, move-ments, activity, and so on. Just notice whatever you notice. Follow your own awareness. Invite your students do the same. . . . Find the connection between observer and observed, and realize that there is no separation, only points along the way that are inter-connected. ("Begin Here," last para.)

In their investigations of award-winning, exceptional postsecond-ary educators, Cohen, Porath, and Bai (2010) noted that the personal grounding and experience of the teacher has been ignored in favor of promoting specific teaching methods. However, they find that ex-ceptional educators don't have a method but rather "enact human and humane qualities," have a deep self-awareness, empathic sensitiv-ity, and a "finely tuned sense of the intersubjective" (p. 2). The authors demonstrated authenticity and congruence of thought, feeling, and somatic awareness; they have an "in the moment demeanor or manner of being" (p. 8).

Meanwhile, students report feeling "truly recognized," safe, and ac-cepted, with a deepened sense of their own "groundedness and connec-tion," encouraged to express themselves freely (Cohen et al., 2010, p. 4). Exceptional educators have an "exceptional ability to be present to stu-dents, and accompany them, side by side or, at times, hand in hand, in their learning journey" (p. 5), and they identify presence as "the ability to be consciously present in-the-moment; to be able to see, feel, know, and notice present experience, which enhances the potential for a strong, felt connection between educator and learners" (p. 5).

## Farber: Teaching and Presence

The presence of the teacher is, for Farber (2008), simply "the condition of being present. Of being fully present" (p. 215). The teaching is "alive," and the teacher also brings forth presence: "Each person there is an absolute center and . . . an emissary: from a family, a set of locales, a set of social contexts, a long history of nights and days" (p. 216). The teacher recognizes and works with the situation and contextual complexity of each individual present, allowing the potential of the student to appear.

Because the classroom is present, immediate, and alive; because of its complexity and multidimensionality; because what takes place in it is physically and socially situated; because it allows a lively and productive interplay between cognition and affect: for all of these reasons, it is a place where learning can reach deep, can establish within each individual a wide range of connections and of kinds of connections, can be integrated, can be memorable, can be transformative (Farber, 2008).

Farber (2008) added that the presence of the teacher allows students to be fully present, to fulfill what Freire (2000) called their "ontological vocation to become more fully human," (p. 75). Farber pointed to the ontology of presence in teaching, noting it "is nothing we can lock up, nothing we can hold on to, nothing we can simply pull off the shelf and run" (p. 223).

## Rodgers and Raider-Roth: Lived Presence and Educational Discovery

Rodgers and Raider-Roth (2006) expressed concern that current standardized and positivistic learning environments take teachers away from the "complex and nuanced notion of what it means to teach" (p. 265), causing teachers to avoid the relational and affective interactions and hospitable class climate that are essential. These authors, too, point to the ontology of presence, conceptualizing it as "alert awareness, receptivity and connectedness to the mental, emotional and physical workings of both the individual and the group in the context of their learning environments and the ability to respond with a considered and compassionate best next step" (p. 265). Stieha and Raider-Roth (2012) suggested presence has cognitive, affective, and relational dimensions, pointing to past research highlighting the significance of meaningful relationships between students and teachers.

The teacher brings her whole self and attentiveness to the moment-by-moment encounter with the student, one "of recognition, of feeling seen and understood, not just emotionally but cognitively, physically and even spiritually" (Rodgers & Raider-Roth, 2012, p. 267). Nel Noddings (2003) similarly noted: "What I must do is to be totally and non-selectively present to the student—to each student—as he addresses me. The time interval may be brief but the encounter is total" (p. 180).

## Integration into the Student Experience

Integration of the presence of the teacher into the online or face-to-face learning experience is both simple and profound: be fully present, whether with the students in a classroom or online. Begin by developing and deepening the dialogical virtues (Scott, 2011) that enhance the ability to engage with students in a learning community.

Deepen awareness (including self-awareness), emptiness, openness—what Cohen detailed as "inner work" (Cohen & Bai, 2008; Cohen, Porath, & Bai, 2010). Rodgers and Raider-Roth (2006) referred to Waks' (1995) work on developing emptiness and keeping the mind open to fully engage with students.

Be willing to let curricular engagements unfold instead of trying to rigidly steer them; by being receptive to students' longings and needs, teachers can better serve them. Farber (2008) created curricular plans that are open and permeable, allowing for student input and direction. Davis and Sumara (2007) championed a willingness to sit with what will emerge, advocating a pedagogy of "interdiscursivity": honoring diverse discourses and reflecting diverse cultures and epistemologies in learning conversations. When the teacher is present, she can "attend, sensitively and vitally, to the living reality of another human being. The teacher's 'fluid center' is ever moving in response to all the conditions of the continuum between the inner . . . and outer worlds" (Davis & Sumara, 2007, p. 6).

And as Farber (2008) stated, to be present is to be willing to be vulnerable and not "out of the picture."

> So we wrap ourselves in whatever insulation comes to hand: a formal and forbidding, or even arrogant, manner; an inflexible agenda; a set of props, videos, PowerPoint presentations, whatever; or workshops or other small-group activities that leave us, day after day, largely out of the picture. (p. 223)

It is important for teachers to confirm and respect the whole presence of the students, including their ideas, cultures, and episteme (Savvidou, 2013; Sung & Mayer, 2012). Caudle's (2013) research pointed to the value of trusting environments in enhancing learning outcomes.

> [assume] a connected stance. In this stance students must have a sense that their teachers can see them and their learning, their strengths and their weaknesses. Not only do they see but they also accept what they see. (Rodgers & Raider-Roth, 2006, p. 278)

Be mindful of the sociocultural, historical, and political contexts of students; everyone is learning in mediated contexts, and everyone is all the time positioning and being positioned (John-Steiner & Mahn, 1996; Morgan, 2011; Wertsch, 1993).

Teachers can be authentic (Palmer, 2007), sharing themselves (Sung & Mayer, 2012) as a means of deepening the relationships with other learners. They can allow themselves to become shaped by the emergent discourses. Sharing the learning outcomes is valuable, allowing students to responsively engage with and modify these (Tsiotakis & Jimoyiannis, 2016).

Finally, following Tsiotakis and Jimoyiannis (2016), developing presence, and through that recognizing an engaged learning community takes time and patience and cannot be forced. Being present requires a willingness to go, step by step, into the unknown, the emergent, and the imaginative.

## Proven Practices, Examples, and Results

Caudle (2013) researched the impact of a mixed-mode approach of working with preservice teachers. Caudle (2013) found that students appreciated her facilitating and caretaking roles in enacting her presence; she disclosed her emotions, gauged students' affective responses, and responded to students' curricular, emotional, and relational needs, working toward a "trusting environment" (p. 119). Dzubinski's (2014) research of a multinational online learning community demonstrated the possibility, through the presence of the teacher, of developing a safe environment in which students feel appreciated; feedback did not separate the curriculum content, instruction, and social and emotional aspects of the learning environment. Brooks and Young (2015) surveyed 268 university students and showed that students felt the teacher's openness and affectively sensitive communication was valuable in their learning. Chakraborty and Nafukho (2015) discovered through an extensive literature review that the teacher's "immediacy"—the teacher's presence and open availability as perceived by the students—was significant in student learning.

As an example, Heesoon Bai and the author once taught an online undergraduate education course with eighty students. As instructors, they made themselves fully open, available, and responsive to the students. They disclosed their goals, values, hopes, and fears. They engaged in the online conversations, facilitating and encouraging responses from students. This course received the highest student evaluations in the history of online and distance education at the university (K. Jayasundera, personal communication); student feedback repeatedly acknowledged appreciation of their presence in the learning community.

## Lessons Learned, Tips for Success, and Recommendations

In applying presence as a way of being, what counts, paradoxically enough, is practice. It includes study and work on developing presence through openness, vulnerability, responsiveness, confirmation of and respect for the other, celebration of otherness and diversity (including epistemic positions different from our own), pedagogic sensitivity to emerging curriculum, a holistic sensitivity to the physical/somatic, aesthetic, emotional, intellectual, and spiritual needs of the students as an ethical response. And along with practice, reflection as a part of praxis.

Gockel (2015) recommended mindfulness practice as a means of developing both awareness and presence. Bai, Cohen, and Scott (2013) have repeatedly advocated contemplative forms of inquiry and engagement in developing one's presence as a teacher (Bai, Martin, Scott, & Cohen, 2016; Bai, Scott, & Donald, 2009).

## Conclusion

The concept and practice of being and becoming fully present as a teacher is nothing new. The roots for presence of the teacher go back as far as Socratic, Confucian, and Daoist principles of teaching. In 1910, John Dewey (Boydston & Hickman, 2003) wrote:

> The teacher must be alive to all forms of bodily expression of mental condition—to puzzlement, boredom, mastery, the dawn of an idea, feigned attention, tendency to show off, to dominate discussion because of egotism, etc.—as well as sensitive to the meaning of all expression in words . . . [and] the state of mind of the pupil. (pp. 338–339)

The presence of the teacher is what Rodgers and Raider-Roth (2006) offered as a "moral imperative, psychological stance, and an intellectual trajectory" (p. 284) in creating a just, democratic society. Bentley, Secret, and Cummings (2015) stated that social presence as manifested by the teacher can transform learning, grounding it in connectivity, exchange, and collaboration. Coming into presence offers teachers and learners the opportunity to become more fully human and then to teach better.

## References

Akyol, Z., & Garrison, D. R. (2008). The development of a community of inquiry over time in an online course: Understanding the progression and integration of social, cognitive and teaching presence. *Journal of Asynchronous Learning Networks, 12*(3), 3–22.

Akyol, Z., & Garrison, D. R. (2011). Understanding cognitive presence in an online and blended community of inquiry: Assessing outcomes and processes for deep approaches to learning. *British Journal of Educational Technology, 42*(2), 233–250.

Akyol, Z., & Garrison, D. R. (2014). The development of a community of inquiry over time in an online course: Understanding the progression and integration of social, cognitive and teaching presence. *Journal of Asynchronous Learning Networks, 12*(3–4), 3–22.

Allen, I., & Seaman, J. (2015). Grade level: Tracking online education in the United States. Babson Survey Research Group. Retrieved from http://www.onlinelearningsurvey.com/reports/gradelevel.pdf

Anderson, T., Rourke, L., Garrison, R., & Archer, W. (2001). Assessing teaching presence in a computer conferencing context. *Journal of Asynchronous Learning Networks, 5*(2), 1–17.

Annand, D. (2011). Social presence within the community of inquiry framework. *The International Review of Research in Open and Distributed Learning, 12*(5), 40–56.

Archibald, D. (2010). Fostering the development of cognitive presence: Initial findings using the community of inquiry survey instrument. *The Internet and Higher Education, 13*(1–2), 73–74. doi:10.1016/j.iheduc.2009.10.001

Bai, H., Cohen, A., & Scott, C. (2013). Re-visioning higher education: The three-fold relationality framework. In J. Lin (Ed.), *Embodied pathways to wisdom and social transformation* (pp. 3–22). Charlotte, NC: Information Age Publishing.

Bai, H., Martin, P., Scott, C., & Cohen, A. (2016). A spiritual research paradigm: Importance of attending to the embodied and the subtle. In J. Lin (Ed.), *Constructing a spiritual research paradigm* (pp. 77–96). Charlotte, NC: Information Age Publishing.

Bai, H., Scott, C., & Donald B. (2009). Contemplative pedagogy and revitalization of teacher education. *Alberta Journal of Educational Research 55*(3), 319–334.

Bentley, K., Secret, M., & Cummings, C. (2015). The centrality of social presence in online teaching and learning in social work. *Journal of Social Work, 51*(3), 494–504.

Boydston, J., & Hickman, L. (Eds.) (2003). *The collected works of John Dewey, 1882–1953* [Electronic edition]. Charlottesville, VA: InteLex Corp.

Brooks, C., & Young, S. (2015). Emotion in online college classrooms: Examining the influence of perceived teacher communication behaviour on students' emotional experiences. *Technology, Pedagogy and Education, 24*(4), 515–527. doi:10.1080/147593 9X.2014.995215

Buber, M. (1947/2002). *Between man and man* (R. Smith, Trans.). London, United Kingdom: Routledge.

Buber, M. (1958/2000). *I and Thou.* (R. Smith, Trans.). New York, NY: Scribner.

Caudle, L. (2013). Using a sociocultural perspective to establish teaching and social presences within a hybrid community of mentor teachers. *Adult Learning, 24*(3), 112-120. doi:10.1177/1045159513489112

Chakraborty, M., & Nafukho, F. (2015). Strategies for virtual learning environments: Focusing on teaching presence and teaching immediacy. *Internet Learning Journal, 4*(1), 8–37.

Cobb, S. C. (2009). Social presence and online learning: A current view from a research perspective. *Journal of Interactive Online Learning, 8*(3), 241–254.

Coburn, T. (2013). Peak oil, peak water, peak education. *New Directions for Teaching and Learning, 2014*(134), 3–11.

Cohen, A., & Heesoon Bai. (2008). Dao and Zen of teaching: Classroom as enlightenment field. *Educational Insights, 11*(3). Retrieved from http://einsights.ogpr.educ.ubc.ca/v11n03/articles/bai/bai.html

Cohen, A., Porath, M., & Bai, H. (2010). Exceptional educators: Investigating dimensions of their practice. *Transformative Dialogues: Teaching & Learning Journal, 4*(2), 1–13.

Cui, G., Lockee, B., & Meng, C. (2013). Building modern online social presence: A review of social presence theory and its instructional design implications for future trends. *Education and Information Technologies, 18,* 661–695.

Davis, B., & Sumara, D. (2007). Complexity as a theory of education. *Transnational Curriculum Inquiry 5*(2), 33–44.

Dzubinski, L. (2014). Teaching presence: Co-Creating a multi-national online learning community in an asynchronous classroom. *Online Learning Journal, 18*(2), 1-16.

Farber, J. (2008). Teaching and presence. *Pedagogy, 8*(2), 215–225.

Freire, P. (2000). *Pedagogy of the oppressed: 30th anniversary edition.* London, United Kingdom: Bloomsbury Publishing.

Garrison, D. R. (2009). Communities of inquiry in online learning: Social, teaching, and cognitive presence. In C. Howard, J. V. Boettcher, L. Justice, K. Schenk, P. Rogers, & G. Berg (Eds.), *Encyclopedia of distance and online Learning* (2nd ed., pp. 352–355). Hershey, PA: IGI Global.

Garrison, D. R., & Arbaugh, J. B. (2007). Researching the community of inquiry framework: Review, issues, and future directions. *The Internet and Higher Education, 10*(3), 157–172.

Garrison, D. R., Anderson, T., & Archer, W. (1999). Critical inquiry in a text-based environment: Computer conferencing in higher education. *Internet and Higher Education, 2,* 87–105.

Gockel, A. (2015). Teaching note—practicing presence: A curriculum for integrating mindfulness training into direct practice instruction. *Journal of Social Work Education, 51*(4), 682-690.

John-Steiner, V., & Mahn, H. (1996). Sociocultural approaches to learning and development: A Vygotskian framework. *Educational Psychologist, 31*(3–4), 191–206.

Lin, S., Hung, T., & Lee, C-T. (2015). Revalidate forms of presence in training effectiveness: Mediating effect of self-efficacy. *Journal of Educational Computing Research, 53*(1) 32–54.

Morgan, T. (2011). Online classroom or community-in-the-making? Instructor conceptualizations and teaching presence in international online contexts. *The Journal of Distance Education, 25*(1). Retrieved from http://www.ijede.ca/index.php/jde/article/view/721/1269

Noddings, N. (2003). *Caring: A feminine approach to ethics and moral education* (2nd ed.). Berkeley, CA: University of California Press.

Palmer, P. J. (2007). *The courage to teach: Exploring the inner landscape of a teacher's life* (10th anniversary ed.). San Francisco, CA: Jossey-Bass.

Rodgers, C. R., & Raider-Roth, M. B. (2006). Presence in teaching. *Teachers and Teaching: Theory and Practice, 12*(3), 265-287. doi:10.1080/13450600500467548

Rourke, L., & Kanuka, H. (2009). Learning in communities of inquiry: A review of the literature. *International Journal of E-Learning & Distance Education, 23*(1), 19–48.

Savvidou, C. (2013). "Thanks for sharing your story": The role of the teacher in facilitating social presence in online discussion. *Technology, Pedagogy and Education, 22*(2), 193–211. doi:10.1080/147593 9X.2013.787267

Scott, C. (2011). *Becoming dialogue: Martin Buber's concept of turning to the other as educational praxis* (Unpublished doctoral dissertation). Simon Fraser University, Burnaby, BC. Retrieved from http://summit.sfu.ca/system/files/iritems1/11608/etd6512_CScott.pdf

Stieha, V., & Raider-Roth, M. (2012). Presence in context: Teachers' negotiations with the relational environment of school. *Journal of Educational Change, 13*(4), 511–534.

Sung, E., & Mayer, R. (2012). Five facets of social presence in online distance education. *Computers in Human Behavior, 28*(5), 1738–1747.

Tsiotakis, P., & Jimoyiannis, A. (2016). Critical factors towards analysing teachers' presence in on-line learning communities. *The Internet and Higher Education, 28*, 45–58. doi:10.1016/j.iheduc.2015.09.002

Vygotsky, L. S. (1978). *Mind in society: The development of higher mental process*. Cambridge, MA: Harvard University Press.

Waks, L. (1995). Emptiness. In J. Garrison & A. Rud (Eds.), *The educational conversation: Closing the gap* (pp. 85–96). Albany, NY: State University of New York Press.

Wertsch, J. V. (1993). *Voices of the mind: A sociocultural approach to mediated action*. Cambridge, MA: Harvard University Press.

# Author Biography

Charles Scott is a Program Coordinator for the MEd Leadership in Education program and an Associate Professor at City University of Seattle. His research interests include contemplative inquiry in education, dialogical models and practices in teaching, curriculum theory and implementation, the spiritual dimensions of leadership, and arts education. He earned his PhD at Simon Fraser University (where he also teaches) in an analysis of the dialogical capacities outlined in Martin Buber's philosophy of dialogue and how they can be implemented in teaching practice.

# 17

# Engaging Pre-service Teacher Candidates in Academic Coursework: Using a Practice to Theory Approach

**Leanna Aker**

## Abstract

Though traditional teacher preparation programs teach education-al theory and ask teacher candidates to put that theory into practice, a practice-to-theory (PtT) approach can more effectively engage preservice teachers. The rationale for such an approach is grounded in research of preservice teachers' perceptions of their preparation programs, theories of situated learning and self-determination in adult learners, and similar innovative teacher preparation approaches. The author dissects two vignettes of successful PtT approaches at a microscale within the classroom, and shares tips for successfully integrating such an approach in preservice teachers' coursework.

## Overview

Using a practice-to-theory (PtT) approach to teacher education can effectively engage preservice teachers in their academic coursework. Improving the cognitive engagement of teacher candidates with educational theory is of great importance, as many perceive their coursework to be irrelevant and disconnected from their classroom contexts. For nontraditional adult learners who enter teacher preparation programs, the theory-to-practice approach is even more problematic from an engagement perspective. These learners often bring a wealth of informal and/or formal experiences with education by way of being a parent, volunteer, or paraeducator. By teaching about instructional theory and then asking candidates to put the theory into practice, we ignore or even devalue their rich educational experiences. A practice-to-theory approach honors the experiences that preservice teachers have in their field placements and prior experiences.

Teacher candidates naturally take a "practice-to-theory" approach when sense making about their classroom experiences. For example, a candidate may share an experience in which he or she brusquely asked a student to sit down, and the student refused to comply. That candidate might draw a conclusion that it is best not to be too brusque in classroom management, based on that classroom experience. Though this initial claim about best practice is naïve and needs development, the salient point is that the creation of theory from practice occurs naturally. Teachers can leverage this intuitive tendency in a PtT approach.

## Review of the Literature

Working to better engage preservice teachers in their academic coursework is important, as there is a consistent body of research suggesting teacher candidates have negative perceptions of this portion of teacher preparation. Some preservice teachers expressed that coursework was irrelevant, or that too much emphasis was placed on the theory of teaching at the expense of more practical concerns (Ashby et al., 2008; Lampert, 2010). Others admitted that they were not sure of the value of their academic coursework (Younger, Brindley, Pedder, & Hagger, 2004), or that there was a disconnect between coursework and what they observed in their field placements (Allen, 2009). As effective teaching requires more than technical "how-to" knowledge, engaging preservice teachers in reflecting on their teaching practice through the lens of educational theories is an important goal.

## Traditional Approaches to Teacher Education

Negative teacher perceptions of academic coursework draw attention to a well-known divide between theory and practice in teacher preparation programs—the "sacred theory-practice story" (Schön, 1983, p. 21). Traditionally, teacher preparation programs adopt a theory-to-practice approach in which teacher candidates learn about theory, and then are expected to put those theories to practice in their coursework. In such an approach, theory precedes practice; teachers are expected to first learn about theory and best practice, and second, to take the best practice and implement it within the classroom.

There are a number of problems with the theory-to-practice approach that contribute to preservice teachers' disengagement with theory in their preparation programs. First, because teacher candidates often see practices within their field placements that conflict with theory, they conclude either that theory is irrelevant or that teaching is idiosyncratic (Allen, 2009). Another problem lies in the conflicting roles of the teacher candidate as both a worker and a learner within their classrooms (Allen, 2009). Being in a high-pressure situation to accomplish a job (the worker role), is in conflict with thoughtful, critical reflection on the experience (the learner role). Faced with a choice of accomplishing the teaching task or slowing down to reflect and analyze, the teacher candidate logically will prioritize the worker role over the learner role.

The worker-learner conflict elucidates a more fundamental readiness mismatch in a theory- to practice approach. This traditional approach presents teacher candidates with theory early in their field experience, when they are focused on basic survival in the classroom (Hutchings, Maylor, Mendick, Mentor, & Smart, 2006). At this stage, the teacher candidate has no need or desire to learn and apply theory. The need for theory emerges only when teacher candidates collect concrete classroom experiences that generate critical reflection and concern (Korthagen, 2011).

Lastly, theory-to-practice approaches adopt an implicit stance that teacher candidates are, or should be, blank slates with respect to educational theory. A broad body of research literature confirms that preservice teachers not only have beliefs about best practices vis-à-vis their own experiences as a student but also these beliefs are resistant to change (Ashby et al., 2008; Raffo & Hall, 2006). Not only is the blank slate approach to teacher education misinformed, but it also disengages teacher candidates by implicitly devaluing the educational experiences they bring to their preparation programs. This problem is particularly pronounced for alternative certification programs that enroll paraeducators with extensive classroom experience.

## Alternate Practice-to-Theory Approach to Teacher Education

An alternative practice-to-theory (PtT) approach offers a solution to the readiness and blank slate issues with traditional teacher education. In a PtT approach, problems of practice from teacher candidates' classrooms serve as the starting point from which candidates generate nascent ideas about educational theory. In other words, rather than putting theory into practice, teachers generate tentative theories from their own classroom practices in a PtT approach. This reverse strategy in teacher education is effective because it foregrounds authentic classroom needs of the preservice teachers. Further, the strategy honors the existing classroom experiences of the preservice teacher by positioning those experiences as relevant data in the discussion. Evaluations of teacher preparation programs show that educational theory is best appreciated and integrated into a teacher's schema when a teacher has classroom experiences to which theory can be compared (Hutchings et al., 2006). Thus, PtT approaches can better engage preservice teachers in the theoretical components of their preparation program.

A PtT approach is grounded in a number of theoretical constructs, including situated learning (SL) and self-determination (SDT) theories. SL posits that knowledge must be situated in a real-life context, and that learning is a social process within a community of practice (Lave & Wenger, 1991; Merriam, 2008). Thus, learning about teaching must be situated or grounded in classroom contexts, and meaning making about teaching is a social process within cohorts or classes of fellow teacher candidates. SDT posits that learners are most motivated when they feel autonomous, competent, and related to others (Deci & Ryan, 1985). A PtT approach enhances all three components: autonomy through the use and valuing of relevant personal experiences, competence through the satisfaction of generating theory that matches existing theory, and relatedness via sharing and interpreting common experiences collaboratively with peers.

## Integration into the Student Experience

Methods to incorporate PtT into preservice teachers' coursework include problem-based learning and other constructivist approaches. Problem-based learning approaches to teacher education involve teachers generating problems of practice from their own experiences, and generating and testing solutions to those problems (McPhee, 2009). Though this approach is similar in ways to the incorporation of case studies in teacher education, it also differs in fundamental ways. Traditionally, case studies have been used as examples of theory, rather than situations from which theory could be generated. Though instructors can empower teacher candidates to make meaning from exemplar case studies, a far more engaging approach would be to generate case studies from problems of practice that originate within the candidates' own field experiences. In this way, teacher candidates are engaged in solving a problem of authentic and immediate concern. Problem-based learning approaches thus situate learning in meaningful context, and support adult learners' self-determination needs.

Rather than beginning with problems of practice, other PtT approaches encourage candidates to categorize personal classroom experiences, generate tentative theories, and then actively test those theories in the classroom. Teacher candidates using the "realistic approach" to teacher education complete a reflective cycle made up of five steps: action, looking back on the action, awareness of essential aspects, creating alternative methods of action, and trial (Korthagen, 2011). The perspective of teacher candidates' peers can be invaluable in terms of increasing awareness and creating alternative methods of action. Similarly, the experiential curriculum project (ECP) promotes teacher candidates' verification of theory generated from both personal experiences and academic theory (Kahne & Westheimer, 2011). Though the active testing of generated theory may seem indistinguishable from putting theory into practice, there are two main differences. In a theory-to-practice approach, students have no personal investment in the theory, and they are also being implicitly or explicitly discouraged to test or question the theory. PtT approaches that encourage active testing of generated theory are also supported by situated learning and self-determination theories.

## Proven Practices, Examples, and Results

Two vignettes are presented here as case studies of successful PtT approaches. Each represents an informal moment confined to a single class session with teacher candidates, although observations about candidates' changing knowledge and approach to self-reflection subsequent to the class meeting were noted. By exploring these brief exchanges, teacher educators can begin to envision a feasible starting point for implementing a PtT approach with their teacher candidates.

## Vignette #1: Rebellious but Highly Capable Student

A teacher candidate expressed that she was having trouble with a student who was judged to be highly capable from testing, but actively misbehaving and distracting others in class. Based on their own experiences with challenging students, the candidate's peers were eager to provide possible solutions including time-outs, choice of work area, or earned computer time rewards. Through the process of sharing, candidates naturally evaluated suggestions, as in the case when one candidate agreed that earned computer time kept one of his students from distracting others, but did not serve to improve the student's academic achievement.

These natural evaluation moments—or "yes, but" moments—in the conversation are pivotal ones in a PtT approach, as they indicate critical thinking that moves beyond the realm of a candidate's personal "gestalt" theories (Korthagen, 2011). At this point, the instructor observed: "You are all proposing solutions that worked in your context . . . let's define 'worked' more carefully . . . What does it mean for a classroom management strategy to 'work'?" Candidates began to thoughtfully reflect on what it means for something to "work" in the classroom. Without much guidance by the instructor, the candidates differentiated between students' passive compliance, obedience, and engagement.

In many PtT exchanges, teacher candidates share personal theories, experience divergent thinking when listening to peers, and then become overwhelmed with the variables that can influence the outcomes. This is another pivotal moment, in which candidates either conclude that teaching is idiosyncratic, or attempt to assimilate diverse experiences into a tentative claim or theory. In this particular vignette, candidates explicitly asked the instructor: "What does the research say about engaging rebellious yet highly capable students?" Because this was an impromptu exchange, the instructor had not preselected theories or scholarly articles to explore. However, two articles were selected for the next class that reflected the tensions among the candidates during the discussion: the use of extrinsic rewards and the selection of classroom tasks with an appropriate level of challenge.

Though this vignette may seem to be a veiled theory-to-practice approach, in that the instructor suggested "correct" answers through the provision of articles, the salient component of this PtT approach is that the candidates expressed readiness and interest in the theory. Theory was introduced once candidates expressed confusion over the variety of peers' experiences and asked to be guided by an external source. Further, the provision of articles was utilized to extend the conversation, rather than to bring it to a close.

## Vignette #2: Group Work Does Not Work for Me

The second vignette highlights a tension a teacher candidate experienced with her mentor teacher about the value and effectiveness of group work. The candidate had experienced multiple perceived failures with group work, and her mentor teacher had tried to explore the issue by explaining the importance and effectiveness of collaboration. Ironically, the mentor teacher's approach represented an exaggerated theory-to-practice-approach failure, in that the candidate's experiences were written off as failures to effectively integrate theory. Subsequently, the candidate developed a persistent theory that group work only works for some teachers.

The facilitation of this PtT exchange was both similar to and different from the first vignette. The main similarities included the instructor clarifying what it meant for group work to be effective and allowing the conversation to develop among candidates. However, this particular vignette exposed personal belief and self-efficacy issues that were more personal than the issues in the first vignette. In this exchange, though the conversation progressed respectfully among the candidates, it was clear that there was a division between candidates who believed group work was best practice and those who believed that group work only worked with teachers who liked such an approach. Throughout the course of the exchange, the instructor made notations on the board about relevant topics (e.g., self-efficacy, personal beliefs, student perceptions of classroom environment, developmental appropriateness) without offering further explanation at that moment. At the conclusion of the class, the instructor explained the notations, and explained that she would provide an article or two for each topic. She suggested that students adopt a jigsaw approach to the issue, with each member exploring one topic in preparation to share with the group. This approach was selected to provide candidates choice and autonomy in what to explore further, as there was discord between candidates' personal theories.

The success of such a PtT approach with controversial topics is often revealed in long-term habit-of-mind changes. Over time, the instructor reported changes in candidates' willingness to question their perspectives and personal theories, and to compare the congruence of their beliefs with research. Additionally, candidates exhibited more vulnerability in their self-reflections, acknowledging that their beliefs could be flawed or biased.

## Lessons Learned, Tips for Success, and Recommendations

The use of a practice-to-theory approach is most successful in classrooms that establish an effective culture of safety and collaboration. To obtain the variety of experiences necessary to generate comprehensive conversations about educational theories, teacher candidates need to feel comfortable sharing both successful and less successful classroom experiences. Instructors can help to establish that safe culture by sharing personal anecdotes about less successful experiences in their classrooms, expressing authentic interest in less successful experiences as learning experiences, modeling how to ask clarifying questions about experiences, allowing candidates the opportunity to share experiences anonymously, and sharing third-party case studies that have less emotional investment for the candidates within the course. Additionally, the instructor can ask if candidates are comfortable with the instructor sharing his or her own personal classroom experiences. In doing this, the instructor can establish a positive class culture by modeling vulnerability in sharing less successful classroom experiences.

Additionally, for an instructor to effectively incorporate a PtT approach, he or she must ensure the inclusion of varied experiences, and illustrative examples of specific conditions—what Mezirow calls the "disorienting dilemma" (1991, p. 168). For example, in a discussion about effective questioning and formative assessment, it would be important to ensure that teacher candidates have examples from both diverse and more homogeneous classrooms, elementary and high school classrooms, introverted and extroverted teachers, et cetera. Even with a variety of experiences available to the candidates—illustrative examples of a particular, critical phenomenon may be missing. For example, experiences with effective higher-order questioning may be absent from the pool of shared experiences. Thus, the instructor must be able to identify the critical issues in defining best practice and theory about a topic, be able to effectively probe candidates for those experiences, anticipate which experiences are less likely to be experienced by teacher candidates, and be prepared to share third-party case studies or personal anecdotes to supplement the pool of experiences. The caveat is to allow teacher candidates, rather than the instructor, to produce the bulk of the experiences. This affords an authentic PtT approach, rather than a veiled theory-to-practice agenda from the instructor.

## Conclusion

A practice-to-theory approach to teacher education can solve a decades-old problem of teacher candidates' perception that academic coursework has no relevance to their practical classroom contexts. Not only does such an approach leverage an intuitive sense-making process candidates use to assimilate classroom experiences, but it also honors and foregrounds the authentic classroom experiences of the candidates. Teacher educators can begin to incorporate such an approach at the course level by adopting the role of facilitator as candidates grapple with complex issues. The facilitator role includes both ensuring a complete range of experiences from which candidates can generate theory, and also selecting appropriate research to generate an appropriate amount of reflection and discord. The defining characteristic of a PtT approach is leveraging candidates' authentic experiences and their collaborative reflections on those experiences prior to theory generation or introduction.

# References

Allen, J. M. (2009). Valuing practice over theory: How beginning teachers re-orient their practice in the transition from the university to the workplace. *Teaching and teacher education*, *25*(5), 647-654. http://dx.doi.org/10.1016/j.tate.2008.11.011

Ashby, P., Hobson, A., Tracey, L., Malderez, A., Tomlinson, P., Roper, T., … Healy, J. (2008). *Beginner teachers' experiences of initial teacher preparation, induction and early professional development: A review of literature.* University of Nottingham, London: Department for Education and Skills.

Deci, E. L., & Ryan, R. M. (1985). The general causality orientations scale: Self-determination in personality. *Journal of Research in Personality*, *19*(2), 109–134. http://dx.doi.org/10.1016/0092-6566(85)90023-6

Hutchings, M., Maylor, U., Mendick, H., Mentor, I., & Smart, S. (2006). *An evaluation of innovative approaches to teacher training on the Teach First programme: Final report to the Training and Development Agency for Schools.* London, United Kingdom. Institute for Policy Studies in Education. Retrieved from https://metranet.londonmet.ac.uk/fms/MRSite/Research/ipse/FINAL%20Report%20Teach%20First%20July06.pdf

Kahne, J., & Westheimer, J. (2011). A pedagogy of collective action and reflection: Preparing teachers for collective school leadership. In E. B. Hilty (Ed.), *Teacher leadership: The "new" foundations of teacher education: A reader* (pp. 145–156). New York, NY: Peter Lang Publishing. http://dx.doi.org/10.1177/0022487100051005005

Korthagen, F. A. (2011). Making teacher education relevant for practice: The pedagogy of realistic teacher education. *Orbis Scholae, 5*(2), 31–50.

Lampert, M. (2010). Learning teaching in, from, and for practice: What do we mean? *Journal of Teacher Education, 61*(1–2), 21–34. http://dx.doi.org/10.1177/0022487109347321

Lave, J., & Wenger, E. (1991). *Situated learning: Legitimate peripheral participation.* Cambridge, United Kingdom: Cambridge University Press.

McPhee, A. D. (2009). Problem-based learning in initial teacher education: Taking the agenda forward. *The Journal of Educational Enquiry, 3*(1), 60–78.

Merriam, S. B. (2008). Adult learning theory for the twenty-first century. *New Directions for Adult and Continuing Education, 119,* 93–98. http://dx.doi.org/10.1002/ace.309

Mezirow, J. (1991). *Transformative dimensions of adult learning.* San Francisco, CA: Jossey-Bass.

Raffo, C., & Hall, D. (2006). Transitions to becoming a teacher on an initial teacher education and training programme. *British Journal of Sociology of Education, 27*(1), 53–66. http://dx.doi.org/10.1080/01425690500376705

## Author Biography

Leanna Aker is an Associate Program Director at City University of Seattle, where she works with preservice teacher candidates as an administrator and professor. She holds a BS from the University of Tennessee in biology, an MS from Walden University in K–8 science education, and is currently working on her PhD in education from Seattle Pacific University. Her interests are intimately tied to engaging students in their learning, whether the learner is a middle-school science student or a pre-service teacher candidate.

# 18

# Moving from Labor to Talent

**Laura Williamson and Monika Petrova**

## Abstract

This chapter is a report on a study-in-process conducted at an institution of higher learning in the western United States. The study examines the degree to which instructional assessment practices, such as the industry analysis paper, affect learning outcomes and student learning results in a graduate business program. Greater numbers of working professionals are in need of professional skills and competencies that will help them immediately excel in their careers. As a result, business faculty and instructional designers are therefore invited to create assessments that utilize industry relevant tools and techniques. Initial results from the study are included along with findings and discussion.

## Overview

The chapter will provide an examination into the degree to which the business programs at an institution of higher education in the Northwest are sufficiently preparing learners to exemplify the needed business skills and competencies that will ensure that they will excel in their careers and meet industry demand. Current instructional assessment practices, while historically effective, do not support the business learner with relevant industry tools to build professional skills and competencies with an immediate and direct effect.

There are several challenges, which include supporting both the employee and the employer. According to Kim and Mauborgne (2014), employees never planned to let their talent lapse, making them irrelevant to their field. The other challenge is that managers struggle with how to support these types of employees. How do you move the discontented, counterproductive, and negative employees toward engagement and finding contentment in their work? Part of the problem lies in poor training of both employees and managers. Both are not always clear on how to create talent within their workforce.

The authors contend that business programs can be part of the solution in creating talent. The key will be in identifying instructional assessment practices that connect learners, including those that are discontented, to a career that draws forth their talent and is connected to a growing industry. The chapter will include an evaluation of business program instructional assessment practices, such as the industry analysis paper, and the degree to which those assignments affect learning outcomes and student learning results in business programs.

## Review of the Literature

The job market has become increasingly competitive. For example, recent MBA graduates are not only competing with one another, they are also competing against other college graduates and against experienced workers (Graduate Management Admission Council [GMAC], 2014). Recruiters look for specific job skills and competencies (Target Jobs, 2014). Further, employers expect job candidates to enter the workforce fully proficient in a wide range of skills and ready to work with software tools relevant to the industry. To be relevant, educational institutions must prepare students to utilize a wide variety of tools and competencies at their workplace (Warwick Institute of Employment Research, 2013). Industrial relevance is important at undergraduate, graduate, and postgraduate levels. The gaps between the abilities of graduating students and those that employers expect them to have can prevent the graduates from succeeding in their careers.

In a recent report from Anderson Economic group, 1.5 million project management–related jobs have been identified for every year for the next ten years (GMAC, 2014). This equals fifteen million jobs around the world. In North America this means around three hundred thousand jobs every year. If students are ready, this is good news, and graduates will qualify for these jobs. However, right now there are not enough talented project and program managers to fill the business needs that these organizations have. Additionally, GMAC (2015) noted that a greater number of working professionals are in need of business skills and competencies that will help them immediately excel in their careers. This means that workers need to be taught and immediately able to utilize industry-relevant tools and techniques.

The typical learner at the institution of higher education under investigation is adult. According to the literature, adults learn best when the material is directly connected to their work (Waight & Stewart, 2005). They noted that this is supported best if the material is identical to elements from the work environment. They also suggested that the material must be clearly explained and reinforced to be effectively learned.

Additionally, there are several major ideas and considerations surrounding the adult business learner. Knowles (1980) suggested use of the term *andragogy*, which he defines as the science of helping adults to learn. In his work he argues that adult learners are self-directed, motivated, goal-oriented, and have extensive life experiences. Merriam, Caffarella, and Baumgartner (2007) agreed with this perspective and further explain the notion of self-directed learning. They claim that adult learners are self-directed in that they take the primary initiative in planning for and carrying out their own learning. Adults also make efforts to evaluate their own experiences and are highly reflective. Delialioglu, Cakir, Bichelmeyer, Dennis, and Duffy (2010) agreed with these ideas about adult learners and additionally suggest that the factors of age and job status strongly influence the achievement that adult learners can experience. The authors claim that these factors influence adult learners, who have greater cognitive development and more life and academic experiences than younger learners and, as such, are likely to perform better.

Delialioglu et al. (2010) further suggested that motivation is a key factor for adult learners as well. Adult learners place a greater value on learning and expect to learn from the material they are studying. Merriam, Caffarella, and Baumgartner (2007) also claimed that, "an adult education activity would have as its main purpose the desire to acquire some type of knowledge, information, or skill and that it would include some form of instruction (including self-instruction)" (p. 103). According to this definition, adult business learners fulfill the role of bringing knowledge, skills, tools, and expertise into whatever they do. For many adults, the context of these roles is the workplace.

As mentioned above, adult business learners tend to have clear goals in mind when enrolling in learning activities. They want to expand their skills and knowledge in an effort to grow professionally and to improve their organizations. Alshebou (2010) supported this notion in a study conducted in Kuwait on the value of continuing education, noting that learners enrolled in the continuing education courses created opportunities for social development and positively influencing their society. They enrolled in the courses for this purpose and were able to attain their educational and professional goals.

Finally, concern is voiced by some authors around creating and developing talent from both the employee and management perspective. According to Kim and Mauborgne (2014), "Most executives—not just those in America—recognize that one of their biggest challenges is closing the vast gulf between the potential and the realized talent and energy of the people they lead," (p. 62).

So the question then becomes one of creating curriculum in business schools that truly supports learners to embody the skills and competencies they need to move from labor to talent in their own careers.

## Integration into the Student Experience

Professional competencies are the skills, knowledge, and qualities gained through work, education, volunteer, and life experience. Currently, the MBA program has the following program-specific outcomes to ensure graduates' excellent performance and fit within the selected industry after completion of their degree:

1. Leverage managerial effectiveness through recognition of individual strengths, values, and leadership strategies.

2. Plan, strategize, and capitalize on business trends and opportunities in a rapidly changing global environment.
3. Apply a broad range of comprehensive business theories, disciplines, and technology.
4. Critically use information and results to identify problems, solutions, and opportunities for continuous improvement.
5. Demonstrate clear, concise, and persuasive communication skills that enable them to lead, manage, and participate in diverse organizations.
6. Identify and develop positive personal traits and ethical awareness.
7. Envision, create, and implement strategies that promote and establish a strong social response and connection to a company, product, idea, or service.
8. Recognize the diversity in global business and cultural practices and respond in a socially appropriate manner.
9. Apply socially responsible and sustainable business practices to an organization.

Considering these skills and competencies, research revealed that employers seek recent graduates who are highly proficient in communication skills, specifically oral communication, followed by listening and writing skills (GMAC, 2014). On average, employers rank communications skills twice as important as managerial skills. The top four skills employers seek in new hires fall within the realm of communication: with oral communication and listening skills ranked first and second, followed by written communication and presentation skills. Ranked fifth was adaptability—a teamwork skill.

This hiring outlook for recent graduate business students is one of the key statistics reported in the Graduate Management Admission Council and its annual Corporate Recruiters Survey (GMAC, 2015). A total of 748 employers located in 47 countries worldwide, including 46 companies in the Fortune 100, responded to the survey in 2015, including adequate sample sizes large enough to report details for the Asia-Pacific region, Europe, and the United States (GMAC, 2015).

Desired skill sets for mid-level hires vary across industries. With the exception of manufacturing, employer respondents in each industry sector expect new hires to be highly proficient in communication skills (GMAC, 2014). Oral communication, listening skills, written communication and presentation skills are ranked as the top four desired skills employers seek for mid-level hires. Recruiters in the finance and the accounting sector seek job candidates who are also highly proficient in technical skills, including both quantitative and qualitative analysis skills (GMAC, 2014). According to the GMAC survey in 2015, employers continue to set a high bar when choosing graduate business candidates to interview—nine in ten cite proven ability to perform, strong communication skills, and strong technical or quantitative skills as their top three criteria in their selection process.

ManpowerGroup surveyed more than 41,700 hiring managers in 42 countries to identify the proportion of employers having difficulty filling positions, which jobs are difficult to fill, and why (ManpowerGroup, 2015). The 2015 Talent Shortage Survey reflected on the fact that worldwide the percentage of employers who are experiencing difficulties filling job vacancies continues to rise (ManpowerGroup, 2015). Among employers who feel that talent shortages are affecting their ability to meet client needs, the most likely consequences are a reduction in the ability to serve clients (42 percent) and reduced competitiveness/productivity (42 percent).

The results reported in these surveys illustrate that employers more than ever are seeking and recruiting new talent that will be a solid match with their corporate culture and organizational needs. The increased hiring estimates for business students are linked to the value that employers place on the talent level of students and their strategic fit within the organizations (GMAC, 2015):

> *We are a Fortune 500 company with global operations and incredible complexity. We need diversity of background, including individuals with formal business training in order to ensure long-term success.*
> —US health-care employer

> *Our company is currently experiencing a transformation, and business students possess most of the skills and competencies required to enable it succeed.* —Technology employer in Middle East/Africa

While business can and should invest in bridging the talent gap, it is clear that success will depend on adopting an approach that engages all the stakeholders, especially educators.

## Proven Practices, Examples, and Results

The business programs at the university reviewed in this study went through a review process in which current instructional assessment practices were compared to industry needs based on relevance (as defined previously). Three local high-technology employers and nearly forty business students were surveyed. The survey asked employers to consider the requirements associated with jobs in their industry. The survey asked students to review the job market and reflect upon their academic qualifications to determine the degree to which the instructional assessments in their courses prepared them for the job market in the industry of their choosing.

Results indicated that although current practices were thought provoking and difficult in some cases, they were determined to be insufficient as they did not adequately connect learners to what they would be doing on the job. The research participants suggested that the business programs move toward the assessment of specific job-related skills and the inclusion of additional industry tools as listed below in Table 1.

## Table 1:

*Industry Tools*

| Project Management Course | Business Foundations Course |
|---|---|
| Responsibility Assignment Matrix (RACI) Network Diagrams | Capsim Business Strategy Simulation |
| Gantt Chart | Contribution Scorecard |
| Microsoft Project | Competitive Analysis |

To address the limitations of the current instructional assessment practices and the talent shortage, the program has launched the Shells Review project and faculty have created the *Skills and Tools* checklist for business programs. All of the MBA master shells have been modified in an effort to create consistency and instructional depth within the content of the shell itself for each business area discipline. The aim is to provide as much support and resources as possible to ensure instructional quality that is more industry relevant and engaging. Faculty members also believe that students will benefit from content that is offered, using a variety of delivery methods such as video, audio, and text.

The *Skills and Tools* checklist serves to guide students and program and enrollment staff. In particular, the checklist will help in advising and supporting students to understand what they will learn in each course with even more specifics. This checklist goes well beyond the course syllabus in detailing exact tools, skills, and theories that students will obtain in taking each course and completing the Business Program degree. It enables students to conduct self-assessment and track their progress. Overall, the *Skills and Tools* checklist is a tool for continuous development process.

## Conclusion

The research is clear that current instructional assessment practices, while historically effective, can support the business learner with even more relevant industry tools to build professional skills and competencies with immediate and direct feedback. The Shells Review project and the *Skills and Tools* checklist have resulted in improved instructional quality and student engagement. Based on findings from the survey, faculty members have integrated additional technology tools such as Microsoft Project and Visio in the curriculum. Following this approach consistently will allow business students to move into a better position to possess the skills and competencies required to enable organizations to succeed and meet industry demands.

## References

Alshebou, S. (2010). The benefits of adult learning: Continuing education and development process in the state of Kuwait. *College Student Journal, 44*(4), 860–877.

Delialioglu, O., Cakir, H., Bichelmeyer, B. A., Dennis, A. R., & Duffy, T. M. (2010). Factors impacting adult learner achievement in a technology certificate program on computer networks. *The Turkish Online Journal of Educational Technology, 9*(2), 97-107.

Graduate Management Admission Council. (2014). 2014 Corporate Recruiters Survey report. Retrieved from http://www.gmac.com/market-intelligence-and-research/research-library/employment-outlook/2014-corporate-recruiters.aspx

Graduate Management Admission Council. (2015). 2015 Corporate Recruiters Survey report. Retrieved from http://www.gmac.com/market-intelligence-and-research/research-library/employment-outlook/2015-corporate-recruiters-survey-report.aspx

Kim, W. C., & Mauborgne, R. (2014). Blue ocean leadership. *Harvard Business Review, 92*(5), 60–72.

Knowles, M. S. (1980). *The modern practice of adult education*. Englewood Cliffs, NJ: Prentice-Hall.

ManpowerGroup. (2015). 2015 Talent Shortage Survey. Retrieved from http://www.manpowergroup.com/wps/wcm/connect/manpowergroup-en/home/thought-leadership/research-insights/talent-shortage-2015

Merriam, S. B., Caffarella, R. S., & Baumgartner, L. M. (2007). *Learning in adulthood: A comprehensive guide* (3rd ed.). San Francisco, CA: John Wiley & Sons, Inc.

Target Jobs. (2014). The top 10 skills that will get you a job when you graduate. Retrieved from https://targetjobs.co.uk/careers-advice/career-planning/273051-the-top-10-skills-thatll-get-you-a-job-when-you-graduate

Waight, C. L., & Stewart, B. L. (2005). Valuing the adult learner in e-learning: Part one—a conceptual model for corporate settings. *Journal of Workplace Learning, 17*(5), 337–345.

Warwick Institute of Employment Research. (2013). *Higher skills develop-ment at work*. Retrieved from http://www.tlrp.org/pub/docu-ments/HigherSkillsComm.pdf

## Author Biographies

Laura Williamson is the Associate Dean and Director of business programs at City University of Seattle and has served as a faculty member and program director in the School of Management. Her industry experience includes private sector work with several West Coast firms including Data I/O and L-3 Corporation, supporting such clients as the LAPD, the US Coast Guard, and KTLA News in Los Angeles, California, to name a few. Dr. Williamson holds a BA in philosophy from Gonzaga University, an MBA from City University of Seattle, and an EdD in instructional technology and distance education from Nova Southeastern University.

Monika Petrova is an Associate Program Director at City University of Seattle in the School of Management. She has worked in the project management, marketing, and finance fields for companies including L'Oréal Paris and Mutual of Omaha. Monika serves on the Puget Sound Project Management Institute Board of Directors as vice president of membership and community and provides the vision and leadership necessary to increase membership and retention of members. She holds a BS in international management from the University of Manchester, United Kingdom, and an MBA from City University of Seattle.

**Part III**

# Proven Practices in Advising and Retaining Adult and Online Learners

# 19

# Four Strategies Institutions of Higher Learning Can Leverage to Help Returning College Students Succeed

**Arron Grow and Paula Grow**

## Abstract

This chapter reviews four successful strategies for returning college students. These four strategies include (1) making meaningful connections with one or more teachers (Kennamer & Campbell, 2011), (2) involvement in student peer groups (Zinger & Cohen, 2010), (3) counselor or student advisor support (Smith & Allen, 2014), and (4) access to discrete point learning such as technical assistance or help with accessing library resources (Henson, 2014). The authors will explore how these activities promote student success and how institutions of higher education can more fully incorporate these strategies.

## Overview

According to the American Council on Education, nontraditional adult learners have been a growing presence in college settings since the 1970s (Soares, 2013). Institutions have been gradually adapting to this reality with multiple updates to both college culture and services that colleges provide. In a study of nontraditional students, Wyatt (2011) identified eight strategies that stand out as more likely to help nontraditional students succeed in higher education. Additional studies support four of these strategies for making a difference in the success of students who are returning to college. These strategies are listed above. This chapter explores these four strategies in greater detail, both how these strategies can help drive returning student success and how institutions of higher education can incorporate them more fully into their practices.

## Review of the Literature

## Meaningful Connections with Teachers

Students need to feel that their teachers are in place to help them succeed. Teachers need to create opportunities to form bonds with students. Rosenberg (2003) posited that in higher education, teachers should no longer be seen only as dispensers of knowledge, but facilitators in the learning process, using compassionate communication. It is not expected that each teacher will develop a connection with each student, but teachers need to create an open environment and a willingness to view each student as a unique individual. In effect, what's being discussed here is engagement. Wyatt (2011) pointed out that college educators can serve as the front line for student engagement, which can have a positive impact on student success.

## Involvement in Student Peer Groups

The notion of the traditional student in higher education is changing (Wyatt, 2011). In past decades, most who attended college were recent high school graduates who came ready to form new peer groups and had the discretionary time to do so. This allows peer groups to form organically. In today's college classes, returning students usually do not have these luxuries. Still, the benefits that peer groups can have for student success have not changed. Recognizing this, Zevallos and Washburn (2014) promoted the facilitation of peer groups as part of a formal, program-wide initiative. More details about this will be provided later in the chapter. The bottom line is this: schools that want their returning students to have the known advantages of camaraderie, socialization, and a sense of teamwork through positive group experiences will take steps to encourage the formation of peer groups in their programs.

## Counselor or Student Advisor Support

Individual students have individual needs. This has been documented by a number of higher education researchers (Smith & Allen, 2014). To the degree school counselors and student advisors can assist with the needs of returning students, it will determine how likely students will find success in their academic efforts. Colleges can more fully leverage counselors and advisors to improve success for returning college students.

## Access to Discrete Point Learning and Student Services

In a review of what Northeast Alabama Community College has done to improve academic success for its returning students, Kennamer and Campbell (2011) asserted that the more services institutions can provide for students, the better off students will be. Services that universities can offer include library and research services, technology assistance, health services, financial aid officers, career placement or tutoring services, and disability services. These are just some examples of specific services institutions can make available to students. The question is: How many of these service areas do students use, or even know about? Kennamer and Campbell (2011) encouraged colleges to do two things: (1) provide as many support services as makes sense for the institution, and (2) ensure returning students are aware of these services and use them when they are needed.

## Integration into the Student Experience

Institutions of higher learning have a vested interest in guiding returning students toward positive learning experiences in their classes, which, in turn, improve their chances of completing the programs in which they enroll. Each of the four strategies discussed in this chapter can be integrated into the student experience. To accomplish this, each of these strategies will need to be integrated into the student experience in different ways.

According to Wyatt (2011), instructors can have a profound influence on student experience. Stes, DeMaeyer, Gibels, and VanPetegem (2012) affirmed this notion and build on it by calling for teachers to have a clear notion of how they approach their teaching and to make this approach known to students. They found that teachers who are open with students about their approach and offer their assistance will have more success with students. Stes et al. (2012) further asserted that students' perceptions of satisfaction and success can be directly tied to their experiences with teachers, making it all the more important that teachers connect not only with returning students but with all students.

In the area of peer group formation, schools can take a more active role in making this happen. In years past, colleges found their numbers were predominately made up of recent high school graduates. The new traditional students for today are more experienced individuals, who have been in the work world for some time and are now returning to school. For these students, time is at a premium. They do not attend college to increase their social circle. What they don't realize, according to Zevallos and Washburn (2014), is that the time put into peer efforts such as mentoring and socialization can improve student success. To help facilitate this, Zevallos and Washburn (2014) recommended colleges encourage programs that make specific tasks of students helping students and then provide either in-class time or other space resources where partners and groups can meet. Adding in a component that has peer groups report back to teachers and to classes can increase accountability even more and lead to even greater student success.

In the arena of counselor, advisor, and student interaction, Smith and Allen (2014) encouraged institutions to give counselors and advisors higher visibility with students. They suggested that making advisors a specific topic in student orientations, promoting advising services through school newsletters, on-campus advertising strategies, and through student-connected media channels can help increase awareness of the services available, and help students become more comfortable in using these services.

Advising and counseling services are two of the many services and learning centers that colleges can offer to returning students. According to Kennamer and Campbell (2011), returning students will use the service and learning centers they most need. Similar to what will work with advising and counseling centers, colleges should look to make these opportunities known and then encourage students to take advantage of them as needed. Increasing awareness can be done through in-class announcements and discussions, hallway advertising, and use of student-wide communication channels such as e-mail or advertising on web-based student portals.

## Proven Practices, Examples, and Results

In many ways, institutions of higher learning are not different than any other organization. Certainly this is true regarding the initiation and propagation of change within an organization. For any organization, the literature is consistent on this one point: organization-wide initiatives have a much higher chance of success when higher-level leaders provide their support (Rankinen et al., 2009; Suciu & Petrescu-Prahova, 2011; Kim et al., 2013). Support can be demonstrated in many ways, but those that connect with a clear use of a leader's time, attention, and the distribution of organizational resources to specific goals will have the greatest influence on incorporation and continuation of initiatives (Church & Rotolo, 2013).

For university leaders, the application is the same. Initiatives designed to help returning students find academic success—be they campaigns for increased teacher/student connectedness, encouraging student peer groups or counselor and advisor support, or leveraging multiple college service centers—have the best chance when higher-level officials support them. University leaders can show this support by giving their time, prolonged attention, and the organizational funds necessary to create influential, sustainable, student-success-oriented operations. These actions, coupled with organizational member buy-in, and a clear mission-related purpose will help these strategies succeed (Church & Rotolo, 2013).

Success through this pattern has been documented in the literature. In this chapter, this pattern with respect to peer group formations has been highlighted (Zevallos & Washburn, 2014) through leader support of specific school service centers (Kennamer & Campbell, 2011) and in the positive impact that college advisors can have on returning student success (Smith & Allen, 2014).

## Lessons Learned, Tips for Success, and Recommendations

To support new initiatives or improvements to current college practices for helping returning college students invites conversation in two subject areas, both related to change: first, how change in one area may affect other areas (systems-related considerations) and, second, factors that influence change success.

Senge (2005) discussed organizations as systems made up of individual parts that often interconnect. Therefore, change made in one area is likely to have an impact in another area. In this respect, institutions of higher education are no different than any other organization—what happens in one area of the organization, or how team members are asked to change, is likely to affect other parts of the operation. In this chapter, four recommendations were set forth for helping returning students succeed: developing meaningful connections with teachers, involvement in student peer groups, encouraging counselor or student advisor support, and access to discrete point learning and student services. Though on the surface, each of these areas might seem somewhat disconnected; they are, in fact, connected, in that they all center around helping students succeed.

As resources, time, and attention are devoted to these different areas, it will be important to understand that additional support to one initiative will help all parts of the organization. To assist with buy-in, it will help if leaders remind all organizational members of this fact: that what benefits students, benefits all parts of the organization. Support, therefore, should

230

be provided by all areas of the school: student services, registration, testing, security, et cetera. The key is that whatever school officials choose to focus on to help returning students succeed will be seen as important to the entire organization. Attempts made to help returning students succeed are to be supported by all college staff and faculty.

This leads to the second tip for success in organizational improvement. When it comes to overseeing organizational improvements, Church and Rotolo (2013) have identified four recommendations for organizations to improve chances that efforts will last beyond an initial "high energy start phase." Though Church and Rotolo (2013) discussed improving diversity and inclusion in organizations, their recommendations make sense for any organization working to improve the chances for success. The four ingredients they cite as necessary for creating lasting change are (1) clear and persuasive business reasons for the effort(s), (2) full employee engagement, (3) committed leadership, and (4) an embedded approach. Each of these will be discussed briefly in reference for higher education administrators and what can be done to help returning students succeed.

As stated earlier, helping not only returning students but *all* students succeed should be at the forefront of every decision that college leaders make. School leaders and faculty need to see the value of this as the foundation of their work. Why do institutions exist if not to help students, all students, learn from classes and move through an academic program? This can be seen as a clear and persuasive business reason to support the four strategies for success discussed in this chapter.

Full employee engagement will follow from clear and persuasive business reasons for the effort. Experience, however, tells us that this is not always the case. If a school, for example, initiates a program to bring in new students, but in this program the state requires additional testing or registration services, it will be important for all offices involved to be on board with this, to be a part of the transition and want to help rather than seeing this as "additional work" that has to be done. Seeing service to students, any service to students, as that which benefits the entire school in achieving its mission is critical. Helping staff and faculty members make this mental transition can be a challenge, but it is a challenge that must be met to improve the chances that high-quality support will continue for any improvements school leaders wish to make.

For higher education administrators who want to help returning students succeed, committed leadership is reflected in the time, attention, and direction school officials give. Leaders may say they want certain things to happen, but as the saying goes, "talk is cheap." If leaders do not show focused, lasting support for actions that can help returning students succeed, the chances that these initiatives continue will be limited.

The last item on Church and Rotolo's (2013) checklist for improving the chances for success in change efforts is what they call using an "embedded" approach. What this means is incorporating transitions in a way that makes them part of the regular work flow. This is as opposed to having things seen, once again, as "additional work" to be done. An example that illustrates this with respect to one of the success traits discussed herein is the student/teacher connection. For teachers to do what can be done to help foster better connections between returning students and themselves could be seen as a given and not as an additional work requirement. Faculty should be selected that have this as their philosophy of education. In the area of encouraging peer groups, school facilities personnel could be looking to identify and dedicate space that facilitates this behavior. This is just one example of what should be a natural inclination for those who oversee this part of a school's operation.

## Conclusion

Certain practices have been shown to help returning college students succeed, including (1) making meaningful connections with teachers, (2) involvement in student peer groups, (3) counselor or student advisor support, and (4) access to discrete point learning such as technical assistance or help with accessing library resources. Research is clear that colleges and universities that put resources, policies, and systems in place to facilitate these four strategies will see increases in both student satisfaction and student success.

## References

Church, A. H., & Rotolo, C. T. (2013). Leading diversity and inclusion efforts in organizations: Should we be standing behind our data or our values (or both)? *Industrial and Organizational Psychology, 6*(3), 245–248.

Henson, A. R. (2014). The success of nontraditional college students in an IT world. *Research in Higher Education Journal 25*, 1–19.

Kennamer, M. A., & Campbell, J. D. (2011). Serving adult and returning students: One college's experience. *Techniques, 86*(2), 44–47.

Kim, J., Song, E., & Seongsoo, L. (2013). Organizational change and employee organizational identification: Mediation of perceived uncertainty. *Social Behavior & Personality, 41*(6), 1019-1034. DOI: 10.2224/sbp.2013.41.6.1019.

Rankinen, S., Suominen, T., Kuokkanen, L., Kukkurainen, M. L., & Doran, D. (2009). Work empowerment in multidisciplinary teams during organizational change. *International Journal of Nursing Practice, 15*(5), 403-416. DOI: 10.1111/j.1440-172X.2009.01768.x.

Rosenberg, M. B. (2003). *Nonviolent communication: A language of life.* (2nd ed.). Encinitas, CA: PuddleDancer Press.

Senge, P. M. (2006). *The Fifth Discipline: The Art & Practice of the Learning Organization.* New York, NY: Doubleday.

Smith, J. L., & Allen, J. M. (2014). Does contact with advisors predict judgments and attitudes consistent with student success: A multi-institutional study. *National Academic Advising Association, 31*(1), 50–63.

Soares, L. (2013). Post-traditional learners and the transformation of post-secondary education: A manifesto for college leaders. American Council on Education. Retrieved from https://www.acenet.edu/news-room/Documents/Post-traditional-Learners.pdf

Stes, A., DeMaeyer, S., and Gibels, D., & VanPetegem, P. (2012). Instructional development for teachers in higher education effects on students' learning outcomes. *Teaching in Higher Education, 17*(3), 295-308.

Suciu, A., & Petrescu-Prahova, M. (2011). Social networks as a change management strategy for performance excellence and innovation. *Journal for Quality & Participation, 34*(1), 16-20.

Wyatt, L. G. (2011). Nontraditional student engagement: Increasing adult student success and retention. *Journal of Continuing Higher Education, 59*(1), 10–20.

Zevallos, A. L., & Washburn, M. (2014). Creating a culture of student success: The SEEK scholars peer mentoring program. *About Campus, 18*(6), 25–29.

Zinger, L., & Cohen, A. (2010). Veterans returning from war into the classroom: How can colleges be better prepared to meet their needs. *Contemporary Issues in Education Research, 3*(1), 39–51.

# Author Biographies

Arron Grow is an Associate Program Director in the School of Applied Leadership at City University of Seattle. Over the past twenty years he has served as a faculty member and administrator in multiple university programs both in the United States and internationally. In business and industry he has supervised training and development work with several companies including Microsoft and Green Mountain Coffee Roasters (GMCR). He holds a BS from Western Oregon University, an MA in English from Colorado State University, and a PhD in adult education and training from Mississippi State University.

Paula Grow is an integrated basic education and skills training (I-BEST) instructor in the Biomedical Technician program at Bates Technical College in Tacoma, Washington. For fifteen years she worked in adult education in the US Armed Forces, where she served as an education counselor and supervisor of training services in the Soldier and Family Assistance Center and a testing center supervisor and instructor in the Basic Skills education program at Joint Base Lewis-McChord. She holds BS and MS degrees in education from Western Oregon University.

# Diverse Credit Transfer: Student Opportunity vs. Higher Education Tradition

**Kathleen Yackey**

## Abstract

Because today's students are taking advantage of educational opportunities in multiple settings to earn an academic credential, maximization of transfer credits for all students has become critical. To serve the students, it becomes increasingly important for postsecondary institutions to consider nontraditional credits for transfer as legitimate forms of learning, while also maintaining academic standards. This chapter will examine a variety of transfer credit types such as the College-Level Examination Program (CLEP), portfolio assessment, competency-based credits, and more. Many exams have become standardized and have been included as acceptable transfer credit substitutes to aid students' educational goals. However, other types of learning assessment have not been regularly included as transferable, which can create the need for students to duplicate prior learning. It has become imperative for postsecondary institutions to work together to identify and accept a larger variety of transfer credits to aid in student success and remove any barriers in attaining educational goals.

## Overview

Today's students are taking advantage of educational opportunities in multiple settings to earn an academic credential. Due to the use of multiple education settings, maximization of transfer credits for all students has become critical. The utilization of prior learning credits, whether from other institutions, testing organizations, or challenge examinations and assessment portfolios, has become an important topic of conversation. Students encounter significant challenges moving these diverse credits to the credential-awarding institution. Each institution sets its own policy of acceptance around transfer credits, tests, and learning assessment. Due to the variance, students with highly mobile lives can have difficulty when seeking to complete an academic credential. It has become imperative for postsecondary institutions to work together to identify and accept common forms of legitimate transfer credits to aid in student success and remove any barriers in attaining educational goals.

Expanding and clarifying alternative forms of earning credit is being mandated by state legislators, in part to recognize the need to assist students in the process of completing degrees. Washington State law RCW 28B.77.230 entitled "Academic credit for prior learning—Goals—Work group—Reports" creates a series of goals for all institutions of higher learning, private and public, in Washington to "increase the number and type of academic credits accepted for prior learning and the number of students who receive credit for prior learning that counts towards their major or towards earning a degree, certificate, or credential, while ensuring that credit is awarded only for high-quality, course-level competencies" (Washington State Legislature, n.d.). The RCW continues to request metrics, support, and faculty development and articulation agreements among other areas to accomplish these goals.

## Review of the Literature

## Transfer Students

Students are becoming increasingly itinerant during their time of study. Of the students attending postsecondary institutions in 2010/11, 18.4 percent transferred from another state or territory. In the academic year 2013/14, Washington institutions, for example, awarded 13 percent of postsecondary credentials to students who began studies outside of Washington State (National Student Clearinghouse, 2015a).

According to the National Student Clearinghouse Research Center data, for the period of 2013–14, "46 percent of students who completed a degree at a four-year institution were enrolled at a two-year at some point in the previous 10 years" (National Student Clearinghouse, 2015b). For students who make the move from a two-year to a four-year college, the Washington four-year schools showed a 70 percent student retention rate at the four-year level. However, this does not include movement between four-year institutions. "About one in nine students who start college in any fall term, transfer to a different institution by the following fall" (National Student Clearinghouse, 2015b). Nationwide, between 2008 and 2014, 2.4 million institutional transfers in higher education occurred (Education Commission of the States, 2015).

These statistics support the reality that students are on the move between higher education institutions, and are likely to make multiple moves throughout their academic career. With the numbers of students seeking transfer credits between colleges, institutions face challenges in reviewing and awarding transfer credits toward completion of a credential. Institutions must balance reviewing credit for program requirements, general education requirements, and school residency while maximizing the use of a student's available credits.

## Common Types of Institutional Student Transfer

Institutional transfer patterns can take many forms. The most common three are vertical transfer, horizontal or lateral transfer, and reverse transfer. Vertical transfer occurs when a student completes coursework in a two-year institution and then transfers to a four-year college. Horizontal or lateral transfer occurs when a student moves from a two-year college to another two-year college or four-year to a four-year, et cetera. And reverse transfer occurs when a student transfers coursework from a four-year college back to a two-year institution (National Center for Education Statistics, 2014).

## Integration into the Student Experience

### Transfer Credit

Because of this high mobility rate for students, clear transfer criteria easily interpreted by students from diverse backgrounds is essential. Students and institutional staff must plan ahead to be sure that credits taken and awarded at one institution can be transferred toward a credential at another institution whenever possible.

### Veterans

This issue has long existed with students in the military since they are repositioned so often. The Veterans Administration utilizes a preauthorization letter to accomplish transfer credit approval between schools. When a student, using VA benefits, chooses to take a course from another institution (known as a "guest school") and wishes to receive benefits for the enrollment, s/he must gain permission of the main school (known as the "parent school"), which includes transferability requirements and authorization that the course being completed at the "guest" school will be transferable into the "parent" school program. (United States Department of Veterans Affairs, 2009). This process, called the VA Once system, ensures transferability once the official transcript is received and evaluated by the "parent school."

### Common Exams and American Council on Education Recommendations

However, utilizing the VA Once system for non-VA students is not a viable option. Streamlining this process for all students through clear transfer policies can make academic goal setting and evaluation of credit more accessible. For example, the College-Level Examination Program (CLEP), Defense Activity for Non-Traditional Education Support (DANTES), and Subject Standardized Tests (DSST) examinations also come with American Council on Education (ACE) college-level credit recommendations, as do Joint Services Transcripts (JSTs) and a variety of work-related training. Having a policy that plainly states that ACE credit recommendations and ACE score thresholds are honored for transfer can achieve the acceptance of a variety of credits without having to create intricate policies for each exam/hours/type.

## Advanced Placement Examinations

Advanced Placement (AP) exams are typically taken by secondary school students who are seeking either placement into a higher-level college course, or who are seeking college credit. (College Board, 2015). Again, students are faced with varying school policies, in which some schools will take the AP exam as a placement exam, while others will award college-level credit and place the student in higher levels within the discipline. Generally, many schools accept an AP score of three (3) or higher for college credit, but again this varies by institutional policy. Similar to the exams covered by ACE recommendations, a clear policy stating transferability of AP credit that is accessible to transferring student groups would be helpful.

## Articulations

Another important aspect of transfer is the use of articulation agreements. An articulation agreement creates a bridge between one college's program to another college's program or from course to course, or even nontraditional learning environment to college credit. These agreements set clear expectations and parameters for the receiving institution. For example, an articulation agreement may include which department or individual within an organization may report internal training, how to officially present documentation to the receiving institution, which particular training experiences may result in an elective credit, and what college credit value that elective would earn. Articulations are particularly helpful if a student identifies that s/he will be attending multiple schools in advance so that the agreement can be used to advise the student on a pathway to success for all institutions/organizations while minimizing paperwork for both the sending and receiving institution.

## Challenge Exams/Learning Assessments for Credit

Some students return to school with knowledge from work or independent learning, which is not officially noted on a transcript. Often the DSST or CLEP exams are recommended if they have an exam in the field, but if no exam is available for the field of experience, a school challenge exam or learning assessment process may be used if permitted by school policy. Challenge exams are typically for courses offered at the college (the college should not assess for a class it does not offer) and usually carries a fee, which is less than the regular tuition rate for the course. A qualified instructor designs the exam or papers that will be used to prove competency and awards credit if competency has been proved. Successes and failures are recorded on the official transcript. Similarly, the learning assessment process is a way in which a student works more directly with an instructor on proving competency for earned credit, usually through a written portfolio on the topics being assessed.

Currently, challenge exams and learning assessments generally are not transferable to other institutions, although this should change. For example, in the state of Washington, some groups have begun discussions around transferring these types of credit. The acceptance of these credits for transfer is reliant upon the idea that the institution initially awarding credit is using its expertise to assess the course outcomes, just like it might in a classroom setting, but using a differing pathway to collect the information from the student. It is simply a different assessment process than that of the traditional classroom/online setting. Therefore, the credit is valid and may be transferable. However, while this conversation continues, these types of credits are not yet commonly accepted as transfer.

## Competency Learning Transfer

The newest challenge is that of transferring competency-based credits to traditional programs. Competency-based credits are often recorded on the transcript as individual competencies. While traditional college courses typically have multiple competencies combined for a course learning outcome, competency-based coursework breaks the learning out to smaller achievable goals and may have partial credit values per competency. Additionally, competency-based coursework does not yet have a common standard of recording student knowledge on an official transcript, making translation of the credits even more perplexing for a traditional school. Further, competency-based work may or may not designate upper or lower division credits, as the knowledge is focused on reaching competency in a set of required knowledge, not on levels of coursework associated more closely with Bloom's taxonomy. All of these factors create a challenge for a student seeking transfer from a competency-based program to a traditional school/program.

In these cases, it is key for the credential evaluators and faculty to work closely together, utilizing the expertise in credit transfer and content, respectively. Faculty can review competency-based areas to see if combinations of the learning meet particular course outcomes, while credential evaluators review the documentation needed to support the credit transfer within a specific plan.

The option of waivers is a real possibility in these types of transfers. Faculty may determine a student meets the course outcomes for a particular course, and yet the credits are not at the desired level (for example, upper division is required, but the competency-based credits may not be not considered upper division). The faculty may waive the upper division class, giving students the option to take new coursework at the upper level of their choice. Of course, the best option is to find direct equivalencies, but this can present a challenge when translating competency-based work into traditional credits.

In some cases, students may have proven competency in three or four required learning outcomes for a class but still be missing a vital piece that does not allow for the waiver. In such cases, another option is to offer an individualized learning contract for the missing learning area. In this way, the student gains the missing knowledge while also being able to make use of the credits taken previously under the competency-based program.

## Lessons Learned, Tips for Success, and Recommendations

Postsecondary institutions often use peer consultation groups to learn about changes that influence higher education. Membership to groups such as the American Association of Collegiate Registrars and Admissions Officers

(AACRAO), and similar state/regional groups, allows institutions to consult with colleagues when a new mode of credit delivery/transcription is developing and moving into general use. Representation on state-level boards and committees can also enhance the depth and timeliness of knowledge with anticipated changes in higher education. Additionally, it remains important to be mindful of accreditation standards, which may differ across accrediting bodies. How the accrediting agency may define some credits, such as competency-based credits, and how the home institution may transcript these credits, can affect how colleges and universities in other regions review and transfer credits. Due to the complexity and levels of stakeholders, maintaining ongoing open communication with peers, government oversight, and accreditors can be critical when these shifts in higher education occur.

# Conclusion

Postsecondary students are utilizing credits from diverse sources to fulfill educational requirements. The government is encouraging postsecondary institutions to consider ways in which they can support students who are transferring credits earned in multiple alternative settings. This situation calls upon postsecondary institutions to review how they accept credits from examinations, experience, traditional credits, and the newer competency-based credit model and how those experiences become credits within a conferred credential. Institutions that work together using a variety of methods, such as articulations and standardized policies, will be able to better serve students by accepting credits, without the student needing to re-prove knowledge at each institution or take additional credits when one institution refuses what another institution has previously accepted. As new conversations continue, it will be crucial for credential-granting institutions to work in concert with students, professional organizations, state and national government, and accrediting bodies to form a network that better serves today's mobile students.

# References

College Board. (2015). AP credit and placement—AP student—How to earn credit for your scores. Retrieved from https://apstudent.

collegeboard.org/creditandplacement/how-to-earn-credit-for-your-scores

Education Commission of the States. (2015). One-third of college students transfer at least once. Retrieved from https://nscnews.org/over-one-third-of-college-students-transfer-at-least-once/

National Center for Education Statistics. (2014). Transferability of postsecondary credit following student transfer or co-enrollment. US Department of Education. Retrieved from http://nces.ed.gov/pubs2014/2014163.pdf

National Student Clearinghouse Research Center. (2015a). Snapshot report—Interstate mobility. Retrieved from https://nscresearchcenter.org/snapshotreport-interstatemobility16/

National Student Clearinghouse Research Center. (2015b). Snapshot Report—Contribution of Two-Year Institution to Four-Year Completions. Retrieved from https://nscresearchcenter.org/snapshotreport-twoyearcontributionfouryearcompletions17/

United States Department of Veterans Affairs. (2009). VA ONCE. Retrieved from https://vaonce.vba.va.gov/vaonce_student/default.asp

Washington State Legislature. (n.d.). RCW 28B.77.230: Academic credit for prior learning—Goals—Work group—Reports: subsection (a). Retrieved from http://apps.leg.wa.gov/rcw/default.aspx?cite=28B.77.230

## Author Biography

Kathleen A. Yackey has worked in different capacities of higher education for over fifteen years. She has performed registrar-related functions, been a member of the board of directors for a seminary, and currently serves as the university registrar at City University of Seattle. As a lifelong learner, she has sought additional credentials in management, counseling, and ordained ministry. Ms. Yackey holds an AA in business from South Seattle Community College, a BA in history from the University of Washington, a master of divinity from the Claremont School of Theology, and an MA in counseling psychology from City University of Seattle.

# A Partnership Between Advising and Academics: Best Practices for Student Support

**Melissa Myers and Pressley Rankin**

## Abstract

The Doctor of Education (EdD) in Leadership program at City University of Seattle instituted an alternative advising program separating the roles of enrollment advising and academic advising. Faculty program directors are responsible for advising students regarding academic success and concerns while enrollment advisors provide support pertaining to administrative functions. This team approach to academic advising is associated with an average increase of 11 percent in the student satisfaction scores related to the overall advising experience. This chapter presents a case study of how pairing a dedicated enrollment advisor with a faculty academic advisor has become a best practice in the advising model.

## Overview

Mentorship, access to New Student Orientation, and creating a community are key factors related to student success of online learners (Hanover Research, 2015). Additionally, Barnes, Williams, and Archer (2010) asserted that students value a connection to faculty members that will help them socialize to the profession. At City University of Seattle (CityU), enrollment advisors consistently find that students, specifically those who have been out of school for a significant period of time, are positively affected by a close relationship with their advisors.

At CityU, once an enrollment advisor makes contact with prospective students, the advisor is responsible for building a relationship and rapport, guiding the students to the best program, and walking them through the application process. Upon admission to the program, the enrollment advisor is responsible for course registration and ensuring the student is prepared to start class. Once the student is enrolled, the academic advisor also begins working with the student. Examples of academic advising may consist of creating a long-term academic plan, dealing with student-instructor frustrations, and providing student success tips associated with prioritization and time management.

Most academic departments at CityU implement a full-cycle advisor model that takes on the roles of both an enrollment and an academic advisor. However, the doctoral program in the School of Applied Leadership (SAL) chose to create a team-approach model. By creating a team consisting of a dedicated enrollment advisor and a faculty academic advisor (e.g., a program director, a course manager, or a doctoral student support faculty), the function is split, allowing advisors to focus on their specialty. Thus, the student receives the best-possible support from the person most qualified to give that support.

Both Spaulding and Rockinson-Szapkiw (2012) and Golde and Dore (2001) found that students need information about aspects of the academic program, about the mechanics of registration, and about the use of academic technology. Failure to provide that information causes the students stress and leads to dropouts. The combination of the enrollment advisor working closely with an academic advisor creates an environment of strong support for students on all aspects of their university experience. This chapter will present a discussion illustrating how the combination of an enrollment advisor, focused on one program, coupled with an academic faculty advisor from that program can create a supportive student environment that increases retention and creates high levels of student satisfaction.

## Best Practices in Online Student Support

Attrition is an issue in higher education. This is especially true for online programs, which typically see an average of 10 to 20 percent higher attrition rates than face-to-face programs (Rovai, 2002). To combat attrition, students must have their expectations managed to lessen the stress and anxiety associated with understanding program requirements and registering for classes (Spaulding & Rockinson-Szapkiw, 2012). To provide needed information on both enrollment and academics, enrollment advisors are often required to perform both functions. Without the specific program information available to them, they often lack detailed knowledge to provide successful academic advising. This lack of specific program knowledge has been shown to increase the likelihood of students to withdraw from a program (Golde & Dore, 2001).

Within most programs, faculty advisors are most knowledgeable about program specifics. Connecting students to faculty advisors as early as possible is important because it provides a support system to effectively manage program expectations. Additionally, there are other benefits for a student-faculty connection. Barnes, Williams, and Archer (2010) examined graduate students and found that the students valued having a connection to a primary faculty member. Further research showed that a connection to a faculty member provided needed professional socialization and was shown to prevent attrition (Spaulding & Rockinson-Szapkiw, 2012). Online universities that serve a primary population of graduate students must provide faculty support to follow these best practices and limit student attrition.

It is important to distinguish between a faculty academic advisor and a nonfaculty academic advisor. Ivankova and Stick (2007), in a mixed-methods study of doctoral students in a leadership program, found that academic advisors had little statistical impact on persistence with online doctoral students. Faculty interaction, however, did significantly contribute to academic persistence with students being more likely to complete their degree (Ivankova & Stick, 2007). The model presented here represents a nonfaculty enrollment advisor paired with a faculty academic advisor.

Studies have shown many factors that support persistence: external program factors such as family support, self-motivation, prior computer skills, and self-efficacy and internal program factors such as course design and course relevance (Hart, 2012; Ivankova & Stick, 2007; Park & Choi, 2009). However, one similar factor in all studies is the need for students to connect to their faculty. Park and Choi (2009) found that "adult learners are more likely to drop out of online courses when they do not receive support from their family and/or organization while taking online courses, regardless of learners' academic preparation and aspiration" (p. 215). They go on to say that instructor support can replace missing external support from family (Park & Choi, 2009). Therefore, creating a strong enrollment and academic team can overcome other external challenges that a student may be facing.

## Practical Application of Best Practices

The following section presents a case study of CityU's School of Applied Leadership program and its practice of having a dedicated enrollment advisor in addition to a separate faculty student support advisor for the doctoral program. The case study outlines the typical support for a doctoral student.

## First Contact

During the first phone call after receiving a request for information, the enrollment advisor spends twenty to thirty minutes asking questions and getting to know the student. Questions include who they are, lifelong goals, value for education, why a degree is beneficial, what is necessary in a school for student success, and what will hold the student back from completing a degree. After learning about the student, the enrollment advisor will spend the next twenty to thirty minutes discussing the program of interest, and why CityU is the student's best option. While taking the time to break down the degree program, which is a doctorate of education in leadership, the enrollment advisor takes advantage of initiating the idea of an online community.

Setting up the concept of the community at CityU and specifically in the doctoral program, the enrollment advisor provides details related to the wide range of student demographics in the classroom and how students have the opportunity to learn cross-industry tips and techniques to improve leadership within their own work setting. The enrollment advisor places value on discussion boards in the online learning environment as the exciting process of learning from others. For example, the enrollment advisor will let new students know:

> You will be in class with leaders across a multitude of industries including corporate VPs, superintendents, principals and administrators, police chiefs, military service members, and other community leaders. This provides a unique opportunity to learn from one another. It also gives you an opportunity to help others learn by bringing and learning fresh perspectives from different industries that may be applicable to your field. It's so exciting to be able to meet so many new people that otherwise you may never have had the chance to do so!

This begins the process of creating a community environment in which students anticipate the prospect of connecting with one another. Through the process of this initial socialization, the enrollment advisor communicates a sense of excitement that helps the student become energized to be a part of our community of leaders across the nation.

Initial conversations with students establish the primary student-advisor relationship and begin the process of building a community within the university setting. The doctoral enrollment advisor at CityU has found in her experience that some adult learners, specifically those who have not previously participated in an online learning environment, need help in learning how to connect with peers, how to manage homework efficiently, and how to get in the proper mindset for being in school. The first quarter is the most hands-on from an advising perspective and in terms of providing support.

During these initial discussions, the faculty advisor is not connected to the students unless he or she has specific program questions. The enrollment advisor knows to refer students to the faculty advisor should the students need in-depth information about the program requirements, classroom culture, or academic expectations. Typically, however, first contact between the faculty advisor and the students happens when the students are interviewed for the doctoral program. The students and the faculty advisor have extended one-on-one conversations to evaluate the students for the program, to socialize the students to the culture at City University of Seattle, and to answer the students' questions about the program. This interview begins the students' relationship with their faculty advisor.

## Initial Enrollment

Prior to class beginning, the enrollment advisor requires students to complete a New Student Orientation, even though the orientation is not required by the university. Rarely are students unable to attend at least one of the four New Student Orientations available. However, if this occurs, the enrollment advisor and student will schedule an appointment to do a one-on-one orientation covering the basics of using Blackboard and the student portal. The New Student Orientation reviews numerous resources available, ranging from tutoring, library services, and student success tips. Hanover Research (2015) found that an introduction to the online learning environment and resources may help prevent future frustration and ultimately increase student retention.

The enrollment advisor implements strategies both before and after New Student Orientation to ensure each student is fully prepared to start courses. Prior to New Student Orientation, the advisor walks the student through the process of locating books and how to find the best deals on textbooks, how to use the bookstore, and how to prepare financial aid. After orientation, the enrollment advisor and student review any student questions and important dates for the upcoming quarter.

In addition to the orientation, the doctoral program also has an introductory class that students are required to take prior to their first academic class. This class is run by a different faculty advisor every quarter and provides students with a chance to practice their skills and learn more about the culture of their doctoral program. Students in this quarterly introduction often form bonds with fellow students that last throughout the program. Angelino, Williams, and Natvig (2007) asserted that introductory orientations are considered a best practice for preventing online student attrition.

## First Quarter

Throughout the first quarter, the enrollment advisor provides personalized tips for student success based on the student's concerns and issues while in class. For example, the enrollment advisor recently worked with a student who was not able to complete the reading prior to answering her discussion question. The student was stressed out about how she would get through all the required and supplemental materials each week while working full-time and taking care of her family. The enrollment advisor said:

> For a situation like this, I provided mentorship and support to encourage the student to try new techniques and maintain a positive demeanor toward school. We reviewed the process of prioritizing using the professor's rock analogy. First, the student must focus on getting the required reading done for her assignments (stones); we reviewed using the glossary in her textbook to find exactly what she needed to answer the discussion question. Once the assignment is out of the way, she can begin to fill in her time by reading the remaining chapters (pebbles). Then she can attack the supplemental materials (sand). Lastly, she can search for her own supplemental materials (water). By creating building blocks of importance, she is able to turn her assignments in on time, complete the necessary reading, and distinguish the difference between necessary and supplemental materials for prioritization purposes all with much less stress than she previously encountered.

This type of tip for success illustrates the balance that must occur between enrollment advising and academic advising. While this is clearly an academic issue, the fact that it occurred during the first quarter means the student is more closely involved with the enrollment advisor and, therefore, help is more appropriate coming from that person. Issues like this represent a gray area where the student is transitioning into the program. A student should never feel that she or he is without support.

Once the student is established, questions like this are referred to the faculty advisor to provide tips related specifically to working at the doctoral level.

## Ongoing

The advising position is a fine balance between mentorship, student advocacy, and boundaries. The purpose of an enrollment advising position is to perform administrative functions for and with the student, but also to provide a single point of contact available for support throughout a student's entire academic career. This includes knowing when a student needs to be referred to a faculty advisor to get needed support.

The relationship between the enrollment advisor and the faculty advisor is reciprocal. The faculty advisor should not attempt to advise students about administrative issues. To accomplish this, the student must see the enrollment and academic advisors as a supportive team. The student should not be made to feel they are being passed around. To accomplish this, clear boundaries need to be set between what each advisor handles once the student is established so that the student is aware of which advisor to contact. Should students contact the wrong advisor that person will get the answer for the student and let them know to contact the other advisor about that topic the next time.

Ongoing student support then falls between both advisors. The faculty advisor is responsible for sending academic tips, conducting quarterly webinars on academic topics, interacting with students on social media, and fielding students' questions about current or future courses they are taking. The faculty advisor is also responsible for following up when students have stopped attending the program. The faculty advisor checks in with the student and maintains records documenting the reasons for the break to be able to notify the enrollment advisor when the student is ready to return. The faculty advisor also maintains a database, which includes information on the students' progress in the program, their grades, their program plans, and a history of contact with each student. This database is separate from the enrollment contact database maintained by the enrollment advisor.

The enrollment advisor works then to make the enrollment process run smoothly. Checking in on students and reminding them about deadlines and other administrative issues. The enrollment advisor is also responsible for handling incoming inquiries from new students. Keeping the advisor focused on these important tasks by shifting the ongoing student support to the academic advisor helps to make sure no students are falling through the cracks with a lack of support. It also encourages university-wide growth by allowing an enrollment advisor to focus on prospecting and recruitment.

## Recommendations

The doctoral program in the School of Applied Leadership has been able to increase student satisfaction scores for advising by an average of 11 percent over the average for the rest of the university (City University of Seattle, 2015). While there may be other factors in this difference, the partnership between enrollment and academics is the main factor that differentiates the Ed.D. in Leadership program from others in the university. The enrollment advisor dedicated to the doctoral program was able to work with the faculty advisor dedicated to that student. It is recommended that graduate programs connect academic faculty with a program-specific enrollment advisor. Working together as a team increases student support and persistence beyond what one or the other department could accomplish on its own as indicated by our higher student satisfaction scores and our 80 percent persistence rate (City University of Seattle, 2015). Having an academic advisor who is a faculty member in the program allows the type of professional socialization that has been shown to increase persistence and completion of graduate programs (Barnes, Williams, & Archer, 2010).

## Conclusion

Attrition is an ongoing concern for online higher education programs. It would seem that one possible way to avoid this would be for universities to commit to creating partnerships between faculty advisors and enrollment advisors. These partnerships must work to provide the student with support, socialization, academic guidance, and a real-world anchor that will build a strong attachment to the university and increase the students' perception of personal value by the university. By coordinating the outreach from both the academic side and the enrollment side, students can receive all the information they need without feeling overwhelmed by a constant flood of communication. Having a program director–level faculty member as a point of contact also mitigates the enrollment advisor from being the point of contact for program issues. The direct feedback to the program director allows for quicker decision making and continuous program improvement, ultimately creating a satisfied and persistent student.

# References

Angelino, L. M., Williams, F. K., & Natvig, D. (2007). Strategies to engage online students and reduce attrition rates. *Journal of Educators Online, 4*(2). Retrieved from http://eric.ed.gov/?id=EJ907749

Barnes, B. J., Williams, E. A., & Archer, S. A. (2010). Characteristics that matter most: Doctoral students' perceptions of positive and negative advisor attributes. *NACADA Journal, 30*(1), 34–46.

City University of Seattle. (2015). Student satisfaction survey results. Unpublished data.

Golde, C. M., & Dore, T. M. (2001). *At cross purposes: What the experiences of today's doctoral students reveal about doctoral education.* Philadelphia, PA: Pew Charitable Trusts.

Hanover Research. (2015). Best practices in online student retention. Retrieved from http://www.hanoverresearch.com

Hart, C. (2012). Factors associated with student persistence in an online program of study: A review of the literature. *Journal of Interactive Online Learning, 11*(1), 19–42. Retrieved from http://www.ncolr.org/jiol/issues/pdf/11.1.2.pdf

Ivankova, N. V., & Stick, S. L. (2007). Students' persistence in a distributed doctoral program in educational leadership in higher education: A mixed methods study. *Research in Higher Education, 48*(1), 93–135. http://doi.org/10.1007/s11162-006-9025-4

Park, J. H., & Choi, H. J. (2009). Factors influencing adult learners' decision to drop out or persist in online learning. *Journal of Educational Technology & Society, 12*(4), 207–217. Retrieved from http://www.jstor.org/stable/jeductechsoci.12.4.207

Rovai, A. P. (2002). Development of an instrument to measure classroom community. *The Internet and Higher Education, 5*(3), 197–211.

Spaulding, L. S., & Rockinson-Szapkiw, A. J. (2012). Hearing their voices: Factors doctoral candidates attribute to their persistence. *International Journal of Doctoral Studies, 7*, 199–219.

## Author Biographies

Melissa Y. Myers is a Senior Enrollment Advisor at City University of Seattle. She has worked in higher education for four years in which she has served as a full-cycle enrollment advisor, academic advisor, team lead, and doctoral enrollment specialist. She has experience outside higher education in event coordination and logistics. She holds a BS in psychology with a Helping Skills certification from Washington State University, an MEd in adult education and training from the University of Phoenix, and is currently pursuing an MA in leadership through City University of Seattle.

Pressley Rankin IV is an Associate Professor and Academic Program Director at City University of Seattle's School of Applied Leadership. He has a PhD from the University of San Diego in leadership studies and an MS in counseling from San Diego State University. His degree in counseling helps him understand the student from a systemic perspective. Balancing multiple life roles is both rewarding and challenging, and he is committed to helping students achieve their own personal goals around balance. Dr. Rankin also has a background in organizational leadership and management including corporate, retail, and nonprofit environments.

# 22

# The Impact of Information Services on Student Retention

**Mary Mara**

## Abstract

Universities, including support departments such as the library, are increasingly called on by the government, accreditation, and professional organizations to provide data demonstrating impact on education outcomes such as student retention. While modern, digital libraries serving nontraditional students distributed across locations are rarely touched on in retention research, qualitative and quantitative data can be combined to portray activities that increase student engagement, a major factor identified as a positive influence for student retention. City University of Seattle's Library & Learning Resource Center has adopted a framework for gathering and analyzing student engagement data organized by the categories of library facilities, library collection, library instruction, and library people. This framework is effective in communicating the depth and range of resources and services library staff deliver to key stakeholders.

## Overview

Utter the words "academic library" and the vision likely to emerge is one of a large, impressively designed building located, perhaps, near the center of campus. The building is filled with rows and rows of shelves housing print journals and books. A handful of study carrels or rooms scattered throughout the stacks are filled with students working independently or in small groups, putting the finishing touches on a class presentation or project. Students may be using their own laptops, or waiting for a chance to log on to a computer. This is a traditional vision of an academic library, where the library is imagined as a quiet and relatively passive place for users who seek out its print resources and services. When the expansion of access to digital content is included in the vision, it is commonly assumed that librarians play an increasingly minor role facilitating access to online content. This traditional academic library is primarily adjacent to, rather than integrated into, the academic work of the university. In this vision, library users are traditional-aged students who are primarily self-guided while library employees focus on checking books in and out, shelving materials, answering a handful of research questions, and sometimes teaching library-use skills through orientations or one-shot instruction sessions at the invitation of faculty.

Historically, it has been sufficient for academic libraries to cite usage data including materials checked out, study rooms reserved, computer log-ins, instruction sessions or research questions answered as evidence that the library's resources and services support outcomes such as student achievement and retention. However, as government, accreditation agencies, and local administrators call for increasing accountability in higher education, and as economic pressure to reduce costs increases, support departments such as the library are seeking more sophisticated methods for assessing and communicating the range and depth of support they provide and its positive impact on university-level concerns such as student retention.

This chapter presents initial steps that CityU's library is taking to measure and communicate the depth and range of support it provides to influence student retention. An overview of current student retention research from higher education and academic libraries, including thoughts on best practices and sample frameworks, will be provided. Steps academic library leaders can take to provide evidence of their positive impact on nontraditional student retention, with specific examples from CityU's library experience, will be shared.

# Review of the Literature

Student retention is defined as "a measure of the rate at which students persist in their educational program at an institution," typically expressed as "the percentage of first-time degree/certificate-seeking students from the previous fall who either re-enrolled or successfully completed their program by the current fall" (National Center for Education Statistics [NCES], n.d., para. 1). Student retention is an area of focus in higher education with federal and local governments calling for increased transparency around higher education outcomes, regional and specialized accreditation agencies calling for evidence of data-driven decision making, and an understanding that it is more cost-effective to retain existing students than recruit new students (Kuh, 2009). Scarcity of funding is also increasing pressure on support departments, including academic libraries, to demonstrate their contribution to educational outcomes.

Student retention is a complex outcome to measure and influence, with multiple cultural, social, and environmental conditions factoring into students' decisions on whether to persist toward their academic goals. Family background, academic aspirations, work status, finances, and a university's delivery method(s), support services, programs, and policies may all influence retention rates (Bean & Eaton, 2001; Hagel, Horn, Owen & Currie, 2012; Kuh, 2009; Murray, 2014; Tinto, 2005).

Research and practice on student retention originated over forty years ago, has focused primarily on traditional freshmen, and has shifted from an original focus on blaming the student for a lack of skills or motivation, to one that includes the role of the university with a particular emphasis on interactions and engagement between students and faculty or staff they encounter (Bean & Eaton, 2001; Murray, 2014; Singletary, 2010; Tinto, 2005;). Kuh's (2009) research focused on actions with proven results that universities can take to positively affect student retention, commonly referred to as high-impact practices, including first-year seminars and experiences, common intellectual experiences, learning communities, writing-intensive courses, collaborative assignments and projects, undergraduate research, diversity and global learning, service and community-based learning, and capstone courses or projects (Association of American Colleges & Universities [AAC&U], n.d.; Kuh & Schneider, 2008; Kuh, 2009).

Nontraditional students, broadly defined as students over the age of twenty-five who have experienced a gap between high school and university, work full- or part-time, serve multiple life roles including employee or parent, represent an increasing percentage of the student population in the United States and continue to experience lower retention rates than traditional students (Kuh, 2009; Markle, 2015; Ross-Gordon, 2011; Singletary, 2010). While some nontraditional students are degree-seeking, others are more focused on skill development and reasons for pursuing education include technology changes, shifting demands of the workplace and global economy, a desire to increase earning potential, or fulfillment of a lifetime goal (Markle, 2015; Ross-Gordon, 2011; Singletary, 2010). Factors identified as important for nontraditional student retention include confidence and belief in the ability to achieve academic goals, the meaning degree completion holds for career or financial advancement, the meaning of personal goal achievement, access to flexible delivery modes or time-to-degree completion, active learning strategies with real-world application, a clear road map of academic expectations, and access to relevant support services (Markel, 2015; Ross-Gordon, 2011).

The Association of College and Research Libraries (ACRL) provides support for libraries that are shifting assessment from a reliance on traditional input/output measures toward methods that demonstrate impact on educational outcomes (Oakleaf, 2010). ACRL recommends libraries document participation in high-impact practices, increasing interactions or engagement with students, increasing collaboration with student support services such as advising, and aligning library assessment with university student retention initiatives (Oakleaf, 2010). Libraries participating in ACRL's Assessment in Action program have completed twenty-four studies investigating the library's impact on retention, focusing specifically on instruction programs, research assistance, academic support, student engagement, library use, and first-year experience integration. The program and body of research produced are important first steps to document library contribution to student retention, but they represent early research stages with many studies reporting insufficient data, incomplete findings, or non-generalizable results.

Other recent library studies have built on traditional input/output data, finding positive relationships between increased expenditures for library resources or professional staff positions and student retention (Emmons & Wilkinson, 2011; Mezick, 2007). Studies that examined student use across multiple library resources and services found positive associations between library use and student retention, particularly early in the first semester of enrollment (Haddow & Joseph, 2010; Soria, Fransen, & Nackerud, 2013; Soria, Fransen, & Nackerud, 2014). Haddow and Joseph (2010) recommended that libraries respond to their findings by offering carefully targeted programs and services, while Soria, Fransen, and Nackerud (2013; 2014) cautioned that results are not causal. It may be that students with higher retention rates are already academically motivated and predisposed to accessing support services such as the library.

Some leaders in the library profession have focused on strategies to build relationships with students such as proactively reaching out early and often to new students, particularly as the students who most need assistance may not seek it, and seeking ways to support fulfillment of students' academic aspirations (Bell, 2008; Blackburn, 2010; Hagel, Horn, Owen, & Currie, 2012; Lankes, 2012). Bell's (2008) five-point strategy included an emphasis on research assistance and personal attention, highlighting data that links student retention to the library's services and people, while others emphasize developing close partnerships with instructors, catering to diverse students in the conception and design of services, anticipating trigger points for withdrawal that can be influenced by point-of-need library support, and collaboration with other support services for integrated academic support (Hagel, Horn, Owen, & Currie, 2012). The focus on relationship development can be framed as a standard of care that aligns with the American Library Association's (ALA) *Guidelines for Behavioral Performance of Reference and Information Service Providers* (2013) and research on the ethic of care. Characteristics of care include approachability, listening/inquiring, interest in the student's needs, accepting responsibility to act on what is noticed, patience, honesty, trust building, and follow-up (ALA, 2013; Keeling, 2014; Kyriacou & Constanti, 2012).

# Integration into the Student Experience

The common thread throughout retention research for traditional and nontraditional students and within library literature is student interaction and engagement, with no clear method identified for how a library director can move beyond traditional input/output measurements to document the department's positive impact on student retention. The form of activities identified by research to increase student engagement are noted to vary widely based on the context of the university in which they are adopted, even when aligned with the AAC&U's leading model of high-impact practices (AAC&U, n.d.; Tinto & Pusser, 2006).

Given no clear research-based strategy, a balanced approach could include intentional selection of formal and informal qualitative data enhanced with relevant quantitative data points from traditional input/output measures. This balanced approach adds meaning to the story shared with academic leadership that may be more familiar with a traditional vision of academic libraries than the depth and range of services delivered by modern academic libraries. Murray (2014) noted that the perception library directors hold of the department's contribution to student retention is not generally backed by data, but presents a useful framework for organizing the range of work libraries engage in to which data could be added. This framework includes the library facility, library collection, and library instruction. The inclusion of library people adds depth to the library's story.

Examples of starting points utilizing this framework for the collection of qualitative and quantitative data, grounded in student retention research and best practices identified by library leaders, are listed in the following table.

| Framework | Qualitative Data Sources | Quantitative Data Sources |
|---|---|---|
| Library facilities | In-person/online feedback | Front desk/online usage Use of study rooms Website usage data |

| Library collection | Open-ended survey questions In-person/online feedback | Survey response data Collection data Usage data |
|---|---|---|
| Library instruction | End-of-Course Evaluations In-person/online feedback | Number of sessions offered Number of students taught Tutorial usage data Student achievement data Number of research consults |
| Library people | Standards of care Collaboration with faculty Collaboration with support departments In-person/online feedback | Outreach data Number of orientations attended Number of students reached Users/non-users data |

## Proven Practices, Examples, and Results

City University of Seattle Library & Learning Resource Center serves primarily nontraditional and online learners in the United States and abroad. For several years the library has been exploring strategies to gather meaningful and actionable data, to align its work with university goals, and to increase academic leadership's understanding of the range and depth of work its staff members provide. Examples of how the CityU library blends qualitative and quantitative data, utilizing the framework of library facility, library collection, library instruction, and library people, are provided below.

## Library Facility

In the context of CityU's distributed student community, the library facility includes a physical location in Seattle, presence in the learning management system, and the library website. A combination of in-person and online feedback combined with usage data portrays student engagement with the library facility.

With a move to a consolidated Seattle campus in 2013, the library was repositioned from a remote building apart from classrooms and faculty to the center of campus. Engagement with students at the service desk has soared from approximately 5 per week to an average of 247. Now serving as a primary gathering space for the university community, demands for library study rooms and booths and computer workstations have steadily increased.

A primary point of contact with online students and students at non-Seattle locations is CityU's learning management system (LMS). CityU library has maintained a virtual presence in the LMS for nearly ten years. The nature of this presence has evolved, based on student feedback, to include a direct link to the full range of resources and services students can access on the library website. Within the LMS, liaison librarian profiles have recently been co-located with faculty profiles inviting students to reach out for assistance and describing the nature of support they can expect. In academic year (AY) 2015 an average of 153 questions per week were received through these LMS connections by librarians.

Student feedback also informed a substantial redesign of the library's website. The site changed from a student portal requiring multiple clicks to access basic content, to a graphically designed and easily navigable website from which most content can be accessed with one to three clicks. Visits have increased from 97,656 in AY 2012 to 159,751 in AY 2015, and students' navigation complaints on the satisfaction survey have entirely disappeared.

## Library Collection

A relevant, accessible collection provides critical support of student learning and supports student retention (Soria, Fransen, & Nackerud, 2014). Even as online content increases, libraries play a role in curating content aligned with academic programs and future workplace needs.

In response to an increasingly distributed student body and complaints about lack of access to resources, CityU's library collection has changed from primarily print in 2008 to one that is 98 percent digital and is enhanced by a patron-driven-acquisition eBook program. Over 152 million international resources in the collection support student assignments outside the United States, and a global focus by programs within the United States. The most recent student survey indicates that 87 percent of respondents use the library's resources and services to support their studies, up from only 13 percent in 2008. Further development of the collection is guided by usage data and direct feedback from students and faculty, and evidence of student engagement with the collection is revealed through usage data.

## Library Instruction

Over the past ten years, CityU's library instruction program has transitioned from ad hoc inclusion in one-shot instruction sessions and orientations, to one that is fully integrated across academic programs at the students' point of need in support of the university's information-literacy learning goal. Instruction is augmented by tutorials accessible 24/7 on the library's website. In AY 2015, librarians led 131 required instruction sessions reaching 1,091 students, and gathered baseline data on the use of instruction materials in the learning management system. Participation in ACRL's *Assessment in Action* program assisted with a pilot to align data on student use of library instruction materials and student performance on the university's information-literacy rubric with student achievement. Modifications to the library's plan for data collection related to instruction are under way.

## Library People

While student engagement is composed of interactions between students and people, interaction in and of itself is not equivalent with engagement. For engagement to be effective, the quality of care within interactions is what will, in the end, have the most significant impact on engagement. Quality of care that includes listening, patience, trust, and more is also difficult to gather quantitative data on.

CityU librarians focus on outreach and on respectful and supportive engagement with students in each interaction that encourages and fosters their confidence in learning. Librarians know these efforts support student retention through explicit feedback they receive from students and increases in research support requests. Examples of feedback include:

- A fifty-year-old aeronautic employee returning to earn his bachelor's degree, anxious about online courses, who was ready to drop out before starting his first course until he received the help from a librarian that he needed to access a required online simulation.
- A thirty-something student reporting she would not have completed her master's thesis research to earn her degree had she not received support from her liaison librarian.

For each student who takes the time to share his/her experience in engaging with the library, librarians know that there are many more students who could use their support who never engage with the library. Initial outreach focused on increasing faculty awareness of library resources and services, based on student survey results indicating 42 percent of students learned about the library from their instructor and through the university's focus on implementing an integrated information-literacy instruction program. With operational maturation of instruction and faculty outreach, focus has turned to increasing direct outreach to new students and on developing collaborative relationships with advising staff. Data on the number of welcome e-mails sent to students and faculty is now tracked, and timing for sending messages has been modified to align with likely due dates for first assignments resulting in increases in student responses and requests for help.

## Lessons Learned, Tips for Success, and Recommendations

From a deep dive into student retention research and initial efforts to seek more sophisticated methods for articulating the depth and range of the library's engagement with students to support retention, CityU's library has learned that:

- research-proven activities that increase student retention are highly dependent upon the specific context of universities and their students' needs;
- selection of qualitative and quantitative data to understand and communicate the library's impact on student retention is a good place to begin local research, and is an iterative process; and
- collaborative relationships can take three or more years to mature.

Each year CityU library works to identify more sophisticated methods for understanding and communicating the impact of its services to stakeholders, with future strategies informed by the previous year's findings. Library directors are encouraged to start with the data at hand and collaborate with other departments, including information technology, institutional effectiveness, and advising. Next steps for CityU's library include gathering and analyzing student-specific library use and instructional engagement data with a goal to identify patterns that inform more effective outreach to non-users and impact on student achievement, and to pilot a low-middle-high need student framework based on practices in CityU's doctoral programs. Collaborations with the advising team will expand, and a pilot comparing the library's instruction data with program retention data will be started.

## Conclusion

Student retention is influenced by many complex factors, and specific research-proven activities to increase retention allow for variations based on individual universities' cultures. Library directors who wish to apply more sophisticated methods for demonstrating the range and depth of the modern library's work and its impact on student retention may use a balance of qualitative and quantitative data to convey the connection between resources, services, student engagement, and thus, student retention.

## References

American Library Association (ALA). (2013, May 28). Guidelines for behavioral performance of reference and information service providers.

Retrieved from http://www.ala.org/rusa/resources/guidelines/guidelinesbehavioral

Association of American Colleges & Universities (AAC&U). (n.d.). High-impact educational practices: A brief overview. Retrieved from http://www.aacu.org/leap/hips

Association of College and Research Libraries (ACRL). (n.d.). Assessment in action: Academic libraries and student success. Retrieved from http://www.ala.org/acrl/AiA

Bean, N., & Eaton, S. B. (2001). The psychology underlying successful retention practices. *Journal of College Student Retention, 3*(1), 73–89.

Bell, S. (2008). Keeping them enrolled: How academic libraries contribute to student retention. *Library Issues, 29*(1). Retrieved from http://www.libraryissues.com/sub/pdf2901sep2008.pdf

Blackburn, H. (2010). Shhh! No talking about retention in the library! *Education Libraries, 33*(1), 24–30.

Emmons, M., & Wilkinson, F. C. (2011, March). The academic library impact on student persistence. *College & Research Libraries, 72*(2), 128–149.

Haddow, G., & Joseph, J. (2010). Loans, logins, and lasting the course: Academic library use and student retention. *Australian Academic & Research Libraries, 41*(4), 233–244.

Hagel, P., Horn, A. Owen, S., & Currie, M. (2012). "How can we help?" The contribution of university libraries to student retention. *Australian Academic & Research Libraries, 43*(3), 214–230.

Keeling, R. P. (2014). An ethic of care in higher education: Well-being and learning. *Journal of College & Character, 15*(3), 141–148.

Kuh, G. D. (2009). What student affairs professionals need to know about student engagement. *Journal of College Student Development, 50*(6), 683–706.

Kuh, G. D., & Schneider, C. G. (2008). High-impact educational practices: What they are, who has access to tem, and why they matter. Association of American Colleges and Universities. Retrieved from https://www.aacu.org/leap/hips

Kyriacou, M., & Constanti, P. (2012). "Why should I care?" Facilitating learning in higher education. European Conference on Research Methodology for Business and Management Studies.

Lankes, R. D. (2012). Beyond the bullet points: Bad libraries build collections, good libraries build services, great libraries build communities [Blog]. Retrieved from http://quartz.syr.edu/blog/?p=1411

Markle, G. (2015). Factors influencing persistence among nontraditional university students. *Adult Education Quarterly, 65*(3), 267–285.

Mezick, E. M. (2007). Return on investment: Libraries and student retention. *Journal of Academic Librarianship, 33*(5), 561–566.

Murray, A. L. (2014). *The academic library and high-impact practices for student retention: Perspectives of library deans* (Doctoral dissertation). Retrieved from http://digitalcommons.wku.edu/diss/57

National Center for Education Statistics (NCES). (n.d.). Retention rate. Retrieved from https://nces.ed.gov/ipeds/glossary/index.asp?id=772

Oakleaf, M. (2010). *The value of academic libraries: A comprehensive research review and report*. Chicago, IL: American Library Association. Retrieved from http://www.ala.org/acrl/sites/ala.org.acrl/files/content/issues/value/val_report.pdf

Ross-Gordon, J. M. (2011). Research on adult learners: Supporting the needs of a student population that is no longer nontraditional. *Peer Review, 13*(1). Retrieved from https://www.aacu.org/publications-research/periodicals/research-adult-learners-supporting-needs-student-population-no

Singletary, G. (2010). *Predicting academic achievement of nontraditional college students* (Doctoral dissertation). Available from ProQuest Dissertations & Theses Global database. (UMI No. 3492798)

Soria, K. M., Fransen, J., & Nackerud, S. (2013). Library use and undergraduate student outcomes: New evidence for students' retention and academic success. *Portal: Libraries and the Academy, 13*(2), 147–164.

Soria, K. M., Fransen, J., & Nackerud, S. (2014). Stacks, serials, search engines, and students' success: First-year undergraduate students' library use, academic achievement, and retention. *Journal of Academic Librarianship 40*, 84–91.

Tinto, V. (2005). *Student retention: What next?* Presentation at the National Conference on Student Recruitment, Marketing, and Retention. Washington, DC. Retrieved from https://vtinto.expressions.syr.edu/wp-content/uploads/2013/01/Student-Retention-What-Next.pdf

Tinto, V., & Pusser, B. (2006, June). *Moving from theory to action: Building a model of institutional action for student success.* National Postsecondary Education Cooperative. Retrieved from https://vtinto.expressions.syr.edu/?page_id=36

## Author Biography

Mary Mara is the Director of the Vi Tasler Library & Learning Resource Center at City University of Seattle with experience leading the design and implementation of an integrated information-literacy instruction program, developing a digital library to serve students located worldwide, and modernizing data collection and analysis strategies within the library. She holds a BA in Norwegian from the University of Washington and a master's degree in library and information science from the University of Washington's iSchool.

# 23

# Building Resilience in Adult Online Students

**Pressley Rankin**

## Abstract

Student resilience has been shown to increase persistence in online academic programs. Resilience is a skill that can be developed (Tugade & Fredrickson, 2004). One method, the broaden-and-build theory, focuses on building positive thought repertoires in students to help them combat negative thought repertoires that can lead to downward spirals of negative emotions (Jackson, Firtko, & Edenborough, 2007). Thought repertoires are the connections our brain makes between events, actions, and emotions (Garland, Frederickson, Kring, Johnson, Meyer, & Penn, 2010). Creating more positive emotional connections between the student and the program in the online classroom can build positive thought repertoires, which can be used during times of adversity to combat stress (Fredrickson, 1998, 2001; Fredrickson & Branigan, 2005).

# Overview

Resilience is the ability to adjust to adversity using positivity and a flexible set of attitudes (Jackson et al., 2007; Klibert, Lamis, Collins, Smalley, Warren, Yancey, & Winterowd, 2014). Tugade and Fredrickson (2004) in a study of college students found that having a positive mindset allowed for positive emotions that in turn aided students in recovering from adverse events. Putting a positive spin on negative events is an important skill that helps students become more resilient. Another study suggests that resilience can be created when faculty build relationships with students especially when they give the students opportunities to become more reflective during their program (Jackson et al., 2007).

Much of the current research into the student experience in higher education does not consider the importance of resilience, motivation, and the student's life experiences in helping students avoid stress (Brewer, 2010). Moreover, a more recent study by Klibert et al. (2014) indicated student depression and anxiety are often linked to socially prescribed perfectionism, which was shown in their study to be mediated by resilience. Finding ways to increase resilience in students, especially in an online environment, can help students combat the increased anxiety often associated with online learning. This chapter explores the literature on resiliency to identify best practices that can be specifically implemented in an online environment to help develop student resilience and maintain high rates of student persistence.

# Review of the Literature

Resilience is a relatively new concept in the research related to student learning and the concept of adaptability under stress (Hartley, 2011). Resilience in this context is defined as the ability to handle adversity and adjust to it in a positive manner (Jackson et al., 2007). Adversity in distance learning can result from issues with technology, the lack of direct interaction with the faculty, and feelings of loneliness (Park & Choi, 2009). Adversity can also lead to stress, which is known to affect academic performance and, ultimately, persistence (Hartley, 2011). Additionally, students who experience disconnection from a program are more likely to experience stress and anxiety (Hartley, 2011). Klibert et al. (2014) have also shown that stress can be a result of perfectionism known to be partially mediated by increased resilience. Increasing the feeling of connectedness, and increasing students' resiliency in the process, benefits students by decreasing stress and promoting persistence, which will help them achieve their personal educational goals (Hart, 2012).

Increasing resiliency has been studied for some time in the psychological community. Fredrickson (1998, 2001) developed the leading theory on building resiliency over seventeen years ago. The broaden-and-build theory was created after research showed a strong connection between positive emotions and resiliency. Fredrickson (1998, 2001) posited that positive emotions broaden thought-action repertoires, helping people to be more resilient by building personal resources. Thought-action repertoires are the scripts that lead thoughts to become emotions or actions: "joy sparks the urge to play, interest sparks the urge to explore, contentment sparks the urge to savor and integrate" (Fredrickson, 2001, p. 1). Negative emotions can also trigger responses; however, those responses are more often narrow such as attacking or fleeing (Fredrickson, 2004).

The broaden-and-build theory predicts that focusing on positive emotions builds psychological resilience by broadening thinking and building more thought repertoires that help people cope (Fredrickson, 2004). Broadening resilience has also been shown to increase the ability of students to pay attention to the subject they are learning by limiting distracting emotions (Fredrickson & Branigan, 2005). Resilience then is seen as a key for helping students control their emotions.

Garland et al. (2010) asserted that emotions are systems that maintain a set organization. For example, fear of failing becomes connected to anger, and then when a grade is not what was expected, that anger can lead to an outburst. Students can feel bad about what they have done and then they can spiral downward into self-hatred and other negative thoughts or behaviors, reinforcing the negative experience. By broadening someone's positive scripts and creating more upward positive spirals, the student is better able to recover from negative events and therefore becomes more resilient. Pulling from the existing literature on the broaden-and-build theory, the next section will apply broadening principles to online classroom experiences that can help build resilience in students.

# Broadening Student Resilience

Many psychological studies have shown that resilience can be built and influenced by others (Abbott, Klein, Hamilton, & Rosenthal, 2009; Fava & Tomba, 2009; Fredrickson 1998, 2001, 2004; Fredrickson & Branigan, 2005; Garland et al., 2010; Luthans, Vogelgesang, & Lester, 2006; Stallman, 2011; Tugade & Fredrickson, 2004; Vacharkulksemsuk & Fredrickson, 2013). Broadening students' resilience by building up positive thought repertoires can help students recover from stressful and adverse life events, getting them back on track faster (Fredrickson 1998, 2001). In the online academic setting, there are limited opportunities for face-to-face connections with students. Therefore, it is important to be mindful of opportunities where negative thoughts can lead to downward spirals (e.g., low grades on papers, large assignments due, past due work, sickness, negative life events, and boundaries, such as final exams and projects or the end of the quarter). These opportunities present a chance to build positive thought repertoires by changing the dialogue from a negative story to a positive one.

It is possible to build positive thought repertoires by creating new stories around studying, reading, completing assignments, discussion boards, and faculty feedback on assignments. For instance, associating a sense of accomplishment or prestige to reading an entire book in one week creates pride that can lead to a greater sense of self-worth. If this happens enough times, it becomes part of the student's thought repertoire associated with required readings. This positive association will combat the negative thoughts and stresses students feel when looking at their reading requirements, making them more resilient and better able to handle future classes. The student will brag about being able to read a whole book in one week instead of complaining about the workload.

Creating positive associations requires online faculty to do more than just grade students' work. Faculty must make connections with their students. One method for creating a sense of connection is the use of class videos. Fredrickson and Branigan (2005) found that students who viewed a funny or happy film before a negative film recovered faster from the adverse event. The use of video (film) allows for a more personal connection with students. Including instructional or general feedback videos wherein the faculty member gets personal, is smiling, and showing concern can build resilience, especially in situations where the students may be receiving criticism such as in a grading situation. Adding humorous videos or comics along with the lesson can also set a positive mood in the online space. Making a connection with the student builds the relationship; the more positive the student relationship with the professor, the more resilience can be generated.

In addition to creating videos for the classroom at large, faculty can create personal grade feedback for students, particularly when they have many issues to address in a paper. Recording grade feedback either with video or with audio-only files has been shown to create a greater connection between the student and the faculty member, allowing for more complex ideas to be exchanged (Marriott & Teoh, 2012; Wolff-Hilliard & Baethe, 2014). In a study of over one hundred students, Marriot and Teoh (2012) found that students who received video and audio feedback for writing assignments felt that the feedback was more personal than written feedback. They also overwhelming felt that the feedback was clear and easy to understand. The connection that audio or visual feedback gives the student during what is typically a negative experience can create a more positive response in students (Marriott & Teoh, 2012). Critically thinking about ways in which you can build students up and change the script from a negative interaction to a positive interaction begins to change the scripts in students' minds, therefore broadening their thought repertoires and increasing resiliency.

Another method to increase positivity in the classroom is through reflective or stress-relieving fun assignments. Creating an assignment designed to make the learning more fun using multimedia, alternative assignment formats, or time to play with the learning allows students to begin associating learning with play, which can elicit joy and happiness (Garland et al., 2010). The sense of play can create new thought repertoires when connected to the online environment. Using the same week for this playful exercise in every class gives students something to look forward to in each class. Over time these moments build a student's resilience by creating happy thought repertoires. For variety, a sense of surprise can be added by hiding the assignment until the week before, which gives the students something to look forward to. Fava and Tomba (2009) asserted that the distance from a goal can often increase a student's negative thoughts and stress. Therefore, another method to build resilience in students is to create short-term goals that allow them to accomplish non-graded tasks that can be acknowledged. For example, the first student to finish all the readings and post on the discussion board wins the Reader of the Week Award. Rewarding students along the path and moving the focus beyond grades also helps to rewrite thought repertoires around what the classroom is about. Face-to-face classes offer many opportunities for connections and special moments. Online classes must specifically create those opportunities by planning them into the curriculum process. The tips listed above are only the beginning. There are still many ways to connect and build student resilience to be explored.

## Recommendations

Pulling from the chapter discussion, there are ways in which online faculty can currently begin to build resiliency in their students. By following the recommendations listed below, faculty can begin to create moments of positivity in the classroom. These moments can start to broaden students' thought repertoires and expand their capacity for resilience. Based on the current literature in online learning and resilience, the following is a list of specific recommendations for online programs:

- Create moments of fun in the classroom.
    - Have students create a meme from the weekly readings.
    - Allow students to watch a funny video that connects to what is being learned.
- Use videos and audio files to connect with students.
    - Record a weekly lecture.
    - Offer tips on upcoming assignments or feedback for the class on prior assignments.
- Use video or audio files to give students feedback on assignments. Record audio or video while grading the paper, discussing both strengths and weaknesses.
    - Be sure to smile and use language to build up student confidence when giving feedback.
    - Be aware of the stress points in class and prepare to build student confidence; upon completion of that phase of the class, be prepared to cheer the students' accomplishments.
- Use goal setting within the class to give students smaller points to work toward and achieve projects that aren't grade related.

- o Note when the weekly readings are particularly long or detailed.
- o Set goals for readings and assignments as markers toward completion.
- o Use discussion boards as markers toward a larger assignment. Let students build up to that assignment so they feel they are making progress.
- Plan for holidays or events that may distract students outside of the class; look for opportunities to connect classroom assignments to those events.

## Conclusion

The process of creating resilience in online students revolves around the ability to broaden their thought repertoires by including more positive repertoires for them to use in times of crisis. Creating these repertoires requires careful planning when designing an online class. The goal is to build opportunities for positive interactions between the student and the faculty member. Online learning can no longer be restricted to reading and writing. To build up student resistance and therefore persistence in the program, faculty must discover innovative ways to reach out to students and build positive thoughts and experiences. Building these positive thought repertoires requires faculty to make positive connections with students. Taking time to set short-term goals, reward challenging requirements with accolades, use video and audio resources from the Internet, and create self-recorded videos helps to deepen the bonds with the student. The recommendations listed here are just a start. More research needs to be done into the application of the broaden-and-build theory to the online classroom.

## References

Abbott, J. A., Klein, B., Hamilton, C., & Rosenthal, A. J. (2009). The impact of online resilience training for sales managers on well-being and performance. *Sensoria: A Journal of Mind, Brain & Culture, 5*(1), 89–95.

Brewer, G. (2010). Resilience and motivation in higher education: A case study. *Psychology of Education Review, 34*(1), 55–60.

Fava, G. A., & Tomba, E. (2009). Increasing psychological well-being and resilience by psychotherapeutic methods. *Journal of Personality, 77*(6), 1903–1934. http://doi.org/10.1111/j.1467-6494.2009.00604.x

Fredrickson, B. L. (1998). What good are positive emotions? *Review of General Psychology, 2*(3), 300–319.

Fredrickson, B. L. (2001). The role of positive emotions in positive psychology: The broaden-and-build theory of positive emotions. *American Psychologist, 56*(3), 218.

Fredrickson, B. L. (2004). The broaden-and-build theory of positive emotions. *Philosophical Transactions of the Royal Society B: Biological sciences, 359*(1449), 1367–1377. http://doi.org/10.1098/rstb.2004.1512

Fredrickson, B., & Branigan, C. (2005). Positive emotions broaden the scope of attention and thought-action repertoires. *Cognition & Emotion, 19*(3), 313–332. http://doi.org/10.1080/02699930441000238

Garland, E. L., Fredrickson, B., Kring, A. M., Johnson, D. P., Meyer, P. S., & Penn, D. L. (2010). Upward spirals of positive emotions counter downward spirals of negativity: Insights from the broaden-and-build theory and affective neuroscience on the treatment of emotion dysfunctions and deficits in psychopathology. *Clinical Psychology Review, 30*(7), 849–864. http://doi.org/10.1016/j.cpr.2010.03.002

Hart, C. (2012). Factors associated with student persistence in an online program of study: A review of the literature. *Journal of Interactive Online Learning, 11*(1), 19–42.

Hartley, M. T. (2011). Examining the relationships between resilience, mental health, and academic persistence in undergraduate college students. *Journal of American College Health, 59*(7), 596–604.

Jackson, D., Firtko, A., & Edenborough, M. (2007). Personal resilience as a strategy for surviving and thriving in the face of workplace adversity: A literature review. *Journal of Advanced Nursing, 60*(1), 1–9. http://doi.org/10.1111/j.1365-2648.2007.04412.x

Klibert, J., Lamis, D. A., Collins, W., Smalley, K. B., Warren, J. C., Yancey, C. T., & Winterowd, C. (2014). Resilience mediates the relations between perfectionism and college student distress. *Journal of Counseling & Development, 92*(1), 75–82. http://doi.org/10.1002/j.1556-6676.2014.00132.x

Luthans, F., Vogelgesang, G. R., & Lester, P. B. (2006). Developing the psychological capital of resiliency. *Human Resource Development Review, 5*(1), 25–44. http://doi.org/10.1177/1534484305285335

Marriott, P., & Teoh, L. K. (2012). Using screencasts to enhance assessment feedback: Students' perceptions and preferences. *Accounting Education, 21*(6), 583–598. http://doi.org/10.1080/09639284.2012.725637

Park, J. H., & Choi, H. J. (2009). Factors influencing adult learners' decision to drop out or persist in online learning. *Journal of Educational Technology & Society, 12*(4), 207–217.

Stallman, H. M. (2011). Embedding resilience within the tertiary curriculum: A feasibility study. *Higher Education Research & Development, 30*(2), 121–133. http://doi.org/10.1080/07294360.2010.509763

Tugade, M. M., & Fredrickson, B. L. (2004). Resilient individuals use positive emotions to bounce back from negative emotional experiences. *Journal of Personality and Social Psychology, 86*(2), 320–333. http://doi.org/10.1037/0022-3514.86.2.320

Vacharkulksemsuk, T., & Fredrickson, B. L. (2013). Looking back and glimpsing forward: The broaden-and-build theory of positive emotions as applied to organizations. In A. B. Bakker, *Advances in positive organization* (pp. 45–60). Bingley, United Kingdom: Emerald Group Publishing.

Wolff-Hilliard, D., & Baethe, B. (2014). Using digital and audio annotations to reinvent critical feedback with online adult students. *Delta kappa Gamma Bulletin, 80*(2), 40–44.

# Author Biography

Pressley Rankin IV is an Associate Professor and Academic Program Director at City University of Seattle's School of Applied Leadership. He has a PhD from the University of San Diego in leadership studies and an MS in counseling from San Diego State University. His degree in counseling helps him understand the student from a systemic perspective. Balancing multiple life roles is both rewarding and challenging, and he is committed to helping students achieve their own personal goals around balance. Dr. Rankin also has a background in organizational leadership and management including corporate, retail, and nonprofit environments.

# 24

# Improving Doctoral Student Retention

**Tony Dixon**

## Abstract

Retention and degree completion at the doctoral level are ongoing challenges for program and university stakeholders. In this chapter the topic of retention practices at the doctoral level is addressed. Three student engagement mechanisms specifically targeted toward online doctoral students and aimed at increasing engagement, program retention, and degree completion rates are presented. A literature review is provided in addition to detailed information relating to each student engagement mechanism. Finally, recommendations are proposed for the successful integration of the student engagement mechanisms into all academic programs where they might provide valuable results to the university and students.

# Overview

University administrators, program faculty, and other stakeholders are routinely confronted with questions surrounding the topics of retention and degree completion (ACT, 2015; Hart, 2012; Law, 2014; Mendoza, Villarreal, & Gunderson, 2014; O'Keeffe, 2013; Rankin, 2015; Sowell, 2008; Tobin, 2014). While retention and degree completion at the baccalaureate and master's level is one of concern, the doctoral level has also proved challenging (ACT, 2015; Barnes, Williams, & Archer, 2010; Grasso, Barry, & Valentine, 2007; Mendoza et al., 2014; Rankin, 2015; Sowell, 2008; Spaulding & Rockinson-Szapkiw, 2012), especially in the online environment (Angelino, Williams, & Natvig, 2007; Di Pierro, 2012; Hart, 2012).

Students enter a doctoral program with personal and professional needs, expectations, and desires influencing retention and degree completion rates. The ability of university leaders to understand and provide what is most useful to students increases a program's value to the student; therefore, supporting higher retention and completion rates. Providing terminal education to working professionals who may also have children and are completing a program online presents additional risks to attrition and graduation rates (Angelino et al., 2007; Di Pierro, 2012; Hart, 2012; Law, 2014; Mendoza et al., 2014; Rankin, 2015; Spaulding & Rockinson-Szapkiw, 2012).

This chapter addresses the topic of retention practices at the doctoral level for online students and provides three suggested practices specifically aimed at increasing engagement, and in turn, program retention and degree completion rates. A review of literature is provided to deliver background and context on the topic. Three specific research-supported engagement mechanisms are recommended for integration into the student experience to support student success: increased career and academic advisement, assignment submission liberty, and research and teaching assistantships and fellowships. Additionally, four recommendations are made for the successful integration of each engagement mechanism. Finally, it is suggested the mechanisms proposed in this chapter be extended into lower-level academic programs should they provide valuable results to the university and students.

# Review of the Literature

Sowell (2008) found a 56 percent completion rate of PhDs in the social sciences comprising many of the programs offered at schools such as

City University of Seattle, National University, Amherst College, and many other private universities with a significant liberal arts influence.

PhDs in social sciences comprise 21 percent of all PhDs completed (Sowell, 2008). According to a report by ACT (2015), on a macro level PhD retention rates at private universities, such as those mentioned, are encouragingly high at 81.7 percent, outperforming the public universities at 78.6 percent. The graduation rate for PhD programs at private universities also outpaces the public universities rate by 13 percent with rates of 62.5 percent and 49.5 percent, respectively (ACT, 2015). Taken together, retention at the doctoral level among all universities nationally indicates that two out of every ten students will not persist, and approximately 5.5 out of every ten students will graduate. Every student who does not persist or graduate carries associated costs.

# Costs of Attrition

Three primary costs are associated with attrition (Grasso et al., 2007). The first cost is borne by society of not receiving the benefits the graduate may produce in the way of practice, research, or teaching. The second cost is to the individual student who will most likely be required to pay for the education received without the benefits of the degree. The third cost is to the university in having an additional student not complete after the faculty invested time and resources in the pursuit of the student's educational goal. Grasso and colleagues (2007) promoted four conditions for optimal doctoral completion: the right people apply, the right people are admitted, students and faculty foster productive working relationships, and students experience social support from other students. Doing more to increase retention and graduation rates creates global economic benefits as well.

# Global Economic Implications

China and Europe are global competitors to the United States in terms of doctoral graduates (Di Pierro, 2012). This carries with it the economic consequence of the United States being less competitive in the global marketplace for highly skilled, well-paying jobs and a reduced internal talent base for educating future doctoral students (Di Pierro, 2012). Di

Pierro (2012) also recommended that universities adopt a just-in-time orientation to provide a welcoming and supportive initial doctoral student experience. This practice has already been adopted in the two doctoral programs available at CityU, the Doctor of Business Administration and Doctor of Education in Leadership programs.

## Case Example: City University of Seattle

City University of Seattle has proactively taken steps to ensure the strongest retention and completions rates are attained. After creating its first online doctoral program in 2011, City University of Seattle decided to create a new position, the doctoral student administrator (DSA), to provide the support needed to ensure the greatest levels of doctoral student retention and completion (Rankin, 2015). This action demonstrates leadership and genuine concern for student success by CityU.

## Career and Academic Advisement

Creating a stronger connection between career and academic advisement has proven successful at increasing retention and graduation rates (Law, 2014). Some students may enter a doctoral program still unsure of their specific career path. Delivering concentrated advisement on the relationship between career trajectory and academic achievement are in line with the findings of Barnes and colleagues (2010) who found helpfulness, caring, and professional socialization among the most valued attributes of a primary faculty advisor. These findings are also in clear alignment with Hart (2012) who identified satisfaction, relevance, self-efficacy, personal growth, and social connectedness as factors associated with student persistence in online programs.

## Assignment Method Liberty

According to Collins and Halverson (2010), technological advances have caused roles to change within the workplace where individuals are routinely charged with finding and using information from a variety of technological formats, which has in turn forced educational entities to adapt. In the current age of technology a person can learn via free college courses through massive online open courses (MOOCs), YouTube videos, blogs, vlogs, and a host of other knowledge-sharing platforms (Collins & Halverson, 2010). Tobin (2014) suggested academic institutions provide greater assignment submission liberty, relying less on structured academic writing and tests and instead letting students use formats more relevant to their professional requirements. The practice proposed by Tobin (2014), and supported by Collins and Halverson (2010) and Hart (2012), provides increased creative freedom, allowing students the ability to take greater control of how their assignments are completed, adding to the relevance and personalization of their educational experience.

## Research and Teaching Assistantships and Fellowships

Mendoza and colleagues (2014) examined the within-year retention rates of doctoral students finding the use of research and teaching assistantships and fellowships to have significantly positive correlations with retention. In part, the use of such programs according to Hart (2012) and O'Keeffe (2013) builds stronger social connectivity between students and the university, thus creating a sense of belonging found to be positively correlated with student persistence (Spaulding & Rockinson-Szapkiw, 2012). Moreover, the creation of social bonds in online programs has proven challenging (Angelino et al., 2007), further suggesting the potential benefits of teaching and research assistantships and fellowships in online doctoral programs.

## Integration into the Student Experience

Three practices can be integrated into the student experience of doctoral students in traditional, online, and hybrid programs that will enhance their learning. First, increase integration between career and academic advising to help students better align educational and career goals (Di Pierro, 2012; Hart, 2012; Law, 2014; O'Keeffe, 2013). Second, provide increased flexibility in assignment submission, allowing students to enhance work-related skills in the program (Tobin, 2014). Third, as Mendoza and colleagues (2014) have suggested: include teaching and research assistantships and fellowships to provide significant and positive effects on retention at the doctoral level.

## Increased Integration of Career and Academic Advisement

The first mechanism allows doctoral students to further explore how their degree and career align beyond program completion. It may be argued that students entering doctoral programs do not require as much in terms of career and academic advising. Some students enter doctoral programs with several years in a specific field and have a clear career path. Other students, however, enter doctoral programs with diverse work experiences ranging in different industries, functions, and organizational sizes and, therefore, do not have a clear career path (Law, 2014). Law (2014) explained that focusing on students with unsure or unclear career paths over several advising sessions produces significantly positive results for student motivation and retention.

Students at all levels need a strong connection between the time and cost of educational attainment and career prospects. Factors outside of a university leader's reach, such as changing economic conditions, or a lack of advisor knowledge of certain industries, geographical areas, or demand expectations may cause some to err on the side of caution by not advising too deeply into career advisement. These factors encourage academic advisors to be more informed so as to create greater value for students. It may also be argued that a doctoral student most likely has sufficient ability to research the factors in question and will then be capable of making an independently informed decision. The interactions between the advisor and student foster social connection (O'Keeffe, 2013), a sense of belonging, satisfaction, and relevance between the university faculty and the student (Hart, 2012).

## Assignment Submission Liberty

The second mechanism allows students to incorporate skills that may be required on the job. Examples of this may include the use of certain technologies or public speaking in the form of presentations or videos (Collins & Halverson, 2010). Technological issues such as files being submitted in an inaccessible way to a professor due to a student's choice of program will occur. Modern work and educational institutions increasingly leverage technology to communicate, collaborate, and learn. Students and professors in online programs already work through technological issues. Additional technological issues will be reduced through effective guidelines set by the university.

Students in doctoral programs have a variety of experiences and expertise, therefore opening the door to unique and creative ideas. Granting students liberty to determine the method and medium of completing assignments based on instructor-designated objectives allows students to lead their own learning, use methods they are more familiar with, and express creativity (Tobin, 2014). Some may argue the use of traditionally preferred, formal methods such as essays and tests require greater academic skill compared to less formal means. With the development and accessibility of technology today, students can address assignment criteria thoroughly and effectively by creating podcasts, videos, websites, mock interviews, or video slide shows (Collins & Halverson, 2010; Tobin, 2014). These factors support increased program relevance (Hart, 2012) and personalization of students' educational experience, factors with a significantly positive correlation with increased retention and graduation rates.

## Research and Teaching Assistantships and Fellowships

The benefits of this mechanism to the university outweigh the drawbacks. The university benefits from a larger talent pool that is more affordable than faculty members. However, research and teaching programs may not be viewed as strategically or financially valuable to the university. This mechanism supports existing retention and graduation efforts by developing stronger working relationships between online students and faculty, given the lack of face-to-face interaction available on traditional campuses (Rankin, 2015). Providing merit-based teaching and research opportunities has significantly positive effects on retention while elevating the students' status, responsibility, and experience (Mendoza et al., 2014), therefore reducing attrition costs.

This mechanism allows students to reinforce learned content through teaching and research. Research assistantships and fellowships enhance program satisfaction, self-efficacy, personal growth, and social connectedness (Hart, 2012; O'Keeffe, 2013) by giving students opportunities to gain recognition as published authors and raise the university's status. Logistically, some may argue this mechanism would be difficult to implement and effectively manage online. It is in the university's interest to work through the logistical challenges as this mechanism encourages student persistence and graduation by giving online doctoral students experience teaching and participating in academic research, and offers an additional source of financial assistance.

Research fellowships and teaching assistantships gives online doctoral students benefits associated with traditional campuses. Some students participate in doctoral programs strictly online due to their life situation, personal preference, or because a program is only available online, such as the Doctor of Business Administration and Doctor of Education in Leadership programs. Tanner and Allen (2006) cited a prevalence of teaching assistantship practices within graduate science programs, while other programs require internships to gain experience; these two practices are associated with on-campus programs. Online students should not be denied opportunities available at traditional universities such as student teaching and assisting with research simply because they study online. Extending these programs to online graduate students makes them more fluent in the process of research and publication (Mendoza et al., 2014).

## Lessons Learned, Tips for Success, and Recommendations

There are four recommendations for the successful implementation of the mechanisms described in this chapter. First, it is recommended that integration of career and academic advisement is a team effort comprising members of the career center, student services, and faculty and that advising should occur throughout the duration of the program. Second, with respect to increasing student submission liberty, it is recommended that doctoral faculty with the advisement of their respective deans be responsible for deciding what criteria to use and what assignments to allow for submission liberty. Third, it is recommended that school deans and university administration work together to identify funding availability, program details, and competitive criteria for assistantships and fellowships. Finally, it is recommended that analytics related to each mechanism's interest, adoption, and impact on retention and completion rates should be measured to inform each mechanism's value and potential expansion to baccalaureate and master's level programs.

Twenty-first-century doctoral students need flexibility and support that meet the demands of the modern economy. Still, many of the same support mechanisms offered at traditional campuses like integrated career and academic advisement, assistantships, and fellowships are also desired, as they are a highly valuable part of the learning experience. Research supports the role of the three proposed mechanisms for increasing engagement, retention, and online doctoral program completion rates.

## Conclusion

Retention and degree completion at the doctoral level are continuous challenges for program and university stakeholders. This chapter addressed the topic of retention practices at the doctoral level for online students by suggesting three specific practices specifically aimed at increasing engagement, and in turn, program retention and degree completion rates. A literature review was provided in addition to detailed information relating to each student engagement mechanism. Finally, recommendations were proposed for the successful integration of the student engagement mechanisms into all academic programs where they can provide valuable results to the university and students.

## References

ACT. (2015). 2015 Retention/completion summary tables. Retrieved from http://www.act.org/research/policymakers/pdf/2015-Summary-Tables.pdf

Angelino, L. M., Williams, F. K., & Natvig, D. (2007). Strategies to engage online students and reduce attrition rates. *Journal of Educators*

*Online, 4*(2). Retrieved from http://www.thejeo.com/Archives/ Volume4Number2/V4N2.htm#Volume_4,_Nu mber_2,_July_2007

Barnes, B. J., Williams, E. A., & Archer, S. A. (2010). Characteristics that matter most: Doctoral students' perceptions of positive and negative advisor attributes. *NACADA Journal, 30*(1), 34–46.

Caffarella, R. S., & Barnett, B. G. (2000). Teaching doctoral students to become scholarly writers: The importance of giving and receiving critiques. *Studies in Higher Education, 25*(1), 39–52. doi:10.1080/030750700116000

Collins, A., & Halverson, R. (2010). The second educational revolution: Rethinking education in the age of technology. *Journal of Computer Assisted Learning, 26*(1), 18–27. doi:10.1111/j.1365-2729.2009.00339.x

Di Pierro, M. (2012). Strategies for doctoral student retention: Taking the roads less traveled. *The Journal for Quality and Participation, 35*(3), 29–32.

Grasso, M., Barry, M., & Valentine, T. (2009). A data-driven approach to improving doctoral completion. Retrieved from http://cgsnet.org/ ckfinder/userfiles/files/Paper_Series_UGA_FrontMatter.pdf

Hart, C. (2012). Factors associated with student persistence in an online program of study: A review of the literature. *Journal of Interactive Online Learning, 11*(1). Retrieved from http://www.ncolr.org/jiol/ issues/pdf/11.1.2.pdf

Law, B. (2014). 5 strategies to improve student retention and success. *Community College Journal, 84*(6), 10.

Mendoza, P., Villarreal, P., & Gunderson, A. (2014). Within-year retention among Ph.D. students: The effect of debt, assistantships, and fellowships. *Research in Higher Education, 55*(7), 650–685. doi:http:// dx.doi.org/10.1007/s11162-014-9327-x

O'Keeffe, P. (2013). A sense of belonging: Improving student retention. *College Student Journal, 47*(4), 605–613.

Rankin, P. (2015, March). Exemplary practices in student support. Paper presented at the City University of Seattle Faculty Development Workshop retrieved from https://www.academia.edu/11380602/Exemplary_Practices_in_Student_Support

Sowell, R. (2008, March). Ph.D. completion and attrition: Analysis of baseline data. Paper presented at the NSF Workshop: A fresh look at Ph.D. education, retrieved from http://www.phdcompletion.org/resources/cgsnsf2008_sowell.pdf

Spaulding, L. S., & Rockinson-Szapkiw, A. J. (2012). Hearing their voices: Factors doctoral candidates attribute to their persistence. *International Journal of Doctoral Studies, 7*, 199–219.

Tanner, K., & Allen, D. (2006). Approaches to biology teaching and learning: On integrating pedagogical training into the graduate experiences of future science faculty. *Life Sciences Education, 5*(1), 1–6. Retrieved from http://www.lifescied.org/content/5/1/1.full.pdf+html

Tobin, T. J. (2014). Increase online student retention with universal design for learning. *Quarterly Review of Distance Education, 15*(3), 13.

## Author Biography

Tony Dixon is an online doctoral student in the Doctor of Education in Leadership program at City University of Seattle. Tony is a training and development professional who specializes in leadership development for the Navajo Tribal Utility Authority. Prior to studying at CityU, Tony earned an MS in organizational leadership and a BS in business administration from National University. His primary research interest is leadership development.

# 25

# Retaining the Struggling Adult Learner

**Liz Bertran**

## Abstract

As a goal of higher education, faculty and staff members can aid in retention of both the struggling and non-struggling adult learners by integrating a few simple practices into their interactions with students. The approach begins with understanding that this population has identifiable characteristics. Since childhood, their learning struggles and confidence levels may have been undermined. Many are right-brained, picture thinkers that do not learn by techniques that focus on standard instructional methods. By recognizing how these students learn and incorporating some simple practices into how to interact with them, students will be free to become confident and successful learners. Application of these techniques will aid those who participate in face-to-face classes and in online formats. The recommendations suggested are designed to embolden this population of adult learners to be more confident and successful so that they can accomplish their goals; and also have the outcome of better retention.

## Overview

"As many as 15–20% of the population as a whole, have some form of dyslexia" according to the American Dyslexia Association (Bardsley, 2015, para. 1); yet it is imperative to understand that they are bright learners. According to Davis (2010), "Dyslexia is the result of a perceptual talent. In some situations, the talent becomes a liability. The individual doesn't realize this is happening because use of the talent has become integrated into the thought process. It began very early in life and by now it seems as natural as breathing" (Davis, 2010, p. 6). Adult students already have ample challenges (family, jobs, finances, etc.) and to add the strain of a learning difference only complicates matters. Since student retention can be associated with the ability to process information and sustain attention, providing understanding support and techniques for faculty and staff to support different learners can enable students to be successful and will ultimately improve retention rates.

## Review of the Literature

Currently, a large portion of the adult population struggles with processing information. Educators in higher education must understand these conditions, and then find and implement strategies so that affected students can be more successful in the classroom. Students who struggle with processing information typically have common elements. Picture-thinking speed is approximately a thousand times faster than word thinking. Where the average brain processes at thirty-two pictures/second; word thinking is at a mere one hundred to two hundred words per minute. According to the Mayo Clinic, "Dyslexia symptoms in adults are similar to those in children" (Smarter, n.d., para. 3). Since childhood, they were told they were slow, lazy, or that they did not try hard enough. Perhaps even worse, they were placed in inadequate, "slow" reading groups, adding to the stigma and providing a message that they were unlikely to be successful as adult learners. All of these elements add up to a loss of self-confidence, which eventually leads to feelings of rejection and isolation. As adults, they often work at jobs where they can hide their difficulties from coworkers.

Although they are easily frustrated at tasks in which they have to use sequential skills, they excel when it comes to using their visual-spatial/kinesthetic abilities. Commonly, they have difficulties with spelling, correct grammar/punctuation usage, concentration, clear handwriting, reading and speaking, reading out loud, note taking, time management, et cetera (The Dyslexia Center, 2016). Contrary to popular belief, language-processing issues are far more complex than the classic letter reversal problems; however, often dyslexics find it hard to recognize words without pictures such as "and" or "the." To some, it appears as if the alphabet is dancing, wiggling, fading in/out, or more frustrating yet, lines seem to appear and disappear. Add to all this the usual challenges that all adults face such as long working hours, family difficulties, financial struggles, and it is understandable why many adult students do not persist in college. Heavy emphasis today is placed on identifying and helping our younger student population, but what about those adults who have slipped through the cracks?

## Integration into the Student Experience

When students (who learn differently) are free to learn in an open and accepting atmosphere, they are more likely to be successful. It's not a matter of catering to them, but instead it's a matter of encouraging them to be the most successful that they can be. When students aren't able to keep up, the stress that occurs creates a continuous downward spiral, and before you know it, they are dropping out of classes and eventually dropping out of their programs altogether. Implementation of the following techniques will aid higher education to retain struggling adult students:

1. Most individuals who struggle with processing information tend to be visual learners. Whenever possible, the practice of making pictorial analogies to make a point will enable understanding.
2. Mind mapping (a simple graphical way to represent ideas) (Litemind.com, n.d.) has proved to be helpful.
3. Since some adult learners experience mental images as reality, instructors who can make comparisons to something tangible in life will be more effective at improving understanding.

4. To reach the curious, intuitive, insightful, "out of the box" thinkers, voice modulation and expressive body language when speaking are useful for the struggling learners.
5. Because verbal dialogue can be confusing, explaining what you plan to convey to them would be a worthy goal at the beginning and at the end of a discussion.
6. Keep messages short and to the point. Break things down into chunks.
7. As much as possible, for handouts, e-mails and tests, usage of larger font sizes, bullet points, and colors will enable struggling students to receive clearer messages.
8. Summarize as often as possible.
9. For advisors, when it's obvious that a student isn't understanding a communication via e-mail, pick up the phone and call. Better yet, have them stop by so that you can talk in person.
10. Coach instructors and staff about how to identify the signs of a struggling student so that the practice of more effective communication skills with their students can occur. Some identifiers are (LoGiudice, 2008, para. 1–4):
    a. Has problems passing tests (SAT, ACT, WEST-B, NES, etc.), which can immobilize them from continuing on with their dream careers
    b. Will often state that they learn best by doing
    c. Often avoid reading out loud
    d. Might talk about struggling in school while growing up
    e. Loud noises can pull them off the tasks at hand
    f. Are embarrassed about previous poor grades
    g. Know what they want to say but often have problems verbalizing it clearly for others
    h. May appear to be understanding verbal communication, but later it is revealed that they did not understand
    i. Can often appear confused in stressful situations
    j. Often unable to show steps of math problems on paper, but can come up with correct answers
    k. Sometimes totally dependent on calculators or counting on fingers
    l. Can be consistently late or obsessively early and struggle with estimating the passing of time

   m. Often dependent on spouses/parents/friends to write papers for them

11. If a student has revealed that he/she has any type of learning disability, ask them if they have checked into receiving accommodations provided by the university.

12. Dyslexia tests—"these days most schools and colleges have made it mandatory for every student to take a dyslexia test. This helps the management to identify those with dyslexia and provide them with proper support and encouragement" (The Dyslexia Center, 2016, para. 11). A quick unofficial test for dyslexia can be found at the following link (www.testdyslexia.com). An official diagnosis can be obtained by finding an educational psychologist, neuro-psychologist, or other learning disability specialist.

13. Encourage these individuals to learn relaxation techniques—such as those used in the Davis method (Davis, 2010).

14. Seeking outside help for dyslexia or other learning disabilities should be encouraged.

The strategies outlined above can best be used in a face-to-face classroom setting, but awareness of these techniques can help students taking classes online as well. Specifically this would be when dealing with discussion boards, e-mails to students, phone calls, et cetera.

## Proven Practices, Examples, and Results

In the quest to determine how to help adult students be successful, it is imperative to understand that they are all learning-abled people. Studies have shown that brain scans of the left and right hemispheres of the brain in a "normal" reader show activation in the left hemisphere (often referred to as the *reading pathway* in the brain). In comparison, the brain scans of students who struggle with processing information (such as those who deal with dyslexia) have greater activation in the right side of the brain during reading. This is the part of the brain that they use to read. Many methods created to assist right-brain readers aim to activate or strengthen the left side, but the best method for working with them is an approach that harnesses the already active pathway in the right side of the brain

(Marshall, 2003). Instead of using rote memorization and drills, these students need to use their unique picture-thinking abilities to get at the root cause of the learning difficulty and correct it by using the natural strengths and talents of their personal learning style.

## Lessons Learned, Tips for Success, and Recommendations

It's exciting to see how attitudes and proven practices are beginning to shift with regards to those who struggle with serious learning disabilities, including dyslexia. Advisors have been learning how to craft e-mails so that learning disabled students and non-LD students can have better understanding. Implementing the usage of bullet points, larger font sizes, and recrafting of e-mails by some of the advisors has enhanced student comprehension. By incorporating such practices as making student communications more succinct, a better understanding is created for the students.

"As many as one in five students may have dyslexia, but not all of these students receive adequate help" (Bardsley, 2015, para. 11). As discussed earlier, those with dyslexia are gifted. According to Davis (2010), "Dyslexics don't all develop the same gifts, but they do have certain mental functions in common. Here are the basic abilities all dyslexics share" (p. 4):

1. They can utilize the brain's ability to alter and create perceptions (the primary ability).
2. They are highly aware of the environment.
3. They are more curious than average.
4. They think mainly in pictures instead of words.
5. They think and perceive multi-dimensionally (using all the senses).
6. They can experience thought as reality.
7. They have vivid imaginations.

If higher education faculty and staff can learn how struggling learners think, then all will begin to serve them more effectively. By incorporating just a few of the techniques discussed, it could change how institutions work with these adults with the goal of maintaining student retention of a significant portion of the attending adult student population.

# References

Bardsley, J. (2015, November 29). Dyslexia is more common than you know. *Daily Herald*, p. D-2.

Davis, R. D. (2010). *The gift of dyslexia* (revised and expanded). New York, NY: Perigee Books.

The Dyslexia Center. (2016). Adult dyslexia test. Retrieved from http://www.the-dyslexia-center.com/

Litemind.com. (n.d.). What is mind mapping? (And how to get started immediately). Retrieved from https://litemind.com/what-is-mind-mapping/

LoGiudice, K. (2008). Common characteristics of adult dyslexia. Retrieved from http://www.dyslexia.com/library/adult-symptoms.htm

Marshall, A. (2003). Brain scans show dyslexics read better with alternative strategies. Retrieved from http://www.dyslexia.com/science/different_pathways.htm

Smarter. (n.d.). How do you test an adult for dyslexia? Retrieved from http://get.smarter.com/qa/health/test-dyslexia-469f03c7aff725d9?qo=contentSimilarQuestions

# Author Biography

Liz Bertran is the campus manager at City University of Seattle in Everett, where she oversees the running of the site in addition to managing the enrollment advisors. She has served as an enrollment advisor since 2009. In addition, she is a Davis Dyslexia Correction Facilitator. Prior to arriving at City University of Seattle, she worked in the Arlington Public School District as a writing instructor for grades 2–12.

# Creating and Embracing a Learning Path for Student Success

**Craig Schieber and Sue Seiber**

## Abstract

Education is evolving greatly in the twenty-first century. The models of education designed in the industrial age are gradually giving way to education built around an information society that operates much differently than a factory. A central theme in this information society is that of personalization. Pedagogical approaches need to change to match the realities of the ever more personalized nature of the information age. As education changes to reflect the trends of the information age, personalization will increase as students are able to identify individualized growth plans in their learning experience. This chapter reviews how pedagogical strategies such as portfolios and rubrics are foundations for building programs that reach deeper levels of personalization in motivating a broad variety of students. The overarching strategy is best conceptualized as each student creating a personal learning path in education of the twenty-first century.

## Overview

All people follow what might be called a learning path on the way to learning a skill or a body of knowledge. That path may be practically subconscious such as learning to walk, or conscious such as learning to play an instrument or sport. Similar to both paths is an intense drive to reach a new state of being. That drive serves to direct the mind and body to find what works best to achieve the final state. It is a personal journey that follows common benchmarks. However, often times in classrooms a clear vision of the learning path is not developed in learners. Learners approach the learning assignment by assignment, achieving the small goals but not understanding the role of the small steps in the context of the overall goal. This makes learners less proactive and more a "consumer" of the activity with no sense of how this builds to their ultimate goal other than it being a grade assigned by an instructor. This chapter will review foundational thinking supporting the concept of a "student learning path" and then give some classroom examples of what it looks like.

## Review of the Literature

The genesis of the learning path comes from many movements in education. In the review of the literature a broad array of some of the major foundations of educational thought are discussed.

## Intrinsic and Extrinsic Motivation

Student motivation can be said to come either extrinsically or intrinsically. Extrinsic motivation uses behavioral-type awards to encourage accomplishment and punishments to discourage not staying on task. Intrinsic motivation uses the inner drive and passion students can have for an action to carry them to completion of tasks (Mirabela-Constanta

& Maria-Madela, 2011; Ryan, & Deci, 2000). Schools through the use of grades, stickers, and punishments have tended to rely mostly on extrinsic motivators. Building effective instruction on intrinsic motivators can be more challenging than creating a series of rewards and punishments.

However, studies have shown that through promoting intellectually stimulating behaviors, student intrinsic motivation can be encouraged (Bolkan, 2015). A more powerful approach is to combine pedagogy to include both intrinsic and extrinsic motivation. In classroom instruction designed to encourage intrinsic motivation, also referred to as autonomy, support and extrinsic motivation, referred to as *structure support*, Jang, Reeve, and Deci (2010) "hypothesized that students' engagement would be highest when teachers provided high levels of both." Their conclusion was that:

> Trained observers rated teachers' instructional styles and students' behavioral engagement in 133 public high school classrooms in the Midwest. . . . Correlational and hierarchical linear modeling analyses showed three results: (a) autonomy support and structure were positively correlated, (b) autonomy support and structure both predicted students' behavioral engagement, and (c) only autonomy support was a unique predictor of students' self-reported engagement. (Jang et al., 2010, p. 588)

These results suggest that teachers can attain best achievement results when they structure their classroom to encourage both extrinsic and intrinsic motivation.

## Student Agency

Students either can be dependent on teacher direction or be more proactive and use their own ideas to drive the learning process. Student agency is that energy that students get when they take charge of their learning and hold themselves responsible for their accomplishments. When students have high agency, they tend to exhibit greater skills of critical thinking, problem solving, and even teamwork: skills that employers want in the employees they hire (Zimmerman, 2015).

## Effective Feedback with Rubrics

High-quality feedback to a student also provides a foundation for piecing together the total concept of a student learning path. Feedback is a strong motivator for students to stay engaged in a course (Martinez-Arguelles, Plana, Hintzmann, Batalla-Busquets, & Badia, 2015). A huge development in design of feedback has been the use of rubrics as part of the instructional and assessment process. Rubrics establish the expectation that clear targets for task accomplishment need to be given at the beginning of instruction (Yoshida & Harada, 2007). A rubric outlines the expectations for different levels of performance a student may deliver (Arter & McTighe, 2001). Students are then able to more clearly identify and perform to teacher expectations (Rochford & Borchert, 2011).

## Portfolios

Portfolios have also provided a valuable extension of bringing student voice and agency into the educational experience. Some portfolios require that student work be collected to meet standards set by the educational program. Other portfolios don't tie the collection of student work to standards, so a more general body of work is included (Worley, 2011). Presented from a growth mindset, the portfolio process can represent an opportunity for students to reflect on their learning and aid them in taking responsibility for their personal growth. Portfolios can even be used as a means for starting deep conversations about the standards to which students are submitting portfolio evidence (Kryder, 2011).

The Purdue University Indianapolis ePortfolio includes four domains: "(1) increasing understanding of self and others, (2) setting self-concordant goals, (3) developing hope, and (4) shaping education career plans with a focus on facilitating students' ability to integrate learning to promote meaning making and the development of purpose" (Buyarski et al., 2015). This kind of framework is exemplary of how these proven strategies of using intrinsic and extrinsic motivation, building student agency, and using comprehensive portfolio structures can work synergistically to create a student learning path to guide and support a student to academic success.

# Integration into the Student Experience

To set the stage for construction of the learning path framework, some analogies to other life learning experiences are helpful. The process of learning to walk illustrates how personal learning can be harnessed by the inner drive that exists in all of us to accomplish personal goals. Our brain tracks small successes and failures in a non-value-laden nature. Each attempt at walking, successful or not successful, is used as a step toward the ultimate goal. The analogy of learning to walk can help students to understand why they must own their learning and ultimately direct it. Helping students see their learning path gives them agency to direct and take responsibility for their learning. They come to understand that learning is not something that a teacher does to them, it is something they accomplish by their own hard work.

In the process of moving to share locus of control between the instructor and student, there should be ground rules. The ground rules should include a process of learning. A generic process can include that the student knows: (1) the learning target, (2) what is next, and (3) the resources needed. For example, for students going through a teacher preparation program, first the instructor should work with the students to define what the learning target is long-term (such as "become an inspiring teacher"), to the short-term (such as "How do teachers get kids' attention after recess?"). The key is to continue to define explicitly what the final target looks like. In the first quarter of a program, most students' understanding of what it takes to be an inspiring teacher will look much different than their view when they get to student teaching. It is helpful to mix abstract and concrete visions in this long-term identification process. In this example, having students focus on how they will answer basic questions about teaching in their interview for a position is a task that matches vision with concrete actions and reality.

Second, students must be able to have a good enough scope of the path to the final target that they can track where they are on that path. Students must be ready for diversions and surprises on the journey. They must learn how to chart and reflect on these diversions and surprises so that the next steps can be modified and adjusted. This is where learning journals or portfolios come in as activities to help learners describe experiences so that they can be seen objectively and analyzed.

Finally, students must know where to go to achieve the next learning steps. Being proactive will be a great advantage to students. If they rely strictly on what the teacher supplies, they may miss the opportunity to personalize elements to their own learning path. The process to identify next steps may be as easy as following assignments in class or reading the textbook. Or it may require students to be creative and find other resources, such as talking with a teacher in a classroom or teaching a lesson to some neighborhood kids. Students, through making their own way through the journey, find their voice, and learn in a constructivist manner, utilizing personalized creative and unique choices to navigate the journey. As J. K. Rowling said, "It is our choices that show who we truly are, far more than our abilities." When students find and make sense of their personal experience in this process, it leads them to gain their professional voice, which guides their becoming an inspirational teacher.

Rubrics are a tool used to chart the journey down a learning path. But current rubrics are limited because they are designed to measure finite tasks as a summative assessment. When applied to a skill, such as critical thinking, they are not effective. A skill or disposition, such as critical thinking, is difficult to measure. More confounding is finding a top end to this kind of ever-developing skill. A skill such as critical thinking continues to develop over a lifetime; it does not fit easily into a four-level rubric. A strategy to adapt rubrics to measure a skill is to think of the standards measured as growing in complexity along a spiral path. In that model, growth in a particular standard is revisited regularly but measured at an ever-greater complexity.

Take for example the critical thinking tool of cause and effect. Children understand cause and effect in concrete terms: if you put your hand on a hot burner, the effect is a burnt hand. As children get older, they are challenged to understand more complex cause-and-effect relationships, such as weather patterns, economic processes, or political events. Understanding cause and effect in these fields is a lifelong learning process. Another analogy is found in the process of learning a skill, such as playing an instrument or a sport. Performers and athletes are always practicing to get better at a particular skill. They never reach a final status of completion at the skill. As Pablo Casals noted when he was in his eighties about his cello practicing, "I think I see some progress. I think I am making some improvement."

## Proven Practices, Examples, and Results

The teacher preparation program at some universities, including as a leader, City University of Seattle, has begun to implement actions that represent the constructs of this learning path approach to education. One example is when education students present their portfolios to fellow cohort members in a formal setting at the end of program. The presentations give opportunity for presenters to choose the most effective work they have done during the length of the program. They get the opportunity to look at their work through a strengths perspective to focus on what they have really done well. Their fellow cohort members are able to see models of other ways to success. The presentations give an opportunity for the entire cohort to review a body of learning on their chosen profession. Through these presentations students are able to put their learning into perspective of a continual learning path on which they are traveling. In addition, from a pragmatic perspective, they are practicing talking about their strengths and approach to school teaching, leading, or counseling, which will directly translate to the answers they will provide in upcoming interviews for positions to which they will be applying. It is this focus on preparing for the imminent interviews for positions that has provided the basis for talking about a long-term learning path. Moving this experience so all students begin this visualization of the interview in the first quarter as part of their formulating their learning path for the entire program will enhance this learning pathway.

Students in the teacher preparation program keep reflective journals in a template format that requires the students to include in their writing the basic levels of Bloom's taxonomy, which includes (1) a level of describing the experience they are writing about, (2) analyzing the experience, and (3) evaluating and putting meaning to the experience. The next evolution with the learning path will be to put this journaling process in the context of the students' learning path and how it reflects on movement along that path. Another activity to keep the focus on tracking growth is the quarterly end-of-course reflection students complete on what they learned in that course to move them along the learning path. This is similar to an End-of-Course Evaluation, but it puts the focus on what the student is doing instead of the instructor. In this way a greater sense of agency is being built in the students, focused on helping students assume responsibility for their learning.

As discussed earlier in review of the literature, it is advantageous to develop pedagogical strategies that utilize both extrinsic and intrinsic perspectives. This process of charting growth along a learning path can do just that. For the extrinsically motivated students, the focus might be more on charting completion of assignments and courses but as part of the total program. In addition, as these students feel ready, they can actually write responses to standardized interview questions they will field in their first interviews. They can check off completion of each answer. And, as in the spiral rubric process, the answer they write in the first quarter about how they will teach most likely will be revised to reflect deeper understanding as they go through the program. For intrinsically motivated students, the quest to understand what kind of inspiring teacher they will be will continually grow and gain depth. The process of becoming the teacher they want to be will be squarely in front of them throughout the program.

## Lessons Learned, Tips for Success, and Recommendations

Incorporating a personalized learning pathway approach continues to expand and affect practice as it is implemented. For example, while portfolios have been used for years, how the portfolios are used and their relationship to the overall program continue to evolve. It seems one change can elicit a cascade effect of changes to other aspects of a program. Deep reflective conversations among faculty are necessary to understand these changes and design appropriate next steps in program and pedagogical design. Second, it is important to understand that the students and faculty all come from different levels of understanding of these changes in pedagogical design. As such, discussions about and even actual implementation are constantly influenced by these vast differences in understanding of pedagogical design among students and faculty. It is critical to approach students from where they are and then move them in their understanding from that point. Finally, with these new activities, it is important to review what elements in an educational program may no longer be necessary. If this is not done, it is easy to have students overwhelmed by the continual addition of activities with none ever taken away. The focus must remain on identifying what is the most effective instruction delivered in the most efficient manner.

# Conclusion

Education is evolving greatly in this new century. The models of education designed in the industrial age are gradually giving way to education built around an information society. A central theme in the information society is that of personalization. Goods and services are all being revolutionized by the way technology is opening opportunities for personalization to the customer. Personalization in education will come as students are able to experience individualized growth in their learning. Pedagogical approaches need to change to match the technologies of the information age. Supporting students in identifying and following their own learning path is just one of the pedagogical changes to come with the twenty-first-century education experience.

# References

Arter, J., & McTighe, J. (2001) *Scoring rubrics in the classroom: Using performance criteria for assessing and improving student performance.* Thousand Oaks, CA: Corwin Press.

Bolkan, S. (2015). Intellectually stimulating students' intrinsic motivation: The mediating influence of affective learning and student engagement. *Communication Reports, 28*(2), 80–91.

Buyarski, C. A., Aaron, R. W., Hansen, M. J., Hollingsworth, C. D., Johnson, A. A., Kahn, S., … Powell, A. A. (2015). Purpose and pedagogy: A conceptual model for an ePortfolio. *Theory into Practice, 54*(4), 283–291.

Jang, H., Reeve, J., & Deci, E. L. (2010). Engaging students in learning activities: It is not autonomy support or structure but autonomy support and structure. *Journal of Educational Psychology, 102*(3), 588–600.

Kryder, L.G. (2011). Eportfolios: Proving competency and building a network. *Business Communication Quarterly, 74*(3), 333–341.

Martinez-Arguelles, M., Plana, D., Hintzmann, C., Batalla-Busquets, J., & Badia, M. (2015). Usefulness of feedback in e-learning from the students' perspective. *Intangible Capital, 11*(4). http://dx.doi.org/10.3926/ic.622

Mirabela-Constanta, M., & Maria-Madela, A. (2011). Intrinsic and extrinsic motivation: An investigation of performance correlation on students. *Annals of the University of Oradea, Economic Science Series, 20*(1), 671–677.

Rochford, L., & Borchert, P. S. (2011). Assessing higher-level learning: Developing rubrics for case analysis. *Journal of Education for Business. 86*(5), 258–265.

Ryan, R. M., & Deci, E. L. (2000). Intrinsic and extrinsic motivations: Classic definitions and new directions. *Contemporary Educational Psychology, 25*(1), 54–67.

Worley, R. B. (2011). Eportfolios examined: Tools for exhibit and evaluation. *Business Communication Quarterly, 74*(3), 330-332.

Yoshida, J. M., & Harada, V. H. (2007). Involving students in learning through rubrics. *Library Media Connection, 25*(5), 10–14.

Zimmerman, M. (2015). The value of student agency. *Phi Kappa Phi Forum, 95*(2), 21.

## Author Biographies

Craig Schieber is the Dean of the School of Education and Division of Arts and Sciences at City University of Seattle. Craig advocates for making the educational system relevant and transformative. His belief in inquiry, project-based learning that empowers the learner is the driving force behind all of Craig's work. He has taught in the public schools where he developed project-based curriculum and a student portfolio system, among other innovations. He holds an EdD in educational leadership from

Seattle Pacific University, an MA in child development from University of Washington and a BA in education from Ohio State University.

Sue Seiber's career has spanned more than forty-five years in education culminating with the position of Director of Teacher Certification programs at City University of Seattle. She has been a classroom teacher, administrator, curriculum developer, professional development trainer, and university faculty member. She has presented conference sessions for the North Dakota Department of Education, International Literacy Association, Council of Exceptional Children, OSPI January Conferences, OSPI Summer Institutes, and many school districts' professional development workshops. Awards include City University Claude Farley Excellence in Teaching, WEA Excellence in Teaching, and the Washington State Christa MacAuliffe Outstanding Educator Award.

# Supporting Student Success with Intuitive, Approachable Data Visualization

**Lindy Ryan and Nathan Snow**

## Abstract

New discoveries surrounding the mechanisms and function of human visual acuity have come with increasing rapidity, each clarifying the astounding pattern recognition, image retention, and processing speed of the human visual cognition system. However, the relationship between institutions of higher learning and data visualization can be classified as embryotic at best. This chapter will examine such a new paradigm in data visualization for higher education, examining obstacles and clearly defining benefits that have been illustrated through real-world case studies utilizing appropriate technologies. For data visualization to offer the most tangible value as student success assets in an educational setting, visualizations need to be made as functionally and cognitively accessible to students and faculty as possible, allowing both to actively share in data prudent for performance improvement and success.

## Overview

In a letter to "Nature," researchers from the Centre de Recherché Cerveau & Cognition presented their findings on the speed of human visual processing (Thorpe, Fize, & Marlot, 1996). Historically, determining how fast human beings visually decode images had been difficult, as any experiments had to not only include processing speed but also monitor motor reaction time. However, utilizing a new technique, event-related potentials (ERP), the team was able to better determine the speed and power of the human visual processing system.

The experiment consisted of flashing a photograph for twenty milliseconds (ms) and then, using ERP analysis, determining how fast human subjects could determine if the photograph contained an animal. The researchers discovered that "the visual processing needed to perform this highly demanding task can be achieved in under 150 ms" (Thorpe et al., 1996, p. 520), with an average proportion of correct responses at 94 percent and one of the fifteen study subjects achieving 98 percent of correct responses. Moreover, the subjects were indeed able to correctly determine whether an animal was in the picture. Essentially, this study provided empirical evidence that human visual processing speed was far faster and more powerful (with regards to accuracy) than had previously been imagined.

Since the mid-1990s, new discoveries surrounding the mechanisms and function of human visual acuity have come with increasing rapidity, each clarifying the astounding pattern recognition, image processing, and visual learning and retention power of the human brain (Stokes, 2002; Toth, 2013; Brinkley, 2014; Borkin, Bylinski, Isola, Sunkavalli, Oliva, & Pfister, 2013; Isola, Xiao, Torralba, & Oliva, 2011). However, seemingly in spite of these new discoveries, the proclivity of data analysis and visualization continues to lag behind, utilizing the same charts and graphs conceived for eighteenth-century shipping manifests. The volume, velocity, and variety of modern data streams occurring in a rapidly data-centric information culture beg for a new method of understanding, one which requires little formal training and takes full advantage of the intrinsic human ability to learn, communicate, and decode information visually. Such methods have often been called transparent due to their clarity and immediate accessibility (Perer & Schneiderman, 2008).

The relationship between institutions of higher learning and data visualization, whether at the organizational or at the classroom level, can be classified as embryotic at best. Traditionally, faculty members and administrators review performance data as rows of raw numbers or in charts and graphs, and usually only after a semester has concluded. The story is even more frustrating for the students, whose interaction with the data is limited to a spreadsheet showing earned grades on assignments, weighted gradebooks per course, or progression through standardized education programs via GPA. However, should more thorough, intuitive, transparent data visualization methods be applied, the results have the potential to be transformative, and early research projects conducted with students in academic environments would support this thesis. For example, by coupling the bimodal distribution of student scores with early warning signs of failure, a grant-based research project conducted at the Michigan Virtual University (Dickson, 2005) successfully performed visual data analyses to gauge student satisfaction with online courseware and lower the barrier to data-driven decision making for faculty in the early intervention of student failure. In areas of future research identified from the study, the researchers encouraged the development of adapted models for visual data representation to fit the specific needs of faculty and students as the previous study had illustrated the applicability of dynamics of student success through visual meta-analysis (Dickson, 2005). A similar undertaking by Canadian researchers successfully developed a Student Success System (S3) by using flexible predictive modeling, machine intelligence, and data visualization as an end-to-end solution for identifying at-risk students and designing interventions to mitigate that risk (Essa & Ayad, 2012).

Additionally, researchers from North Carolina General Assembly, in partnership with JMP Software, a data visualization–based interactive tool for desktop statistical discovery, conducted an experiment to expose students to data in a unique and exciting way by allowing them to engage with information and describe, visualize, and critique data sets from various verticals of industry. With limited focus on materials generally covered in traditional mathematics curriculum, students were invited to explore data critically and visually to structure information for summary analysis. At the end of the program, students had developed a improved capacity to visually work with and understand data, understand the role of data in decision making, and achieve higher individual engagement with visual data (Brinkley, 2014).

Providing guided visualization examples has also been acknowledged as a catalyst for creative thought and problem solving and has been determined to offer innovative pedagogical formats to engage more intimately with higher education students (Honey-Roses, Le Menestrel, Arenas, Rauschmayer, & Rode, 2013).

Thus, a new paradigm exists in data visualization for higher education with clear benefits already being recognized by researchers and realized by early-adopting organizations. For data visualization to be of the most use in an educational setting, visualizations should be accessible to students and faculty, allowing both to share in data that is prudent to improve performance. Fortunately, recent research into the speed and power of human visual processing has given rise to new methods of data visualization that harness this ability, using universal visual language to instinctually highlight areas of improvement with no prior training required and to capitalize on data visualization as a mechanism to support student success.

## Review of the Literature

The case for supporting student success with data visualization begins with understanding the power of pictures, and their impact on memorability, learning, and learning retention. Previous to the research of Thorpe et al. (1996), seminal research from the 1970s tells us that humans are extremely good at remembering thousands of pictures and a vast amount of visual detail. As a measure earmarked in the academic literature, the number of remembered images and context has been estimated to be roughly ten thousand images at an accurate recognition rate of approximately 83 percent (Standing, 1973).

In more recent years, attributes-based visual recognition has continued to receive much attention, particularly in the computer science literature, and numerous in-depth studies have provided clear data and learning opportunities. Thus, we now definitively know visualizations that blend information with influential features (such as color, density, and content themes, like recognizable icons or imagery) significantly and reliably increase learning, memorability, and recall (Borkin et al., 2013). Further, seeing and interacting with an image in combination with traditional written and verbal instruction has, too, been consistently associated with higher levels of retention and understanding of salient ideas. While research into the human cognitive capacity to remember visual stimuli remains ongoing, in the past few years researchers have worked to systematically study the intrinsic memorability of images and the interface between human cognition and computer vision. This body of study is ultimately intended to understand the predictive ability of visual memorability and how visuals can be designed to best leverage our innate visual recognition system.

## Visualization Stimulates Memory Retention

A collaborative research project by computer scientists from Harvard and cognitive scientists from MIT explored cognitive memorability of visualizations to uncover empirical evidence to support the theory that while our memories are unique, we have the same embedded algorithm necessary to convert visual communication into memory and thereby learn and retain learning. To test this theory, researchers used a publicly available memorability data set and augmented the object and scene annotations with interpretable spatial, contextual, and aesthetic image proprieties (i.e., colors, shapes, etc.) (Isola et al., 2011).

The researchers found that, contrary to popular assumption, unusualness and aesthetic beauty are not associated with high memorability and are, instead, negatively correlated with memorability. Instead, a visualization is instantly and overwhelmingly more memorable if it includes a human-recognizable element (i.e., a photograph, person, cartoon, or logo). These items provide our memory with visual cues by which to build a story around, and offer a compelling case for the use of icons in visualizations like infographics that rely on symbols to communicate mass amounts of complex data in simple and meaningful ways.

## Human-Like Symbols Provide Memory and Engagement Cues

Neuropsychology has long associated written word recognition with different functional areas of the brain, known as the visual word form area (VWFA). However, in recent studies, cognitive researchers have provided more modern empirical evidence that the VWFA overlaps with a subpart of the ventral visual cortex that exhibits special sensitivity to line junctions, including symbols and natural scenes (Dehaene & Cohen, 2011). As illustration of this finding, in a subsequent study on what makes a visual memorable, researchers built a broad, static visualization taxonomy to cover the large variety of data visualizations in use today. They then collected nearly six thousand visual representations of data from various publications and categorized them by a wide range of visual attributes.

The images were exposed to participants via Amazon Mechanical Turk to test the influence of features like color, density, and content themes on participants' memorability. The results of the study validated previous findings that faces and human-centric scenes are more memorable than others—specifically, people and human-like objects contributed most positively to the memorability of images. These findings provide further support that certain design principles make visualizations inherently more memorable than others, irrespective of individual context and biases (Borkin et al., 2013).

## Integration into the Student Experience

By synthesizing the implications of the aforementioned research, it can be reasonably assumed that integration of data visualization to support student learning and success can be achieved at the intersection of data and analytic accessibility and the application of known low-barrier visual cognitive engagement elements, particularly human-recognizable visual features. With a proximal goal in place, the question now becomes "How can educational institutions use transparent data visualizations to foster student success?"

Unfortunately, such implementations are somewhat challenging to find as more traditional forms of visualization, such as basic charts and graphs, still largely dominate the field. These basic visualization forms lack the key elements required for memorability and speedy visual consumption and understanding as demonstrated by Isola et al. (2011) and Borkin et al. (2013) and thus lack the required transparency necessary for an untrained student, parent, or faculty member to quickly understand relevant educational data. However, while homegrown academic solutions are still incubatory, commercially available data visualization software platforms exist that make the work of translating tabular, two-dimensional data into transparent visualizations more accessible. While these technologies are still in their nascent stages due to the prevailing reliance on older forms of data visualization, there are case studies provided by higher learning institutions that have implemented available technologies to positive effect, thereby proving the theory that data visualization can be useful in higher education to support student engagement if approached correctly.

## Proven Practices, Examples, Results, and Lessons Learned

As an applied example, VisualCue Technologies LLC is one such software platform. Its technology translates key performance indicators into human-recognizable icons, each resembling in some recognizable way the metric they represent (see Figure 1). Thresholds are then introduced into the data, and these are the parameters by which the colors of the icons change based on educational best practices embraced by the institution. This data visualization technique takes full advantage of the key requirements for memorability put forth in the literature review. Icons provide recognizable, relatable elements with which to ground abstract data sets in visual language, thus making them accessible to the widest-possible range of users. And this approach serves to take full advantage of the speed and processing power in the human visual system as originally described by Thorpe et al. (1996) and reinforced through myriad continued scholarly research endeavors since. In essence, these new visualization techniques make even the largest data sets immediately and intuitively consumable.

*Figure 1. An example of a VisualCue tile, which transforms tabular, raw data into a responsive, icon-driven performance indicator for intuitive visual analytics.*

These transparent visual data techniques have been implemented in a number of educational organizations with positive results. In the interest of fostering practicability, the case studies below provide real-world examples of the value found in theoretical principles regarding the importance of transparent data visualization applied to higher education to support student engagement and success. These institutions have been chosen due to their efforts in using a commercially available data visualization software platform to translate tabular, two-dimensional data into transparent visualizations from which faculty and students can benefit.

## Colégio Notre Dame—São Paulo, Brazil

A large school in one of Brazil's largest cities, the Colégio Notre Dame needed a way for instructors to easily communicate with students regarding educational progress. The school implemented a web portal where instructors input data on grades, absence occurrences, and additional coursework. Students were then able to see performance metrics that were updated daily. Rather than seeing one particular grade (or course) at a time, this visualization showed the students their entire education in context with daily status updates. With real-time data, students were actively able to make course corrections as they were happening.

Both reception and results have been positive. Students feel more included, and due to the transparent nature of the visualization, they are able to spot patterns faster and act on them with more certainty. Due to the frequency of the updates, students were able to successfully make micro-corrections to their learning and improve earlier in each term (G. Barretto, personal communication, January 23, 2016).

## Seminole State College—Sanford, Florida

Located near Orlando, Florida, Seminole State College faced a different set of challenges from Colégio Notre Dame. In what might be a common concern among many institutions of higher education, the college simply did not have enough teachers and administrators to adequately analyze and tailor support for each student. While large class sizes are certainly nothing new to academia, for this smaller university having even fewer faculty and administrative staff exacerbated the problems caused from a lack of analytics. However, this organization decided that its ever-growing student population could benefit just as much from advanced analytics as those at a larger, more well-funded university. As such, its task was not only to analyze the academic performance of its students, but also compare those results with other key performance indicators, such as absenteeism, course history, and enrollment.

Rather than expect real-time feedback, Seminole State was more interested in looking at long-term trends alongside more granular information. Since implementing the transparent data visualization technology, the college has been effectively able to gain a sense of the student's entire educational experience and support that impression with specific details to help improve student success on an individualized basis (K. Gilger, personal communication, January 20, 2016).

## Conclusion

Whether through real-time corrections to student behavior or using more long-term analysis to augment a teacher's skill set, the benefits remain the same. The institutions detailed above, and the scholarly support provided through the analysis of available literature on the positive benefits of student engagement with data visualization, illustrate enormous benefit to student achievement and university data-driven decision making through the use of intuitive, approachable data visualization. Thus, the authors conclude that a combination of both real-time and long-term data analysis utilizing intuitive, pictorial data visualization techniques will produce tangible value for both students and faculty at any institution of higher education where it is implemented.

# References

Borkin, M., Vo, A., Bylinski, Z., Isola, P., Sunkavalli, S., Oliva, A., & Pfister, H. (2013). What makes visualization memorable? Paper presented at IEEE INFOVIS. Atlanta, GA. Retrieved from http://cvcl.mit.edu/papers/Borkin_etal_MemorableVisualization_TVCG2013.pdf

Brinkley, J. (2014). Using JMP as a catalyst for teaching data-driven decision making to high school students. Paper presented at JMP Discovery Summit 2014. Retrieved from https://community.jmp.com/docs/DOC-6690

Dehaene, S., & Cohen, L. (2011). The unique role of the visual word form area in reading. *Trends in Cognitive Sciences, 15*(6), 254–262.

Dickson, W. P. (2005). Toward a deeper understanding of student performance in virtual high school courses: Using quantitative analyses and data visualization to inform decision making. *A Synthesis of New Research in K–12 Online Learning*, 21–23. Retrieved from https://www.heartland.org/sites/all/modules/custom/heartland_migration/files/pdfs/28155.pdf

Essa, A., & Ayad, H. (2012). Improving student success using predictive models and data visualisations. *Research in Learning Technology, 20.* Retrieved from http://www.researchinlearningtechnology.net/index.php/rlt/article/view/19191

Honey-Roses, J., Le Menestrel, M., Arenas, D., Rauschmayer, F., & Rode, J. (2013). Enriching intergenerational decision-making with guided visualization exercises. *Journal of Business Ethics, 122*(4), 675–680.

Isola, P., Xiao, J., Torralba, A., & Oliva, A. (2011). What makes an image memorable? Paper presented at IEEE Conference on Computer Vision and Pattern Recognition. Atlanta, GA. Retrieved from http://web.mit.edu/phillipi/www/publications/WhatMakesAnImageMemorable.pdf

Perer, A., & Shneiderman, B. (2008). Integrating statistics and visualization: Case studies of gaining clarity during exploratory data analysis. Proceedings of the SIGCHI Conference on Human Factors in Computing Systems, 265–274. doi:10.1145/1357054.1357101

Standing, L. (1973). Learning 10,000 pictures. *Quarterly Journal of Psychology, 25*(2), 207–222.

Stokes, S. (2002). Visual literacy in teaching and learning: A literature perspective. *Electronic Journal for the Integration of Technology in Education, 1*(1), 10–19.

Thorpe, S., Fize, D., & Marlot, C. (1996). Speed of processing in the human visual system. *Nature, 381*(6582), 520–522.

Toth, C. (2013). Revisiting a genre: Teaching infographics in business and professional communication courses. *Business Communication Quarterly, 76*(4), 446–457.

# Author Biographies

Lindy Ryan is a researcher in the confluence of data discovery, visualization, and data science. She is a research associate with the Rutgers University Discovery Informatics Institute (RDI2) and an associate faculty member of City University of Seattle's School of Applied Leadership. She is the author of *The Visual Imperative: Creating a Culture of Visual Discovery* (2016), a featured contributor to *Big Data Quarterly* and *Information Management*, and a frequent guest speaker at conferences such as the Data Summit, Teradata Partners, TDWI, and more.

Nathan Snow is a PhD candidate, graduate teaching associate, and adjunct faculty member in the University of Central Florida's School of Visual

Arts and Design. His research in visual language, cognition, and audience reception theory and practice has led him to cofound the Animators Oral History Project and digital archive at the University of Central Florida. In 2014, he became involved with VisualCue Technologies LLC as a data journalist, analyzing their implementations and extrapolating new applications for their unique visual language.

Made in the USA
San Bernardino, CA
21 July 2016